PHILIP MASSINGER

Vera ac Viva Effigies
PHILIPPI MASSINGER. Gen

Emery Walker ph.sc.

J. Crofs fecit

PHILIP MASSINGER

BY

A. H. CRUICKSHANK

SOMETIME SCHOLAR AND FELLOW OF NEW COLLEGE, OXFORD
CANON OF DURHAM, AND PROFESSOR OF GREEK AND CLASSICAL LITERATURE
IN THE UNIVERSITY OF DURHAM

NEW YORK / RUSSELL & RUSSELL

FIRST PUBLISHED IN 1920 BY BASIL BLACKWELL, PUBLISHER

REISSUED, 1971, BY RUSSELL & RUSSELL

A DIVISION OF ATHENEUM PUBLISHERS, INC.

BY ARRANGEMENT WITH BASIL BLACKWELL, PUBLISHER, OXFORD

L. C. CATALOG CARD NO: 72-139914

PRINTED IN THE UNITED STATES OF AMERICA

INSCRIBED TO

FREDERIC G. KENYON

IN MEMORY OF A FRIENDSHIP
OF FORTY-FOUR YEARS

PREFACE

In confessing that the war made me write a book I do not stand alone. Sensible as I am of its defects, I trust it will help to spread the knowledge of Massinger's works, and will invite others to deal on similar lines with the other dramatists of the great age. The design widened as it went on, and was then contracted. In the end I thought it wiser to confine myself to digesting the knowledge which I had of Massinger's text.

The Clarendon Press undertook to publish this book, but as, owing to war-work, they could fix no date, I asked them to release me. There would be no occasion to mention this fact were it not that it was owing to the original arrangement that I received much valuable help and advice from Mr. Percy Simpson. Many other scholars and friends have kindly aided me in various matters, among whom I should like to mention: Mr. J. C. Bailey, Mr. P. James Bayfield (photographer to Dulwich College), Dr. A. C. Bradley, Mr. Robert Bridges, Mr. A. H. Bullen, Mr. A. K. Cook, Professor W. Macneile Dixon, Mr. H. H. E. Gaster, the Dean of Gloucester, Mr. E. Gosse, Sir W. H. Hadow, Archdeacon Hobhouse, Sir Sidney Lee, Mr. C. Leudesdorf, Dr. Falconer Madan, Mr. A. W. Pollard, Dr. P. G. Smyly, the Master of University College, Durham, Sir A. Ward, and Sir George F. Warner. Last, but not least, I thank my wife for her skilful and ready help with the proofs.

A. H. CRUICKSHANK.

CONTENTS

FRONTISPIECE : PHILIP MASSINGER.

	PAGES
PREFACE - - - - - -	V
TEXT - - - - - -	1–143
APPENDIXES - - - - - -	144–225
INDEX - - - - - -	226–228

FACSIMILE OF HENSLOW DOCUMENT AT DULWICH.

FACSIMILE OF "BELIEVE AS YOU LIST" MS. IN THE BRITISH MUSEUM.

References to Webster are made to Dyce's Edition, 1877.

PHILIP MASSINGER

PHILIP MASSINGER

It is interesting to revise the literary judgments of youth; it is pleasant to find them confirmed by a more mature judgment. This train of thought has led me to read Massinger once more; and as I read, the desire arose to treat his works, to the best of my ability, with the attention to detail which modern scholarship requires. A great amount of valuable work has been done in the last fifty years on the writers of the Elizabethan and Jacobean ages; but no one, perhaps with the exception of Boyle, has applied to Massinger the care which Shakspere, Marlowe, and Ben Jonson, to name no others, have secured. There is no reason why any of our great dramatists should be treated with less respect than those of Greece and Rome, of France and Germany.

The first thing to be done was to facilitate references by numbering the lines of Massinger's plays;[1] the next was to investigate once more the facts of his life, and to correlate them with the period in which he lived; the third was to read typical plays of the period, so as to arrive at a just estimate of our author.

His life will not detain us long. We know far less of him than we do of Shakspere. None of his sayings have been preserved to us; hardly any incidents of his career. His father was house-steward to two of the Earls of

---

[1] It is much to be wished that someone would essay the same task for Beaumont and Fletcher, though there the work would be less easy, partly from the looseness of the metres, partly from the corruption of the text, but chiefly from the presence of prose-passages bordering on verse.

1

Pembroke, first to Henry Herbert, then to William Herbert,[1] Shakspere's friend. The elder Massinger was a Fellow of Merton College, Oxford, and for several years a Member of Parliament. Philip Massinger, the dramatist, was born at Salisbury in 1584. In 1602 he went up to St. Alban's Hall, Oxford, where his father had been an undergraduate. We are told by A. à Wood that he went at Lord Pembroke's expense, but that he did not work hard at the University, and took no degree.[2] In or after the year 1606 he seems to have gone to London, and to have speedily engaged in the work of writing plays.[3] The wide reading which his plays presuppose probably began at Oxford.

It was the custom in those days, as in the time of Plautus at Rome,[4] for playwrights to revise old plays; and still more was it usual for them to collaborate.[5] We find Massinger at work in this way with Field,[6] Daborne,[7]

---

[1] A. à Wood's *Fasti Oxonienses*, p. 313.

[2] Herein he resembled F. Beaumont. G. Langbaine, on the other hand, says that the Earl sent Massinger to Oxford, where he "closely pursued his studies." But we must be careful how we believe Langbaine; his account of our poet begins thus: "This author was born at Salisbury, in the reign of King Charles the First, being son to Philip Massinger, a gentleman belonging to the Earl of Montgomery." Here are three gross blunders at once.

[3] Boyle (*N. S. S.*, xxi., p. 472) says that "Massinger's inveterate habit of repeating himself arose probably from his profession as an actor." I know of no evidence for this hypothesis. *Cf.*, however, p. 6, note 1.

[4] *Cf.* Mommsen's *History of Rome*, English translation, vol. ii., p. 440.

[5] Thus in the play of *Lady Jane*, of which *The Famous History of Sir T. Wyatt* is a fragment, we find five authors concerned. It will be remembered that Eupolis contributed to the *Knights* of Aristophanes.

[6] For some account of Field see Appendix XI.

[7] Daborne's letters bulk large in the Henslowe Correspondence. We have two plays of his: *A Christian turn'd Turke*, based on the story of the pirate Ward; and *The Poor Man's Comfort*, a tragi-comedy. Like Marston, he abandoned the stage in middle life and took orders, before 1618. It is therefore unlikely that he collaborated with Massinger in any of the plays which we possess.

Dekker, Tourneur, and above all, with Fletcher. With the latter he worked from 1613 to 1623. In that year, for some unknown reason, he seceded from the service of the leading company of actors of the day, who went by the name of the King's men, and wrote unaided three plays for the Queen's men, *The Parliament of Love*, *The Bondman*, and *The Renegado*. After Fletcher's death, in 1625, Massinger rejoined the King's men, and wrote for them until his death in 1640.

It has been surmised from the vivid colouring of *The Virgin Martyr*[1] and the plot of *The Renegado*,[2] where a Jesuit plays a leading part and is portrayed in a pleasing light, that Massinger turned Roman Catholic. The evidence for this theory is quite inadequate. Indeed, we might as well argue from Gazet's language that the author followed the Anglican *via media*.[3] Plots derived from French, Spanish, and Italian sources would naturally contain Roman Catholic machinery. We might as well infer that Shakspere was a Roman Catholic because Silvia goes to Friar Patrick's cell,[4] or because Friar Laurence is prominent in *Romeo and Juliet*.[5]

---

[1] Such a reference to *Acta Sanctorum* as is contained in these lines might be made by an Anglican:

ANTONINUS.   It may be, the duty
    And loyal service, with which I pursued her,
    And sealed it with my death, will be remember'd
    Among her blessed *actions.—V. M.*, IV., 3, 28.

More stress might be laid on the metaphor contained in these lines:

THEOPHILUS. O! mark it, therefore, and with that attention,
    As you would hear an embassy from heaven,
    By a wing'd legate.—V. M., V., 2, 103.

[2] No doubt it required courage to present a Jesuit in this way so soon after Gunpowder Plot; and the curious argument in *The Renegado*, V., 1, 28-41, in favour of lay-baptism certainly shows a mind interested in ecclesiastical problems.

[3] *The Renegado*, I., 1, 24-32.

[4] *Two Gentlemen of Verona*, V., 1.

[5] Friar Paulo takes an important part in *The Maid of*

We know that Massinger lived a life of comparative poverty; on one occasion we find him, with two other dramatic authors, asking for a loan of £5.[1]

The person who thus obliged the three writers was Philip Henslowe, a dyer, theatrical lessee, and speculator, who acted as a kind of broker between actors and authors, buying from the one and selling to the other; we still possess his diary, containing information as to the prices which he gave for plays.[2] The prologue of *The Guardian* shows us that for two years before 1633 Massinger had been under a cloud, and had abstained from writing. Two of his plays had failed in 1631—*The Emperor of the East*[3] and *Believe as You List*[4]—so he appears to have put forth his full strength in *The Guardian*.

Honour, ad finem. Octavio, disguised as a priest, elicits Alonzo's repentance in *The Bashful Lover*, IV., 2. The same expedient occurs in *The Emperor of the East*, V., 3, where Theodosius, disguised as a friar, convinces himself of his wife's innocence. Shakspere disguises the Duke as a friar in *Measure for Measure*, II., 3, III., 1, 2, IV., 1, 2, 3.

[1] See the photograph at the beginning of the book. *Cf.* also Greg's Henslowe Papers, article 68. Fleay identifies the play referred to in the document as *The Honest Man of Fortune*, acted in 1613. In the first Dublin poem, after referring to the patronage which had befriended Jonson and Fletcher, Massinger goes on thus:

> "These are precedents
> I cite with reverence; my low intents
> Look not so high; yet some work I might frame
> That should not wrong my duty, nor your name;
> Were but your lordship pleased to cast an eye
> Of favour on my trod-down poverty."

[2] *Cf.* W. W. Greg's *Henslowe's Diary*, vol. ii., pp. 110-147. Mr. Greg points out (p. 113) that "there is no record of any speculations of Henslowe's own as far as the evidence of the Diary is concerned. The accounts are company accounts" —*i.e.*, of The Rose and Fortune Theatres.

We have also at Dulwich a bond from R. Daborne and P. Massinger to Philip Henslowe for payment of £3, dated July 4th, 1615. *Cf.* Greg's Henslowe Papers, article 102.

[3] Licensed March 4th, 1631.

[4] Licensed May 6th, 1631.

Mr Hinchlow

you vnderstand oⁿ vnfortunate extremitie and
I doe not thincke you so void of chriftianitie
but that you would throw fo much money into the
Thames as wee request now of you; rather then
endanger fo many innocent liues; you know
there is xⁿˡ more at leaſt to be receaued of
you for the play, wee defire you to lend vs
vⁿˡ of that, wᶜʰ shall be allowed to you whout
wᶜʰ wee cannot be bayled, nor I play any more
till this be difpatch'd, it will loofe you xxˡ
ere the end of the next weeke befide the hin-
-derance of the next new play, pray Sⁱ Confider
our Cafes wᵗʰ humanitie, and now giue vs caufe
to acknowledge you our true freind in time of
neede; wee haue entreated Mʳ Baniſter to
deliuer this note, as well to witnzffe yoʳ loue,
as oʳ promiffe, and alwayes acknowledgment to
be euer

yoⁱ moſt thanckfull; and louing freinds,
Nat: Feild

the mony fhalbe fo abated out
of the mony remaynes for the
play of mⁱ fleonger Court
Rob: Daborne   J haue euer founde yow
a true louinge freind to
mee & in foe fmall a futte ſt
faild bb: lernꝰ louꝰ hope yow will noꝰ

I. HENSLOW DOCUMENT AT DULWICH. See page 4

The dedications of Massinger's plays which have been preserved show that he was often dependent for support on the leaders of what he once or twice calls " the nobility."[1]

The connexion of the poet with the family of which his father was the loyal and trusted servant has been exaggerated by some;[2] in the dedication of *The Bondman,* written in 1623, to Philip, Earl of Montgomery,[3] the poet distinctly states that though the Earl had helped the play at its first performance by his " liberal suffrages " yet he was personally unknown to him.[4] Amongst others to whom we find dedications is George Harding, Baron Berkeley, to whom Webster inscribed *The Duchess of Malfi.* It is pleasant to read in the dedication of *The Picture* " to my honoured and selected friends of the Noble Society of the Inner Temple " that Massinger received " frequent bounties " from them.

The plays give us no clear evidence that Massinger ever travelled abroad,[5] though such a passage as *The Great*

---

[1] See poem "Sero sed serio" (Cunningham, p. 628); *Picture,* II., 2, 37; *City Madam,* I., 2, 116; *Emperor of the East,* II., 1, 45. *Cf. Catiline;* II, 1.

[2] Aubrey, in his *Natural History of Wiltshire* (ed. J. Britton, 1847, p. 31), distinctly says that the poet had a pension of twenty or thirty pounds per annum, which was " payed to his wife after his decease."

[3] Younger brother of William Herbert, Earl of Pembroke.

[4] The dedication begins thus: "However I could never arrive at the happiness to be made known to your lordship," etc.

[5] No doubt he knew some foreign languages. His plays come from various sources, French, Italian, and Spanish, some of which, however, had been translated into English. *The Renegado* is traceable to a comedy of Cervantes, *Los Baños de Argel,* printed in 1615. *The Emperor of the East* is derived from a French translation of Zonaras. If, which is doubtful, *The Duke of Milan* owes anything to Guicciardini, his history had appeared in an English translation by Sir Geoffrey Fenton in 1579. Fleay has a curious theory that where French scenes are found in Fletcher they are due to Massinger.

Much interesting information on the great debt which

Duke of Florence, II., 2, 5-21, rather suggests a visit to
Italy. Nor have we any ground for supposing that he
was, like Shakspere, an actor, unless indeed an obscure
reference in the Dublin poem to the Earl of Pembroke be
so interpreted.[1] In London he lived on the Bankside,
Southwark. The story of his death is told us by our
gossiping old friend Anthony à Wood, in his *Athenae
Oxonienses*.[2] Massinger went to bed one night well, and

Fletcher and other dramatists owed to Spanish literature will
be found in F. E. Schelling's *Elizabethan Drama*, vol. ii.,
pp. 205-218 and 530. Schelling comes to the conclusion
that Fletcher did not know Spanish; but he quotes an unpublished dictum of his friend Dr. Rosenbach, who holds it as
certain that Massinger knew Spanish. *The Island Princess*
is based on a Spanish play, of which no translation is known,
Conquista de las islas Malucas, by De Argensola, 1609. Rosenbach attributes the play to Massinger ! It is clear, however,
that a translation may have been in circulation from which
Fletcher took his materials, or somebody may have seen the
play acted in Spain, and reported it to him. Further, *Love's
Cure* is based on the *Comedia de la Fuerza de la Costumbre*, by
Guillen De Castro, licensed at Valencia, February 7th, 1625,
and published three months later. Fletcher died in August,
1625, and Stiefel thinks that he read Spanish, and that this
is his last work. Rosenbach and Bullen assign the play to
Massinger (*cf.* Appendix III., No. 29). It is highly desirable
that the grounds which led Rosenbach to believe that Massinger knew Spanish should be made public.

[1] Lines 39-45 run thus:

> Let them write well that do this, and in grace.
> I would not for a pension or a place
> Part so with over candour: let me rather
> Live poorly on those toys I would not father;
> Not known beyond a player or a man,
> That does pursue the course that I have ran,
> Ere so grow famous.

Lines 41-42 are interesting as seeming to hint that Massinger preferred to waive publicity as to his collaboration with
Fletcher and others. The poem was published by A. B.
Grosart in *Englische Studien*, xxvi., pp. 1-7, and will be found
with the original spelling and punctuation in Appendix XVII.

[2] *A. O.*, ii., 654-656. A. à Wood includes in the list of
Massinger's plays *Powerful Favourite, or the Life of Sejanus*.
As Massinger was but nineteen in 1603 he cannot have been

was found dead the next morning. He was buried at St. Saviour's on March 18th, 1639/40.[1] The funeral was "accompanied by comedians," a phrase which seems to show that his professional friends did him honour at the last; he is described in the monthly accounts of St. Saviour's as "a stranger "—that is to say, a non-parishioner. His intimate friend Sir Aston Cokaine tells us that he shared the grave of his friend John Fletcher;[2] and in 1896 a window in the south aisle of the nave of Southwark Cathedral was unveiled in his honour by Sir Walter Besant.[3]

What was the atmosphere in which Massinger lived ? The days of James I. and Charles I. were less heroic than those of Elizabeth. In foreign politics England intervened once or twice in an ineffective way, and a good deal of sympathy was shown, much of it in a practical fashion, for the cause of the Protestant King of Bohemia. Gardiner[4] has pointed out that Charles I. gave permission to the Marquis of Hamilton to carry over volunteers in aid of Gustavus Adolphus just as James I. had allowed

---

the "happy genius" referred to in the address "to the readers" of Ben Jonson's play. For the explanation of the mistaken attribution of *The Powerful Favourite, cf.* Appendix XIV.

[1] Gifford was right as to the date and Cunningham wrong. The entry in question is as follows: "March 18th, 1639 [*i.e.*, old style], Philip Massenger, a stranger." The entry about Fletcher runs thus: "Aug. 29, 1625, John Ffletcher [sic], a man, in the church." Entries such as "a man," "a boy," "a girl" are not unusual in the book, and the practice of burial "in the church" was comparatively common at the time.

[2] The stone inscribed with his name in the chancel of St. Saviour's does not mark the place of his burial, which is unknown.

[3] By a charming if undesigned coincidence the Massinger window stands next to that of Shakspere. It represents two scenes from *The Virgin Martyr*, and, unfortunately, repeats the erroneous date (1639) of the poet's death, and gives 1583 as the year of his birth.

[4] *Contemporary Review*, August, 1876.

Vere to carry over volunteers to the Palatinate. Hamilton sailed in July, 1631, and *The Maid of Honour* was printed in 1632. The whole plot of this play recalls the relations of England to the Protestant cause on the Continent. Thus, William, Lord Craven, to whom Ford's *Broken Heart* is dedicated, and who was knighted at the age of seventeen, after his " valiant adventures " in the Netherlands under Henry, Prince of Orange, went to the assistance of Gustavus Adolphus in 1631, when only twenty-two years old.

Wars in the Low Countries are vaguely referred to in various passages, as, *e.g.*, in *The Fatal Dowry*:[1]

NOVALL JUN. Oh, fie upon him, how he wears his clothes !
As if he had come this Xmas. from S. Omer's
To see his friends, and return'd after Twelfth-tide.

The date of the play is uncertain, but it must have been written some considerable time before being printed in 1632.[2] In *The New Way to pay Old Debts* Lord Lovell "has purchas'd a fair name in the wars."[3] In *The Fatal Dowry*, *The Picture*, and *The Unnatural Combat*, we have the familiar type of the brave soldier who is disregarded in time of peace, and has come down to poverty and old clothes.

---

[1] II., 2, 140.

[2] Intercourse with the Low Countries is referred to in the *New Way* (I., 2, 75). The monastery to which Sir John Frugal retires is at "Lovain" (*City Madam*, III., 2, 58). *Cf.* also for the University of "Lovain" *The Elder Brother*, II., 1.

[3] III., 1, 38. *Cf.* also Frank Wellborn's petition, V., 1, *ad finem*. Compare the part played in *Sir John Barnavelt* by the English mercenaries in Holland; and especially IV., 2.

ORANGE. I have sent patents out for the choicest companies
Hither to be remov'd, first Colonel Vere's
From Dort, next Sir Charles Morgan's, a stout Company.

IV., 3. BARNAVELT (*to his daughter*):
What ! wouldst thou have a husband ?
Go marry an English Captain, and he'll teach thee
How to defy thy father and his fortune.

In the wider world of Europe the Turk and the Algerine pirate are still grim realities enough to form an effective scenic background.[1] Indeed, it was not so very long since the Battle of Lepanto. We find constant references to galley-slaves,[2] to the slave market,[3] and to apostates to Islam.[4] In the opening scene of *The Picture* the soldier husband parts from his wife on the frontier of Bohemia " not distant from the Turkish camp above five leagues." One of the objections urged against the new custom of fighting duels is that thereby lives are lost which might have done service against the Turk.[5] The age of chivalry has its faint reflection in schemes to "redeem Christian slaves chain'd in the Turkish servitude" by force of arms, and in the prowess of the Knights of Malta.[6] The wealth and power of Turkey are taken for

---

II., 1. BARNAVELT:

But have you tried by any means (it skills not
How much you promise) to win th' old soldier
(The English Companies in chief I aim at)
To stand firm for us ?

[1] *Unnatural Combat,* I., 1, 243, 278; *Great Duke of Florence,* I., 2, 62; II., 1, 145; *Picture,* I., 1, 3-5; *Guardian,* II., 1, 84; V., 4, 160; *Very Woman,* V., 5, 28. *Cf.* in Marlowe, *Tamburlaine,* Pt. I., III., 3; Pt. II., I., 2; *Jew of Malta.* I., 1; II. 2. For a Christian pirate *cf. Decameron,* II. 4.

[2] *Bondman,* IV., 3, 77; *Renegado,* IV., 1, 99-102; II., 6, 32.

[3] *A Very Woman,* III., 1.

[4] *Cf. The Unnatural Combat* and *The Renegado.*

[5] *Guardian,* II., 1, 84. Similarly in *The Bashful Lover,* V., 3, 110, Matilda warns Lorenzo that "Heaven's liberal hand" has designed him to fight rather against the Turk than a Christian neighbour-king. Compare *The Devil's Law-case* (p. 138*b*).

ERCOLE. When our bloods
Embrac'd each other, then I pitied
That so much valour should be hazarded
On the fortune of a single rapier
And not spent against the Turk.

[6] *Renegado,* II., 5, 24 and 64-73. Bertoldo, the Knight of Malta, is the hero of *The Maid of Honour.* *Cf.* also Fletcher's play of that name; and *Guardian,* V., 4, 143-145.

granted. When Malefort senior vows vengeance on Montreville, he cries out:

> The Turkish Empire offer'd for his ransom
> Should not redeem his life.[1]

At home we find the vices of a prolonged peace lending opportunity for some easy satire. On the whole, we may say that we do not learn very much about our country from the poet which we could not find in the other playwrights of the day. Let us rapidly put together some of his references. There were two Englands at this time, drifting inevitably apart, only to clash in fratricidal war under Charles I. The drama was becoming less and less national, more and more an affair of aristocratic patronage. Massinger does not often refer to the Puritans;[2] there is nothing so amusing in his plays as the passage in Fletcher's *Fair Maid of the Inn*, where the Pedant solicits the advice of Forobosco the quack about "erecting four new sects of religion at Amsterdam."[3] The fashionable love of astrology is satirized in *The City Madam*. The England of Massinger's plays is an England which loves expense,[4] amusements, Greek

---

[1] *Unnatural Combat*, V., 2, 230. We find a similar emphasis on the Turk and pirates in Webster's *White Devil* and *Devil's Law-case*.

[2] The "zealous coblers" and "learned botchers" who preach at Amsterdam are mentioned in *Renegado*, I., 1, 30-32. In *The Unnatural Combat*, III., 1, 75, the "Hugonots" are referred to as using the word "mortified." "Geneva print" is mentioned in *Duke of Milan*, I., 1, 11; "precisians" in *New Way*, I., 1, 6, use the word "verity."

[3] *Fair Maid*, IV., 2.

[4] *Very Woman*, III., 1, 124:

> MERCHANT. They have a city, Sir—I have been in it,
> And therefore dare affirm it—where if you saw
> With what a load of vanity 'tis fraughted,
> How like an everlasting morris-dance it looks,
> Nothing but hobby-horse and Maid Marian,
> You would start indeed.

wines,[1] masques,[2] new clothes,[3] and foreign fashions.[4]
London is a great port, with trade to the Indies and
aspirations after the " North passage." The jealousy of
the City and the Court, the ostentations of the one and
the refinement of the other, point the moral of *The City
Madam*.[5] The high-spirited 'prentices of the City of

---

[1] *Old Law*, IV., 1, 20; *New Way*, III., 2, 169; *Very Woman*,
III., 5, 29 and 70; *Renegado*, I., 3, 74. *Cf. Decameron*, II. 5.

[2] For the influence of the masque on Massinger, *cf. Picture*,
II., 2; *City Madam*, V., 3; *Guardian*, IV., 2.

[3] *Cf.* the characters of Simonides in *The Old Law* and
young Novall in *The Fatal Dowry*, II., 2; *Emperor of the East*,
I., 2, 21; *Picture*, II., 2, 29-36; *Very Woman*, III., 1, 131-2
Compare also *Henry VIII.*, I., 3.

[4] *Renegado*, III., 1, 57; *Guardian*, II., 1, 81. *Cf. Merchant
of Venice*, I., 2, 78-81; *As You Like It*, IV., 1, 34-40.

[5] The play ends thus:

Make you good
Your promised reformation, and instruct
Our city dames, whom wealth makes proud, to move
In their own spheres, and willingly to confess,
In their habits, manners, and their highest port,
A distance 'twixt the city and the court.

Cf. also *Maid of Honour*, III., 1, 84; *City Madam*, III., 2,
153; IV., 4, 43; *New Way*, II., 1, 81 and 88. In *The Renegado*,
I., 2, distinctions are drawn between the country ladies, the city
dames, and the court ladies of England. Compare also
the epilogue to *Henry VIII*:

Others, to hear the city
Abused extremely, and to cry 'that's witty.'

Rape of Lucrece, II., 1; II., 3; *The Devil is an Ass*, III., 1;
Westward Ho! I., 1; "I tell thee, there is equality enough
between a lady and a city dame if their hair be but of a
colour." Ford contrasts the ladies of the city and the court
in *The Broken Heart*, II., 1. In Dekker's *Shoemaker's Holiday*,
I., 1, the Lord Mayor says:

Too mean is my poor girl for his high birth,
Poor citizens must not with courtiers wed.

Cf. also *A Chaste Maid in Cheapside*, I., 1:

MAUDLIN. Besides, you have a presence, sweet
Sir Walter,
Able to dance a maid brought up in the city;
A brave court-spirit makes our virgins quiver.

London take the law into their own hands in days when
there are no police,[1] and their vices are satirized after
the manner of Ben Jonson in the same play. Horse-play,
such as tossing in a blanket, is considered a great joke.[2]
The balladmonger so often referred to in Shakspere is
much in evidence,[3] though indeed it was an age in which
everyone wrote poetry.[4] In rural England we find the
possibility of an unscrupulous local tyrant, such as is
depicted to us in Massinger's masterpiece, Sir Giles
Overreach, aided by his jackal, Mr. Justice Greedy.[5] That
our poet had a keen eye for social evils, for the man who
sells food at famine prices, the encloser of commons, the
usurer, the worker of iron, the cheating tradesman, is

Eastward Ho! deals with the same contrast. *Cf.* also the
Induction to *The Knight of the Burning Pestle*, and *ib.*, IV., 5;
Induction to *Four Plays in One.*

[1] *Renegado*, I., 3, 92-94; *City Madam*, I., 2, 34. *Cf. Henry
VIII.*, V., 4; *Shoemaker's Holiday*, V., 2; *The Honest Whore*,
Pt. I., III., 1; *Sir Thomas More*, II., 1.

[2] *Parliament of Love*, IV., 5, 12; *New Way*, II., 1, 142.
Cf. Epicoene, V., 1 *bis*; *Elder Brother*, IV., 3; *Honest Man's
Fortune*, V., 3; *Thierry and Theodoret*, II., 3.

[3] *Unnatural Combat*, III., 3, 35; IV., 2, 35; *Parliament of
Love*, IV., 5, 125, 126; *Bondman*, V., 3, 245-252; *Guardian*,
III., 3, 8; *City Madam*, IV., 1, 74; *Duke of Milan*, III., 2,
18. *Cf.* 1 *Henry IV.*, II., 2, 49; III., 1, 130; 2 *Henry IV.*, IV.,
3, 52-54; *Winter's Tale*, IV., 3, 181-263; V., 2, 25-27; *Antony
and Cleopatra*, V., 2, 215; *Queen of Corinth*, III., 1; *Spanish
Curate*, IV., 7; *False One*, I., 1; *Elder Brother*, IV., 4; *The
White Devil*, p. 23b; *The Devil's Law-case*, pp. 131b and 143b;
Love's Sacrifice, III., 1; IV., 1; *The Honest Whore*, Pt. I, I., 1;
Bartholomew Fair, Induction; II., 1; and III., 1; *Rape of
Lucrece*, II., 1; *Edward II.*, II., 2; *Orlando Furioso*, IV., 1;
George a Greene, IV., 2; *Parliament of Bees*, ch. v.

[4] *Renegado*, II., 4, 1. *Cf. Much Ado about Nothing*, V., 1, 295-
297; *A King and No King*, I., 2; IV., 2; *Four Plays in One;
Triumph of Love*, 4; *Little French Lawyer*, III., 2; *The False
One*, III., 2; IV., 3; *Lover's Progress*, I., 1; III., 4; V., 3;
Cupid's Revenge, II., 4; *James IV.*, 1, 2.

[5] *New Way*, especially II., 1; for the difficulty of getting
justice done for the poor, *cf. Unnatural Combat*, I., 1; *Fatal
Dowry*, I., 1, especially lines 67-80.

clear from a passage in *The Guardian*.[1] The beautiful description in the same play of the amusements of country life, the hunting and the hawking, with which Durazzo seeks to console his love-sick ward Caldoro,[2] probably takes one back to Massinger's own boyhood in Wiltshire. As we should expect, there is a good deal of riding in the country scenes.[3] The characters of Sir John Frugal, the successful merchant, and Mr. Plenty, the country gentle-man,[4] show us that the "John Bull" type of Englishman existed in those days.

The temptation to give a back-hand blow to one's own country in the course of a plot laid abroad is obvious and irresistible; where Shakspere had set the example others were sure to follow,[5] and Massinger does not spare the female sex of England. To judge by the passage in *The Renegado*,[6] the women of his day loved expense and luxury, and were very independent in their attitude to their husbands.[7] The humiliation of Lady Frugal and her two daughters after their extravagant ambitions is the point of *The City Madam*. The contrast between a uxorious husband and an imperious wife is one of Massinger's favourite effects.[8] Donusa's speech in her own

---

[1] II., 4, 79-106. The reference to the mills is as follows:
Builders of iron mills, that grub up forests
With timber trees for shipping.
Cf. Volpone, I., 1, 33-36.

[2] I., 1, 290-340.

[3] *E.g.*, in *The New Way* and *The Guardian*.

[4] *City Madam*.

[5] Thus Ford, in an interesting passage in *Love's Sacrifice*, I., 1, refers to the national love of self-depreciation among the English. *Cf.* also *Rape of Lucrece*, III., 5.

[6] I., 2, 22-49. *Cf.* also *Very Woman*, III., 1, 133-135; and Webster's *Westward Ho!* I., 1, and III., 3.

[7] *Cf. The Honest Whore*, Pt. II., IV., 1:
MATHEO. England is the only hell for horses, and only paradise for women. Also Lamira's words in *The Honest Man's Fortune*, III., 3.

[8] *Cf. Duke of Milan, Picture*, and *Roman Actor*. The Duke of "Pavy" in Ford's *Love's Sacrifice* is a slighter sketch of

defence in *The Renegado* might have been written by a suffragette of our own day.[1]

We do not get much direct evidence as to the characteristics of the playwright's audiences; Dr. Bradley has some good remarks on this subject.[2] "Nor is it credible that an appreciation of the best things was denied to the mob, which doubtless loved what we should despise; but appears also to have admired what we admire, and to have tolerated more poetry than most of us can stomach;" "the mass of the audience must have liked excitement, the open exhibition of violent and bloody deeds, and the intermixture of seriousness and mirth." Dr. Bradley points out elsewhere[3] that the Elizabethan actor probably spoke more rapidly than our modern actors. This would make soliloquies less tedious.

To turn to the politics of the age; the rift between the dynasty and the nation grew wider as the century advanced. Though Massinger died before the days of the Long Parliament, we can imagine that he would have been one of those who eventually fought under protest for the King. We find evidence in his plays for supposing that he belonged to the Conservative Opposition, like his patron Philip, the fourth Earl of Pembroke and Mont-

---

the same type. The worthlessness of Bianca in the same play is a measure of the moral gap between Massinger and Ford.

[1] *Renegado*, IV., 2, 116-143.

[2] Oxford Lectures on Poetry, pp. 363-365. *Cf.* also pp. 392-3.

[3] *Cf.* op. cit., p. 381. *Cf.* Prologue to *Henry VIII.*, line 13; Prologue to *Romeo and Juliet*, line 12, and Chorus to Act I. in *The Mayor of Queensborough.*

> If all my powers
> Can win the grace of two poor hours,
> Well apaid I go to rest.

Also Prologues to *Two Noble Kinsmen*, lines 28, 29; *Alchemist*, line 1; *Love's Pilgrimage*, line 8; *Lover's Progress*, line 18 ("*three* short hours"); and Shirley's Preface to the Folio of Beaumont and Fletcher.

gomery. He was a lover of liberty, and there are one or
two indications that his plays offended the strict ideas
of Charles I.'s censorship.

Sir Henry Herbert, the Master of the Revels, refused
on January 11th, 1630/31, to license one of his plays[1]
because "it did contain dangerous matter, as the deposing
of Sebastian King of Portugal by Philip II., and there
being a peace sworn 'twixt the Kings of England and
Spain."[2] The same worthy records that King Charles I.
himself read another of his plays,[3] while staying at New-
market, and wrote against one passage, "This is too
insolent, and to be changed." The passage, which is put
into the mouth of a King of Spain, runs as follows:

> Monies! we'll raise supplies what way we please
> And force you to subscribe to blanks, in which
> We'll mulct you, as we think fit. The Caesars
> In Rome were wise, acknowledging no laws
> But what their swords did ratify; the wives
> And daughters of the senators bowing to
> Their will as deities.[4]

These lines clearly reflect on the autocratic methods
which prevailed in England from 1629 to 1640.

There is much in Timoleon's speeches in the senate[5]
which seems to contain covert references to the England

---

[1] *Cf.* Malone's *Shakspere* (edition 1790), vol. i., pt. 2, p. 226.
Believe as You List probably represents an adaptation of this
play, with classical names and setting substituted for the
original plot. *Cf.* Appendix VII.

[2] Chapman had to suppress a considerable part of *The
Tragedy of Byron,* which referred to quite recent events in
France. But the censorship seems to have become much
more stringent in Massinger's days.

[3] *The King and the Subject;* now lost. The play was performed, after alterations had been made, under another title.
Sir H. Herbert wrote, "Received of Mr. Lowen's for my paines
about Massinger's play called *The King and the Subject,* 2nd
June, 1638, £1."

[4] Malone's *Shakspere* (ed. 1790), vol. i., pt. 2, p. 235.

[5] *Bondman,* I., 3.

of the day, and notably in lines 203-213, where the unprepared state of the army and navy is referred to.

It has been thought with much probability that the Duke of Buckingham is satirized in the slight sketch of Gisco in *The Bondman*,[1] and in the more fully drawn character of Fulgentio in *The Maid of Honour*:[2]

ADORNI. Pray you, sir, what is he ?
ASTUTIO. A gentleman, yet no lord. He hath some drops
Of the king's blood running in his reins, derived
Some ten degrees off. His revenue lies
In a narrow compass, the king's ear; and yields him
Every hour a fruitful harvest. Men may talk
Of three crops in a year in the Fortunate Islands,
Or profit made by wool; but, while there are suitors,
His sheepshearing, nay, shaving to the quick
Is in every quarter of the moon, and constant.
In the time of trussing a point, he can undo
Or make a man; his play or recreation
Is to raise this up, or pull down that, and though
He never yet took orders, makes more bishops
In Sicily than the Pope himself.

The grumbling of the professional soldier against the royal favourite inspires a passage in *The Duke of Milan*.[3] A similar freedom of speech is found in *The Maid of Honour;* for instance, in the following passages:

GASPARO.   When you know what 'tis,
You will think otherwise; no less will do it
Than fifty thousand crowns.

CAMIOLA.   A pretty sum,
The price weighed with the purchase; fifty thousand !
To the king 'tis nothing. He that can spare more
To his minion for a masque, cannot but ransom
Such a brother at a million.[4]

---

[1] I., 1, 49-56. *Cf.* also *Great Duke of Florence*, I., 1, 75-84. Sanazarro is one of the better type of favourites.
[2] I., 1, 23-36.   [3] III., 1, 10-17.   [4] III., 3, 135.

CAMIOLA.   With your leave, I must not kneel, sir,
While I reply to this, but thus rise up
In my defence, and tell you, as a man
(Since, when you are unjust, the deity,
Which you may challenge as a king, parts from you,)
'Twas never read in holy writ, or moral,
That subjects on their loyalty, were obliged
To love their sovereign's vices; your grace, sir,
To such an undeserver is no virtue.[1]

There are also passages in *The Emperor of the East*
which seem to attack the Government of the day and its
agents.[2] I will quote the chief of these as a specimen of
honest indignation:

PULCHERIA.   How I abuse
This precious time ! Projector, I treat first
Of you and your disciples; you roar out,
All is the king's, his will above his laws;
And that fit tributes are too gentle yokes
For his poor subjects; whispering in his ear,
If he would have their fear, no man should dare
To bring a salad from his country garden,
Without the paying gabel; kill a hen,
Without excise; and that if he desire
To have his children or his servants wear
Their heads upon their shoulders, you affirm
In policy 'tis fit the owner should
*1st
quarto,
"pole."* Pay for them by the poll; or, if the prince wants
A present sum he may command a city
Impossibilities, and for non-performance
Compel it to submit to any fine
His officers shall impose. Is this the way
To make our emperor happy ? Can the groans
Of his subjects yield him music ? Must his thoughts
Be wash'd with widows' and wrong'd orphans' tears,
Or his power grow contemptible ?[3]

---

[1] IV., 5, 52. *Cf.* also *Great Duke of Florence*, I., 1, 73-84.
[2] *Cf.* especially the offer made by the Informer to Paulinus,
I., 2, 69-89.
[3] I., 2, 236-257.

The Englishman's love of liberty inspires a vigorous speech delivered by the British slave in *The Virgin Martyr*.[1]

Further, the impatience which Englishmen felt from time to time at the poor part played by their country in the Thirty Years' War is reflected in *The Maid of Honour*. Bertoldo there gets leave from the King of Sicily to go to help the beleaguered Duke of Urbin. He is, however, disavowed by the crafty, peace-loving king. In the debate Bertoldo describes Sicily in language which might easily be applied to England, and then proceeds in an eloquent passage to refer to England's glorious naval tradition in the past:

> BERTOLDO.   If examples
> May move you more than arguments, look on England,
> The empress of the European isles,
> And unto whom alone ours yields precedence:
> When did she flourish so, as when she was
> The mistress of the ocean, her navies
> Putting a girdle round about the world ?
> When the Iberian quaked, her worthies named;
> And the fair flower-de-luce grew pale, set by
> The red rose and the white ! Let not our armour
> Hung up, or our unrigg'd Armada make us
> Ridiculous to the late poor snakes, our neighbours,
> Warm'd in our bosoms, and to whom again
> We may be terrible.[2]

Here, at any rate, Massinger differs from Shakspere, who makes no reference to the exploits of our sailors; indeed, it would seem that, like Trafalgar, the defeat of the Armada had no significance for its own generation.[3] But we must not forget that Massinger was the bosom

---

[1] IV., 1, 136-147.   [2] I., 1, 220-233.

[3] Middleton refers to "the great Armada" in *A Trick to Catch the Old One*, III., 4; Dampit: "In Anno '88, when the great Armada was coming." *Cf. The Alchemist*, IV., 2.

friend of Fletcher, in whose plays sailors occur again and again.[1]

The fact that Massinger was a Cavalier " Radical," a free lance and grumbler of the Opposition, may in part explain his struggles and his poverty. His natural patrons may have looked askance at his independent attitude, so alien to the passive obedience preached by Fletcher. But, whatever were his politics, it is clear that he was no Puritan. Brought up in close contact with a noble house, educated at Oxford, and well versed in the classics,[2] as many allusions in his works testify, he shows alike in his merits and his faults the Cavalier mind. To this extent he may be judged " *felix opportunitate mortis*," for of all sections of the nation those whose hearts were with the King, and their reason with the Opposition, had the hardest part to play after 1640.

In the department of literature the talent of the country had concentrated itself more and more on playwriting. Among Massinger's contemporaries we note Jonson, Chapman, Fletcher, Beaumont, Webster, Middleton, Dekker, Heywood, Rowley, Tourneur, Shirley—all keen and able dramatists. Massinger, in his grasp of stagecraft, his flexible metre, his desire in the sphere of ethics to exploit both vice and virtue, is typical of an age which had much culture, but which, without being exactly corrupt, lacked moral fibre.

His plays may be divided into three classes: first, those which have come down to us under his name; secondly,

---

[1] *Cf.* Champernal in *The Little French Lawyer*, and Alberto in *The Fair Maid of the Inn*. Notice too the zest with which Valerio (*A Wife for a Month*, V., 3) describes the sea-action with the Turks.

[2] The question whether Massinger knew Greek is discussed in Appendix II. To take one play only, *The Maid of Honour*, we find classical allusions in I., 1, 240; I., 2, 36, 107-128; II., 1, 48; II., 2, 23; II., 3, 26; II., 4, 17; II., 5, 13, 28; III., 1, 29; III., 1, 194; IV., 4, 13; IV., 4, 97, 108, 109; IV., 4, 140-145.

those which he wrote with Fletcher or other authors; and, thirdly, those which have disappeared. It is not easy to draw the border-line between the first and second classes. In the last forty years the students of English literature have devoted much attention to verse and other tests, and there are those who profess themselves competent to decide which parts of a composite play were written by the various collaborators. It is clear that the use of these tests requires caution. An author may sometimes experiment in the style of somebody else; it has been held that Shakspere wrote *Henry VIII* in the manner of Fletcher, his younger rival; and Delius was of opinion that *The Two Noble Kinsmen* is due to two imitators, one of Shakspere and one of Fletcher. Boyle speaks confidently as follows:[1] " Mr. Fleay used almost exclusively versification to distinguish author from author. Nor is this by any means so bold an undertaking as it seems. I have used other tests apart from the versification, and have almost uniformly found the impressions derived from the latter correct." Our confidence in Boyle is shaken when he attributes[2] the first two acts of *A New Way to pay Old Debts* to Fletcher on the evidence of the double endings. He points out that the allusion to the taking of Breda on July 1st, 1625,[3] is just possible, as Fletcher was buried on August 29th, 1625. This is clearly a case where we must take other than metrical considerations into account. Has the comedy the sparkle, the bustle, and the improbability of Fletcher ?

Again, it is not too much to say that it is a waste of time to apply verse tests to Tourneur; a great part of the *Atheist's Tragedy* is not poetry at all, but prose measured off in engths.

The Virgin Martyr states on its title-page that Dekker was part author. Similarly, *The Fatal Dowry* was partly

---

[1] *N. S. S.*, xxvi., p. 581.   [2] *Englische Studien*, V., 93.
[3] I., 2, 27.

due to Field. Part of *A Very Woman*[1] is held by many critics to be written by Fletcher; certainly the style of the play is in places more tender and more racy than we should expect from Massinger. *The Old Law* is said to have been written by Massinger, Middleton, and Rowley. It was a popular play, and often revived; its first appearance was in 1599,[2] when our poet was but fifteen years old. His share in it must therefore consist of additions or modifications at a later date. Certainly there is little in the play which reminds one of him; original as is its plot, and tender its pathos, both its tragedy and comedy are in a simpler manner than his.[3]

On the other hand, Boyle arrives at some startling results when he investigates the works of Fletcher.[4] He attributes to Massinger parts of *Thierry and Theodoret*, *The Queen of Corinth*, *The Knight of Malta*, *The Custom of the Country*, *The Little French Lawyer*, *The Fair Maid of the Inn*, and of several other plays.[5]

It may appear strange that in order to estimate Massinger we should have to read Fletcher as well; but to this the scientific study of English brings us.[6] Boyle

---

[1] Also called *The Prince of Tarent*. It would have been easier for Fletcher to imitate Massinger than for Massinger to imitate Fletcher. The pathos and comedy of the latter were alike out of our author's range.

[2] III., 1, 39. [3] See discussion on p. 141.

[4] *Cf.* Appendix III.

[5] The question suggests itself at once: Did Massinger ever collaborate with Beaumont ? Mr. Macaulay does not face this problem in his interesting monograph on Beaumont; indeed, he ignores Massinger's undoubted claims to have collaborated with Fletcher, though he makes full amends for this omission in his article in the *Cambridge History of English Literature*. Boyle at one time thought that Massinger worked with Beaumont and Fletcher in *The Honest Man's Fortune* and *The Knight of Malta* (*N. S. S.*, pp. 589-590).

[6] From the nature of the case the idea is not new; thus Weber, in the Preface to the 1812 Edinburgh edition of Beaumont and Fletcher, attributes the completion of *The Lover's Progress, Love's Pilgrimage*, and the character of

declares that "we ought in future to have no more editions of Beaumont and Fletcher, but the plays of Beaumont, Fletcher, and Massinger arranged in nine groups."[1] The verdict of experts cannot be disregarded in this matter; there is a real danger that Massinger's merits will be underrated if we do not attempt to estimate the share which he took in writing the plays attributed to Fletcher. His friend Sir Aston Cokaine might have done us a great service here, but, unfortunately, he missed his opportunity. In a poem[2] relating to Shirley's edition of Beaumont and Fletcher's works published in 1647,[3] he points out that the title is inaccurate for two reasons: first, because many of the plays were written after Beaumont's death; secondly, because Massinger wrote parts of some of them; it is a great pity that he did not tell us which these plays were.

But worse still remains behind; if we are to believe Boyle, it is practically certain that Massinger and Fletcher wrote *Henry VIII*[4] and *The Two Noble Kins-*

Septimius in *The False One* to Massinger. Fleay (*Shakespeare Manual*, p. 152) makes out a list of ten of Fletcher's plays in which he traces Massinger's hand. *Cf.* Appendix III.

[1] *Eng. St.*, VII., 75.

[2] Reprinted 1877. Congleton. A copy of the original book is to be seen at Shakspere's birthhouse, Stratford-on-Avon.

[3] An inauspicious date for such a publication!

[4] There are many touches in *Henry VIII* which remind one of Massinger; and not a few passages in Massinger remind one of *Henry VIII*. Take as an example *City Madam*, III., 2, 111.

> LUKE.   O my lord!
> This heap of wealth, which you possess me of,
> Which to a worldly man had been a blessing,
> And to the messenger might with justice challenge
> A kind of adoration, is to me
> A curse I cannot thank you for; and, much less
> Rejoice in that tranquillity of mind
> My brother's vows must purchase. I have made
> A dear exchange with him: he now enjoys
> My peace and poverty, the trouble of
> His wealth conferr'd on me; and that a burthen
> Too heavy for my weak shoulders.

men.[1] It must be pointed out that there are still good critics who attribute a large part of *Henry VIII* to Shakspere, and a small part of *The Two Noble Kinsmen.* It would take us too far from our subject to enter in detail on these two difficult problems.[2]

Then, in the third place, there are the plays that are lost. In the eighteenth century there was a certain John Warburton, F.R.S. and F.S.A., Somerset herald, who collected no fewer than fifty-five genuine unpublished dramas of the golden period, which he handed over to the care of his cook until he could find someone to publish them. The cook appropriated these plays leaf by leaf for coverings for her pastry, and a certain number of Massinger's—possibly as many as ten—perished among them. Here are the names of some of them: *The Forced*

> LORD LACY.   Honest Soul,
> With what feeling he receives it !

Or this from *The Bashful Lover*, IV., 2, 87.

> ALONSO.   She cause, alas !
> Her innocence knew no guilt, but too much favour,
> To me unworthy of it; 'twas my baseness,
> My foul ingratitude—what shall I say more ?
> The good Octavio no sooner fell
> In the displeasure of his prince, his state
> Confiscated, and he forced to leave the Court,
> And she exposed to want; but all my oaths
> And protestation of service to her,
> Like seeming flames, raised by enchantment, vanish'd;
> This, this sits heavy here.

Cf. also *City Madam*, I., 2, 126-134. I feel inclined to say that Massinger knew *Henry VIII* by heart. *Cf. infra*, pp. 84, 85.

[1] *The Two Noble Kinsmen* is a remarkable play, full of fine poetry and lofty thought. On the other hand, its technique is very immature. The Gaoler's daughter's soliloquies are inartistic, and at times ludicrous. The play has at once the dignity of an early period and the complexity of style with which we are familiar in Shakspere's later manner. One thing is clear: Act I. is by a different hand from the rest. Perhaps Shakspere and Fletcher touched up an old anonymous play.

See, however, discussion *infra*, pp. 84-104.

Lady, a tragedy; *The Noble Choice*, a comedy; *The Wandering Lovers*, a comedy; *Philenzo and Hippolita*, a tragi-comedy.[1]

It may be a consolation when we grieve over this disaster[2] to reflect that many of the fifty-five plays may not have been worth reading; eight of them were early works of Massinger's, and may have been immature or even unsuccessful. There is a presumption in favour of this supposition, for his more famous plays appeared separately in quarto, and most of them can still be procured from dealers in that form; we must suppose that Mr. Warburton had only what are called actors'—*i.e.*, manuscript—copies. If a play never attained the distinction of being printed there may have been some defect which militated against its success.

Colonel Cunningham in his edition gives us the names of thirty-seven plays in all from Massinger's pen; if the many be added to this total in which he joined with other writers, we have a considerable literary output for a life of fifty-five years.

Massinger, like Shakspere, fell into disfavour after the Restoration, when Beaumont and Fletcher carried everything before them. We learn from Malone's Preface[3] that *The Bondman* was acted in 1661 and *The Virgin Martyr* on January 10th, 1662; *The Renegado* on June 6th in the same year. Pepys saw *The Virgin Martyr*, and liked it,[4] more, however, for the music than the words. Dryden and Jeremy Collier never mention Massinger. Selections from *The Guardian* appeared in prose form, with insertions from *A Very Woman*, in

---

[1] *Cf.* Appendix V.

[2] Mr. Halliwell Philipps, in his MS. note to *Believe as You List*, now in the British Museum, expresses himself as sceptical of the Warburton legend. *Cf.* Greg's *Bakings of Betsy* (*Library*, July, 1911).

[3] Shakspere, III., p. 275. *Cf.* Downes' *Roscius Anglicanus*, pp. 18, 52.

[4] Diary, 1848 edition, I., p. 192; IV., p. 373.

1680, under the title *Love Lost in the Dark, or the Drunken Couple*. Adorio and the other names are the same, but the Guardian's part disappears, and his remarks are put in Adorio's mouth. A servant, Calandrino, is brought in, whose name is borrowed from *The Great Duke of Florence*, and Muggulla, a nurse, is added to be Calandrino's bride. The contents are worthy of the title. Monck Mason deplores the fact that Johnson's dictionary does not once quote Massinger or Beaumont and Fletcher. "They are more correct," he says, "and grammatical than Shakspere, and appear to have had a more competent knowledge of other languages, which gave them a more accurate idea of their own." There was a great reaction in the eighteenth century in favour of Massinger. Brander Matthews points out that *The New Way* is the only Elizabethan or Jacobean play, except Shakspere's, which held the stage until the first quarter of the nineteenth century,[1] and gives a good history of its illustrious career on the English and American stages.

The critics have differed much about Massinger. Gifford[2] and Hallam were enthusiastic in their support; Charles Lamb and Hazlitt[3] were against him, perhaps because they disliked his able Tory editor. The eighteenth-century writers regarded him as the champion of female virtue; and in our own time Sir A. Ward has defended his manly and sane morality in unhesitating language.[4] On the other hand, Boyle deems his heroines to be corrupt and his heroes "the victims of one devour-

---

[1] Gayley's *Representative English Comedies*, p. 319.

[2] Gifford's edition of Massinger, in four volumes, is one of the classics of our literature, though careless in details.

[3] To Hazlitt, however, we owe, in his estimate of Sir Giles Overreach, one of the most brilliant pieces of English prose that we possess.

[4] (*E. D. L.*, iii., p. 42) "In Massinger we seem to recognize a man who firmly believes in the eternal difference between right and wrong, and never consciously swerves aside from the canon he acknowledges."

ing passion, often in a state of incipient madness, alternately raging and melancholy."[1]

Like Euripides, Ovid, and Juvenal, Massinger is a writer whose faults are patent; all the more important, therefore, is it to make his merits quite clear. We cannot convince the world if we adopt the famous line of Goethe's heroine:

I cannot reason, I can only feel.[2]

I do not indeed claim to discover much that is new about Massinger, nor to reverse the judgment of time. He is, and he remains, in the second rank of English writers. But it would be a misfortune if undue obscurity were to befall an author who was at once so manly and so skilful. I take up the cudgels for him, partly because the balance of critical judgment has of late gone too far against him; and yet in a sense he has only come into his own in the last thirty years, by reason of the unanimity with which so much good strong work in Fletcher's plays is now deemed to be due to him. He has received much praise and much blame; I should like by careful analysis of the problem to arrive at a juster judgment. But in the main, I must confess, I plead for Massinger because I love him.

What, then, are the chief merits of our author ? They are three: his stagecraft, his style, and his metre. And, first, his command of stagecraft has been universally conceded.[3] This is an important point; it is as much as to say that the plays are readable and would act well;[4]

---

[1] *N. S. S.*, xxvi., p. 586.

[2] *Iphigenia auf Tauris*, IV., 4: "Ich untersuche nicht, ich fühle nur."

[3] **Dr.** Bradley (*Oxford Lectures*, p. 383) points out that " the average play of Shakspere's day has great merits of a strictly dramatic kind, but it is not ' well-built,' it is not what we mean by ' a good play.' " He traces this fault to the multiplication of scenes, which the absence of scenery in those days made easy.

[4] Gayley points out (*R. E. C.*, p. xci.) that, "Shakspere and

when you begin one of them you wish to know what is going to happen. The first act has usually a great breadth and swing; it is admirably proportioned and dignified. The chief characters are introduced, and the train is well laid, without stiffness or delay. Good examples of this fact are to be found in *The Bondman* and *The Emperor of the East*. In *The Renegado* the first scene at once reveals the object of the plot, the rescue of Paulina. In *The Bondman* Marullo enters at line 38, and our attention is called to him by Leosthenes. As the play progresses you feel that it is what the French call *bien charpenté*— well constructed. If, as is often the case, there is a mystery or a secret, it is sufficiently well kept to excite the curiosity. The author does not depend very much on soliloquies or disguises; he does not, as a rule, complicate matters by underplots and cross-interests. The stage is not overcrowded; you do not feel the need of constantly referring to the list of *dramatis personae*. A curious instance of this economy is *The Maid of Honour*, where there is no Queen of Sicily. Minor characters when they reappear are recognized and provided for, as, for example, Calypso in *The Guardian* (IV., 3). The conscientious author forgets no detail in order to round off his plot; thus in the same play the blow struck at the beginning is apologized for in V., 3, 250. Nor is there a reckless change of scene. Moreover, a lifelike effect is given by the fact that speeches generally end in the middle of a line. As so often in Euripides, the people say the sort of things that under the circumstances you would expect them to say in real life.[1] A comparison of Mas-

---

Fletcher excepted, Massinger has been adjudged by posterity the most successful of the practical dramatists of the early seventeenth century." He suggests (*R. E. C.*, p. xcv.) that with slight and judicious modification an enterprising actor-manager might successfully produce *A New Way*, *The Maid of Honour*, *The City Madam*, and perhaps *The Bondman*.

[1] Aristotle, *Rhetoric*, III., p. 1404*b*.

singer with Ben Jonson will make this ease of construction clear at once. Köppel has noted the skill with which the narratives of Suetonius and Dion Cassius are combined in *The Roman Actor*. It may sound obvious to add that the titles of the plays correspond to the chief subject-matter, were it not that in so many of the Elizabethan plays this is not the case. Take as examples Middleton's *Changeling* and *Mayor of Queenborough*.

Yet it would be too much to say that all Massinger's plays are equally successful in this respect. The plot of *The Guardian*, for example, is unusually intricate. Like Shakspere, he occasionally crowds too much into the fifth act—for instance, in *The Unnatural Combat*. The device of the apple which produces so much jealousy and trouble in *The Emperor of the East* is rather trivial for a tragi-comedy.[1] The promise of Cleora to wear a scarf over her eyes until her jealous lover returns from the war is exasperating.[2] Again, Camiola in *The Maid of Honour* (III., 3, 200) forgets that Bertoldo is " bound to a single life," as she had herself pointed out to him (I., 2, 148). Nor does Bertoldo (IV., 3, 100) in his acceptance of her offer say anything about the necessary dispensation. On the other hand, Massinger avoids those scenes on board ship of which Fletcher is so fond, and which on the Jacobean stage must have been ineffective to the spectators, and indeed, are so on any stage.[3]

Similarly, it is clear that torture on the stage can hardly be made effective.[4]

---

[1] IV., 2. On the other hand, we should remember that our author did not invent this incident, but took it from Byzantine history. *Cf.* Gibbon's *Decline and Fall*, chapter xxxii.

[2] *Bondman*, II., 1, 187. *Cf.* ὁ ἄφωνος in Ar. *Poetics*, 1460 a. 32.

[3] *Cf. The Sea Voyage* and *The Double Marriage*.

[4] *Roman Actor*, III., 2, 71; *Virgin Martyr*, V., 2, 206. *Cf.* Dr. Bradley's remarks (*Oxford Lectures*, p. 366, note) on the blinding of Gloucester in *King Lear*. When the Duke in Ford's *Love's Sacrifice* (V., 3) stabs himself and cries aloud:

One of Massinger's favourite devices is to combine subordinates. He has learnt from *Hamlet* the lesson of Rosencrantz and Guildenstern. He has studied the method of such scenes as *Henry V.*, I., 2, 97-135; II., 2; III., 5; III., 7. If something has to be done, two or three people express their eagerness to do it. If someone has to be persuaded, two or three of the characters press home the various arguments. This all works for lucidity and ease, and presents a lifelike combination on the stage.[1] Instances of the device abound; let us take one from *The Picture*.[2] The great soldier Ferdinand, on his return from

---

> Sprightful flood,
> Run out in rivers ! O, that these thick streams
> Could gather head, and make a standing pool,
> That jealous husbands here might bathe in blood;

the words can only produce an anticlimax in the spectator's mind, however effective they may be to the reader. Massinger is more dexterous in *The Fatal Dowry*, IV., 4, 154: "Yes, sir; this is her heart's blood, is it not ? I think it be." There is a similar difficulty about D'Amville in *The Atheist's Tragedy* (V., 2) knocking out his brains with the executioner's axe; and about Scaevola in *The Rape of Lucrece* (V. 4) burning off his hand. *Cf.* also Bajazet and Zabina in *Tamburlaine*, Pt. I., V., 1, and Tamburlaine himself in Pt. II., III., 2.

[1] Needless to say, the idea is not original; it is already a marked feature of Marlowe's *Tamburlaine* and *Faustus ;* but the device does not often work so smoothly as in Massinger.

[2] II., 2, 59-77. *Cf. The Virgin Martyr*, I., 1 (the three kings); *Emperor of the East*, II., 1 (Theodosius and his courtiers); *A New Way*, I., 3, 43 (the servants); *City Madam*, IV., 1 (Luke and the three creditors); IV., 2 (Luke and the two apprentices); *Bashful Lover*, I., 1 (Matilda and the waiting-women); V., 1 (Octavio and three friends); *Bondman*, I., 3 (Timoleon and four senators); *Unnatural Combat*, II., 2 (Theocrine and three attendants); *Great Duke of Florence*, I., 2 (three councillors); II., 2; V., 2 and 3 (Cozimo and courtiers); *Guardian*, IV., 4 (Severino and four banditti); *Maid of Honour*, I., 1 (Bertoldo and the two heirs "city bred"); *Roman Actor*, IV., 1, 98; V., 1, 213 (the three tribunes); V. 2, 1-19 (the conspirators); *Duke of Milan* I., 3, *ad init.* (three gentlemen). We find this method again and again in Webster; *cf. The Duchess of Malfi*, p. 63a; p. 78b; p. 80b; *The White Devil*, p. 56; p. 42a; *The Devil's Law-case*, p. 111b;

the wars, is received courteously by the old Counsellor
Eubulus, but the fashionable young men, Ubaldo and
Ricardo, think they can do the thing better; the passage
runs thus:

> RICARDO.   This was pretty;
> But second me now; I cannot stoop too low
> To do your excellence that due observance
> Your fortune claims.
>   EUBULUS.   He ne'er thinks on his virtues !
>   RICARDO. For, being as you are, the soul of soldiers,
> And bulwark of Bellona——
>   UBALDO.   The protection
> Both of the court and king——
>   RICARDO.   And the sole minion
> Of mighty Mars——
>   UBALDO.   One that with justice may
> Increase the number of the worthies——
>   EUBULUS.   Heyday !
>   RICARDO. It being impossible in my arms to circle
> Such giant worth——
>   UBALDO.   At distance we presume
> To kiss your honour'd gauntlet.
>   EUBULUS.   What reply now
> Can he make to this foppery ?
>   FERDINAND.   You have said,
> Gallants, so much and hitherto done so little,
> That till I learn to speak and you to do,
> I must take time to thank you.
>   EUBULUS.   As I live,
> Answer'd as I could wish, how the fops gape now !
>   RICARDO. This was harsh and scurvy.
>   UBALDO.   We will be revenged,
> When he comes to court the ladies, and laugh at him.

Another of Massinger's effective devices is to sustain
the interest of the spectators by concealing characters

---

p. 116a. Cf. also Cymbal and Fitton in *The Staple of News*,
I., 2; and the three courtiers in *Cupid's Revenge*.

and facts; thus, in *The Duke of Milan* we do not fathom for some time the villainy of Francisco; in *The City Madam* we ponder from the beginning over the obscure character of Luke. The best instances of this expedient are to be found in *The Unnatural Combat* and *The Bondman*. The air of gloom which overhangs the former tragedy is as great in its way as anything which our author has attained; and though the play is what we may call Elizabethan rather than for all time, yet it is in some sense the best specimen of his serious work. The desire of Malefort is that of the father in Shelley's *Cenci;* and perhaps the only way to prevent the theme from being intolerable was to veil it as long as possible, and to raise the spectators' sympathy at first for a man who had fought well for the State, and who to all appearance was badly treated by his pirate son.[1] In *The Bondman*, Marullo and Timandra, the brother and sister, are concealed till the very end, when they reveal themselves to be Pisander and Statilia—thereby bringing to an unexpected conclusion a plot which seemed to offer no solution.[2]

In *The City Madam* the method is varied a little; here we have one of Massinger's greatest creations, the fawning hypocrite, Luke. Indications of his future development are skilfully given from time to time, so that when this alarming person at length shows himself in his true colours we shiver without being surprised. The same idea shows itself in *The Renegado*,[3] in the skill with which Donusa leads up to her proposal that Vitelli should turn Mahometan; and in *The Virgin Martyr*,[4] where Artemia prepares the way for the offer of her hand to Antoninus.

---

[1] The exact cause of the son's anger is the murder of his mother by his father. The secret is not revealed until Act V., 2, 122, though it is hinted at in II., 1, 118-120. The son knows nothing of the other terrible charge.

[2] In *The Renegado* the brother and sister are not revealed until V., 4.

[3] IV., 3.   [4] I., 1.

Massinger is never so happy as when he has an opportunity in his well-proportioned scenes for displays of
rhetoric, such as we find in Euripides, where character
argues against character.[1] These scenes are often thrown
into the form of a trial at law or a debate in the Senate.[2]

The plays end well and effectively; our author excels
in the tragi-comedy, a type much affected by Fletcher.
Like all his contemporaries, he felt that the intermixture
of a lighter element in a play which ended happily was
justifiable.[3] The haste which Shakspere sometimes shows
in his fifth act is, as a rule, not apparent in Massinger.
For example, in *The Virgin Martyr*, the death of the
heroine occurs at the end of the fourth act. To all
appearance there is bound to be an anticlimax in the
fifth act. But there is not; on the contrary, the appearance of the heavenly messenger, bearing the fruits of
Paradise to the cruel persecutor Theophilus, elevates the
mind into a state of surprise and admiration. It has
often been pointed out that the appearance of a deity to

---

[1] The best instance of Euripidean art is the scene in *The
Emperor of the East* (II., 1), where all the arguments for the
Emperor's speedy marriage are cleverly amassed. *Cf.* also
Luke's appeal for mercy to the creditors in *The City Madam*,
I., 3; the long preparation which Sforza makes in *The Duke
of Milan*, I., 3, 268; the skill which leads up to the disclosure
of Marullo's name in *The Bondman* (IV., 3, 124), and the way
in which he persuades the slaves to revolt (II., 3). For other
instances of what we may call the gradual method, compare
The Virgin Martyr, I., 1, 294, and *A Very Woman*, V., 4, 91.

[2] *Cf. Fatal Dowry*, I., 2; IV., 4; V., 2; *Roman Actor*, I., 3;
Bondman, I., 3; *Parliament of Love*, V., 1; *Great Duke of
Florence*, V., 3.

[3] Here he incurs the censure of Milton on such plays
(Preface to *Samson Agonistes*): "This is mentioned to vindi-
cate tragedy from the small esteem, or rather infamy, which
in the account of many it undergoes at this day with other
common interludes; happening through the poet's error of
intertwining comic stuff with tragic sadness and gravity; or
introducing trivial and vulgar persons, which by all judicious
hath been counted absurd, and brought in without discretion,
corruptly to gratify the people!"

cut the knot at the end of a play of Euripides, which sometimes irritates the thinker in his study, and provokes him to write essays on the bad art and theology of the poet, is dazzlingly beautiful on the stage, and raises associations of sublimity and awe; it may in the same way be imagined how effective must have been the procession at the end of *The Virgin Martyr*. The stage directions run as follows: " Enter Dorothea in a white robe, crownes upon her head, led in by Angels, Antoninus, Caliste, and Christeta following, all in white, but lesse glorious, the Angell with a Crowne for him " (*i.e.*, Theophilus). At the sight of the glorious vision the persecutor dies, converted to the Christian faith, and the evil spirit, which has prompted his cruel acts, sinks to his own place with thunder and lightning, while Diocletian and his court look on in amazement. Similarly, in *The Roman Actor* there is no anticlimax; though Paris dies in the fourth act,[1] we feel that the tragedy is incomplete until it is rounded off by the punishment of the Emperor Domitian, which we breathlessly await.

Secondly, Massinger has a beautiful style. This point again is conceded by all the critics. The elegance of his dedications shows that had he wished he could have written excellent prose.[2] One who depreciates him allows that his style is " pure and free from violent metaphors and harsh constructions."[3] It has the grace and balance which one would expect from a well-bred and educated man, owing little to ornament or epithets or images. It serves its purpose, which is to tell a story

---

[1] *Cf.* Shakspere's *Julius Caesar*, where the hero dies in the third act; but the plot is not felt to have exhausted itself until Brutus and Cassius are disposed of.

[2] Massinger is very sparing in his use of prose in his plays, though Fleay goes too far when he says: " Neither Fletcher nor Massinger admits prose " (*Shakespeare Manual*, p. 71). The grace of Massinger's dedications is very marked when compared with the stilted and obscure style of Ford's.

[3] C. Lamb.

rapidly, and to unfold character rather than to display
the author's command of language or subtlety of thought
and expression. Seldom trivial, it is never prosaic, and
yet it is constantly on the border-line of prose. Massinger thought in blank verse because he was a dramatist
rather than because he was a poet. Hence his enemies
might say that his lines are prose in lengths; yet that
would be an unjust accusation. The poetical " colour "
is here, the ideal dignity, the atmosphere, although they
obtrude themselves less on the reader than in most poets.
Like Ovid, Massinger is one whose amazing facility carries
us along like a flood—a writer who should be read in
large quantities at a time,

"Whose easy Pegasus will amble o'er
Some three-score miles of fancy in an hour."[1]

It needs little argument to show that a poet of this
order can easily secure the effect of verisimilitude to life,
and will owe much of his success to that fact. Style
naturally appeals differently to different people; there
are those who are captivated by the glamour of Shelley
and Swinburne, or the pomp of Jeremy Taylor; there are
also those who enjoy the severity of *Paradise Regained*,
and the simplicity of Newman's *Sermons*. In an age
like the present, when many of our poets, like our musi-
cians, whatever else they are, either will not or cannot be
simple, it is refreshing to turn to an author who is always
lucid, and who is content to tell a story to the best of his
ability.

There are times when the style of Massinger rises into
solemn eloquence, especially when he indulges in the
moralizing vein. Unlike some of his literary contemporaries, Massinger wishes to show Virtue triumphant
and Vice beaten. Vice is never glorified in his pages, or
condoned. Honest indignation is perhaps the emotion

---

[1] Lines referring to Massinger quoted by Langbaine.

which he handles best. The uncontrollable anger which meanness and unworthiness provoke expresses itself in lofty language. Forcible and plain-spoken rebukes are found, which show that Massinger could be curt when he pleased. The plays are full of high-spirited passages, affording admirable opportunities for a master of elocution.

Let me give a specimen of just anger in the speech of Marullo. Marullo is the leader of the revolt of the slaves at Syracuse, and he is addressing their former lords and masters:

> Briefly thus then,
> Since I must speak for all,—your tyranny
> Drew us from our obedience. Happy those times
> When lords were styled fathers of families,
> And not imperious masters ! when they number'd
> Their servants almost equal with their sons,
> Or one degree beneath them ! when their labours
> Were cherish'd and rewarded, and a period
> Set to their sufferings; when they did not press
> Their duties or their wills, beyond the power
> And strength of their performance ! all things order'd
> With such decorum, as wise lawmakers
> From each well-govern'd private house deriv'd
> The perfect model of a Commonwealth.
> Humanity then lodged in the hearts of men,
> And thankful masters carefully provided
> For creatures wanting reason. The noble horse
> That, in his fiery youth, from his wide nostrils
> Neigh'd courage to his rider, and brake through
> Groves of opposed pikes, bearing his lord
> Safe to triumphant victory, old or wounded,
> Was set at liberty and freed from service.
> The Athenian mules that from the quarry drew
> Marble, hew'd for the temples of the gods,
> The great work ended, were dismiss'd and fed
> At the public cost; nay, faithful dogs have found
> Their sepulchres; but man to man more cruel,
> Appoints no end to the sufferings of his slave;

Since pride stepp'd in and riot, and o'erturned
This goodly frame of concord, teaching masters
To glory in the abuse of such as are
Brought under their command; who grown unuseful,
Are less esteem'd than beasts. This you have practis'd,
Practis'd on us with rigour; this hath forced us
To shake our heavy yokes off; and, if redress
Of these just grievances be not granted us,
We'll right ourselves, and by strong hand defend
What we are now possess'd of.[1]

In a lower key of manly dignity is the speech of Charalois before the Judges in *The Fatal Dowry*. It begins
thus:

                       Thus low my duty
Answers your lordships' counsel. I will use,
In the few words with which I am to trouble
Your lordships' ears the temper that you wish me;
Not that I fear to speak my thoughts as loud,
And with a liberty beyond Romont;
But that I know, for me that am made up
Of all that's wretched, so to haste my end,
Would seem to most rather a willingness
To quit the burden of a hopeless life
Than scorn of death or duty to the dead.[2]

As an example of a high-spirited passage, a speech may
be given from *The Bondman*. Cleora, the heroine, comes
forward in a meeting of the Senate to urge patriotic effort
on her fellow-countrymen. Timoleon, the general, is in
the chair, and she addresses him first:

CLEORA.   If a virgin,
Whose speech was ever yet ushered with fear;
One knowing modesty and humble silence
To be the choicest ornaments of our sex
In the presence of so many reverend men,
Struck dumb with terror and astonishment,
Presume to clothe her thought in vocal sounds,

---

[1] *Bondman*, IV., 2, 51-88.   [2] I., 2, 147.

Let her find pardon. First to you, great sir,
A bashful maid's thanks, and her zealous prayers,
Wing'd with pure innocence, bearing them to heaven,
For all prosperity that the gods can give
To one whose piety must exact their care,
Thus low I offer.
    TIMOLEON.   'Tis a happy omen.
Rise, blest one, and speak boldly. On my virtue
I am thy warrant, from so clear a spring
Sweet rivers ever flow.
    CLEORA.   Then thus to you,
My noble father, and these lords, to whom
I next owe duty; no respect forgotten
To you my brother, and these bold young men
(Such I would have them) that are, or should be,
The city's sword and target of defence,
To all of you I speak; and if a blush
Steal on my cheeks, it is shown to reprove
Your paleness, willingly I would not say,
Your cowardice or fear; think you all treasure
Hid in the bowels of the earth, or shipwreck'd
In Neptune's wat'ry kingdom, can hold weight,
When liberty and honour fill one scale,
Triumphant Justice sitting on the beam ?
Or dare you but imagine that your gold is
Too dear a salary for such as hazard
Their blood and lives in your defence ? For me,
An ignorant girl, bear witness ! heaven, so far
I prize a soldier, that to give him pay,
With such devotion as our flamens offer
Their sacrifices at the holy altar,
I do lay down these jewels, will make sale
Of my superfluous wardrobe, to supply
The meanest of their wants.[1]

This passage is printed in a broadside (headed "Country-men") relating to the expected invasion of England by Bonaparte, to be found at the British Museum. A short

---

[1] I , 3, 268-306.

statement of the plot of *The Bondman* is followed by a quotation of Act I., 3, 213-368, with one or two slight omissions. Possibly Gifford inspired its publication.

Perhaps the most eloquent passage in Massinger is the speech of Paris, the Roman actor, before the Senate, in defence of his profession:

ARETINUS.   Are you on the stage,
You talk so boldly ?
   PARIS.   The whole world being one,
This place is not exempted; and I am
So confident in the justice of our cause,
That I would wish Cæsar, in whose great name
All kings are comprehended, sate as judge
To hear our plea, and then determine of us.
If to express a man sold to his lusts,
Wasting the treasure of his time and fortunes
In wanton dalliance, and to what sad end
A wretch that's so given over does arrive at;
Deterring careless youth by his example,
From such licentious courses; laying open
The snares of bawds, and the consuming arts
Of prodigal strumpets, can deserve reproof;
Why are not all your golden principles
Writ down by grave philosophers to instruct us,
To choose fair virtue for our guide, not pleasure,
Condemn'd unto the fire ?
   SURA.   There's spirit in this.
   PARIS. Or if desire of honour was the base
On which the building of the Roman empire
Was raised up to this height; if, to inflame
The noble youth with an ambitious heat
T'endure the frosts of danger, nay, of death,
To be thought worthy the triumphal wreath,
By glorious undertakings, may deserve
Reward, or favour from the commonwealth;
Actors may put in for as large a share
As all the sects of the philosophers;
They with cold precepts (perhaps seldom read)

Deliver, what an honourable thing
The active virtue is; but does that fire
The blood, or swell the veins with emulation,
To be both good and great, equal to that
Which is presented in our theatres ?
Let a good actor, in a lofty scene,
Show great Alcides honour'd in the sweat
Of his twelve labours; or a bold Camillus
Forbidding Rome to be redeem'd with gold
From the insulting Gauls; or Scipio,
After his victories, imposing tribute
On conquer'd Carthage; if done to the life,
As if they saw their dangers, and their glories,
And did partake with them in their rewards,
All that have any spark of Roman in them,
The slothful arts laid by, contend to be
Like those they see presented.

    RUSTICUS.   He has put
The consuls to their whisper.

    PARIS.   But, 'tis urged
That we corrupt youth and traduce superiors.
When do we bring a vice upon the stage,
That does go off unpunish'd ? Do we teach,
By the success of wicked undertakings,
Others to tread in their forbidden steps ?
We shew no arts of Lydian panderism,
Corinthian poisons, Persian flatteries,
But mulcted so in the conclusion, that
Even those spectators that were so inclined,
Go home changed men. And for traducing such
That are above us, publishing to the world
Their secret crimes, we are as innocent
As such as are born dumb. When we present
An heir, that does conspire against the life
Of his dear parent, numbering every hour
He lives, as tedious to him; if there be,
Among the auditors, one whose conscience tells him
He is of the same mould, we cannot help it.
Or, bringing on the stage a loose adulteress,
That does maintain the riotous expense

Of him that feeds her greedy lust, yet suffers
The lawful pledges of a former bed
To starve the while for hunger; if a matron
However great in fortune, birth, or titles,
Guilty of such a foul, unnatural sin,

^{1st}
_{quarto,} Cry out, 'tis writ for me, we cannot help it.
"by," Or when a covetous man's express'd, whose wealth
Arithmetic cannot number, and whose lordships
A falcon in one day cannot fly over;
Yet he so sordid in his mind, so griping,
As not to afford himself the necessaries
To maintain life; if a patrician
(Though honour'd with a consulship) find himself
Touch'd to the quick in this, we cannot help it.
Or, when we shew a judge that is corrupt,
And will give up his sentence, as he favours
The person, not the cause; saving the guilty,
If of his faction, and as oft condemning
The innocent, out of particular spleen;
If any in this reverend assembly,
Nay, even yourself, my lord, that are the image
Of absent Cæsar, feel something in your bosom
That puts you in remembrance of things past,
Or things intended, 'tis not in us to help it.
I have said, my lord; and now as you find cause,
Or censure us, or free us with applause.[1]

I will quote three more passages: one to show how life-like in description Massinger can be; the second, to show how he can ennoble the expression of love; the third, to show how tender he is at his best.

The first is from *The Maid of Honour.* A soldier comes in with news for the besieged general, who is standing on the walls of Siena, looking for aid from his friends:

        Enter a Soldier.
FERDINAND.   What news with thee ?
SOLDIER.   From the turret of the fort,

---

[1] I., 3, 49-142.

By the rising clouds of dust, through which, like
  lightning
The splendour of bright arms sometimes brake through,
I did descry some forces making towards us;
And from the camp, as emulous of their glory,
The general, for I know him by his horse,
And bravely seconded, encounter'd them.
Their greetings were too rough for friends; their
  swords,
And not their tongues, exchanging courtesies.
By this the main battalias are join'd;
And if you please to be spectators of
The horrid issue, I will bring you where,
As in a theatre, you may see their fates
In purple gore presented.[1]

The second is from *The Duke of Milan*, where Marcelia
expresses her love for her lord, Sforza, the Duke of
Milan.

MARCELIA.   My worthiest lord !
The only object I behold with pleasure,
My pride, my glory, in a word, my all !
Bear witness, heaven, that I esteem myself
In nothing worthy of the meanest praise
You can bestow, unless it be in this,
That in my heart, I love and honour you.
And, but that it would smell of arrogance
To speak my strong desire and zeal to serve you,
I then could say, these eyes yet never saw
The rising sun, but that my vows and prayers
Were sent to heaven for the prosperity
And safety of my lord, nor have I ever
Had other study, but how to appear
Worthy your favour; and that my embraces
Might yield a fruitful harvest of content
For all your noble travail, in the purchase
Of her that's still your servant; by these lips,

---

[1] II., 4, 22-35.

Which pardon me that I presume to kiss——
SFORZA. O swear, for ever swear !
MARCELIA.　　　　　　　I ne'er will seek
Delight but in your pleasure; and desire,
_{1st}　When you are sated[1] with all earthly glories,
quarto,
'seated."And age and honours make you fit for heaven,
That one grave may receive us.[1]

The third is from *A Very Woman;* the disguised
John Antonio is telling his story at Almira's request:

Not far from where my father lives, a lady,
A neighbour by, blest with as great a beauty
As nature durst bestow without undoing,
Dwelt, and most happily, as I thought then,
And bless'd the house a thousand times she dwelt in.
This beauty, in the blossom of my youth,
When my first fire felt no adulterate incense,
Nor I no way to flatter, but my fondness;
In all the bravery my friends could show me,
In all the faith my innocence could give me,
In the best language my true tongue could tell me,
And all the broken sighs my sick heart lend me,
I sued and serv'd; long did I love this lady,
Long was my travail, long my trade to win her;
With all the duty of my soul I serv'd her.[2]

At times the poet rises to what is not far removed from
inspiration; and such lines as the following from *The
Parliament of Love* make good the claim of English to be
the imperial language of the world.　King Charles seeks
to justify the honours which he, the "most Christian
king," gives to the statue of Cupid; he then continues
thus:

CHARLES. 'Tis rather to instruct deceived mankind,
How much pure love that has his birth in heaven,
And scorns to be received a guest, but in
A noble heart prepared to entertain him,

---

[1] I., 3, 51-74.　　　　[2] IV., 3, 124-138.

Is by the gross misprision of weak men,
Abused and injured. That celestial fire,
Which hieroglyphically is described
In this his bow, his quiver, and his torch,
First warm'd their bloods, and after gave a name
To the old heroic spirits; such as Orpheus,
That drew men, differing little then from beasts,
To civil government; or famed Alcides
The tyrant-queller, that refused the plain
And easy path leading to vicious pleasures,
And ending in a precipice deep as hell,
To scale the rugged cliffs on whose firm top
Virtue and Honour, crown'd with wreaths of stars,
Did sit triumphant.[1]

But there is another characteristic of Massinger's style
and that perhaps more obvious still; it is full of courtliness
and grace. A perusal of *The City Madam*, where the
subject is the absurdity of the ladies of the Mansion House
who ape the manners of the West End, suggests the question whether Massinger was ever attached to the Court.
We do not know. He must, at any rate, have moved
amongst refined and educated people. Napoléon said
that Corneille's plays ought to be performed to an audience of ambassadors and ministers of state;[2] in the same
way, in reading Massinger, we feel that we are moving
freely in the palaces of the great. There is comparatively
little here of dialect[3] or low life; we are at once taken up

---

[1] V., 1, 42-60.
[2] *Cf.* Prologue to *Henry V*, line 4, a passage imitated and
expanded in *The Virgin Martyr*, V., 2, 98-102.
[3] We have a Somersetshire rustic in *The Emperor of the
East*, IV., 2. *Cf.* Schmidt's *Shakespeare Lexicon*, Appendix II.,
p. 1424. "In general it can be said that Shakspere abstains
from the use of provincial dialects, as characteristic of his
dramatical persons. . . . It is only on one occasion that he
seems to imitate the peculiar speech of a certain dialect:
King Lear, IV., 6, 239-251. Concerning the particular
county there referred to English scholars have been of different
opinions. Steevens pleads for Somersetshire, in the dialect of

into high life with all its virtues and its faults. The kings
and courtiers behave and express themselves as we should
expect them to do; the politeness and the compliments
which we hear on every side have the merit of being
entirely natural. And if there is little to remind
us of Dickens, there is still less to recall Thackeray.
There is no air of snobbishness; such is the dexterity of our author that we do not feel like Jeames
Yellowplush, that we are awkward menials watching the
doings of the titled and the great. Not only do the
characters move with an inborn grace which is free
from self-analysis and self-contempt, but they take
the audience up into their company; and as the
gallants of that era used sometimes to sit upon the
stage, close among the actors,[1] so in reading Massinger
we feel that we are unconsciously present at the scenes
he portrays.

This is as much as to say that the stage of those days
responded to a real and living need in the minds of the
audience; there was nothing exotic or artificial about it,
as there seems to have been about our plays ever since
the Puritans turned things upside down. It will be said

---

which rustics were commonly introduced by ancient writers;
Collier inclines to decide in favour of the North." *Cf.* Mr. H.
Bradley's remarks in *Shakspere's England*, II., p. 570. In
Bartholomew Fair, IV., 3, a contrast is drawn between the
dialect of a rustic from the West and one from the North.
Urania's dialect in *Cupid's Revenge* cannot be pronounced a
success, or Antonio's Irish in *The Coxcomb*.

[1] *City Madam*, II., 2, 128. Among the things which Anne
demands from her suitor, is:

A fresh habit,
Of a fashion never seen before, to draw
The gallants' eyes, that sit on the stage, upon me.

Cf. also Induction to *The Malcontent;* Induction to *The
Staple of News;* Induction to *Cynthia's Revels;* Fitzdottrel
in *The Devil is an Ass*, I., 3; Induction to *Knight of the
Burning Pestle;* *Woman-Hater*, I., 3; Prologue to *All Fools;*
and Dekker's *The Guls Horne-booke*, Chapter VI.

that this enchanted atmosphere belongs to all the greater playwrights of the age alike. And this is true; it is one of the secrets of their abiding charm. Brander Matthews, in dealing with the unreality of Massinger's atmosphere, says that "some of Shakspere's most delightful plays, *The Merchant of Venice* for one, and *Much Ado* for another, are charming to us now only because we are quite willing to make believe with the poet" (*op. cit.*, p. 311). And so, when Leslie Stephen asks if we are "invigorated" by the perusal of Massinger's plays,[1] I reply to that apostle of common sense that I am not only charmed and delighted, but invigorated. And why? Because I am admitted to a world of heroism and romance.

But may we not put the matter more broadly still? When we read the Cavalier lyrics of Suckling, Herrick, and Lovelace, when we think of Falkland, when we stand before the portraits of Vandyck, do we not feel that modern England was in danger until lately of losing something? There is an aroma there of chivalry which had almost faded from our ken. And yet there is an element in our shy and dumb English nature to which this atmosphere is congenial, however overgrown with money-making our minds had seemed to be. Nor, as the student of history knows well, had the Puritans in the Civil War the monopoly of religion and duty. Indeed, the Civil War was a true tragedy, because both sides had right, both fought and bled for what they believed to be

---

[1] *Hours in a Library*, ii., p. 171. Leslie Stephen elsewhere (pp. 167-171) does justice to Massinger's "romantic tendency." "The chivalrous ideal of morality involves a reverence for women which may be exaggerated or affected, but which has at least a genuine element in it. The same vein of chivalrous sentiment gives a fine tone to some of Massinger's other plays; to *The Bondman*, for example, and *The Great Duke of Florence*, in both of which the treatment of lovers' devotion shows a higher sense of the virtue of feminine dignity and purity than is common in the contemporary stage."

the truth. To-day, in spite of our many domestic discords, no party spirit discounts the gallant deeds of which we have read daily, and of which of necessity only a fraction has been publicly rewarded. Perhaps the flame of romance will breathe once more in our midst, now the War is over, purified by suffering, and quickened by the memory of those serene yet manly spirits whom we have lost on the battlefield, whose departure in the dayspring of life seems, as it were, to have extinguished so many stars in the vault of heaven. They put aside the calls of culture and pleasure, and the natural ambition to do something in the world before they were abolished by death. They have willingly given for their country all that they had; they have given themselves. If we remember their devotion with gratitude it may purify us from the commonplace, the vulgar, and the selfish. They, at any rate, can address the power of evil, which for the moment seemed to triumph, in the words of Dorothea:

> What is this life to me ? Not worth a thought:
> Or, if it be esteem'd, 'tis that I lose it
> To win a better; even thy malice serves
> To me but as a ladder to mount up
> To such a height of happiness, where I shall
> Look down with scorn on thee and on the world;
> Where, circled with true pleasures, placed above
> The reach of death or time, 'twill be my glory
> To think at what an easy price I bought it.
> There's a perpetual spring, perpetual youth;
> No joint-benumbing cold, or scorching heat,
> Famine, nor age, have any being there.
> Forget for shame your Tempe; bury in
> Oblivion your feign'd Hesperian orchards;
> The golden fruit, kept by the watchful dragon,
> Which did require a Hercules to get it,
> Compared with what grows in all plenty there,
> Deserves not to be named. The Power I serve
> Laughs at your happy Araby, or the

Elysian shades; for He hath made His bowers
Better in deed than you can fancy yours.[1]

As an instance of Massinger's courtliness I will quote
a short passage from *The Great Duke of Florence:* Contarino has come from the court of the Duke to fetch his
nephew Giovanni, who has been brought up by a tutor,
Charomonte by name, in the country. As the prince
comes in, Charomonte addresses Contarino:

CHAROMONTE. Make your approaches boldly; you will find
A courteous entertainment. (CONTARINO *kneels.*)
GIOVANNI.   Pray you, forbear
My hand, good signior; 'tis a ceremony
Not due to me. 'Tis fit we should embrace
With mutual arms.
CONTARINO.   It is a favour, sir,
I grieve to be denied.
GIOVANNI.   You shall o'ercome;
But 'tis your pleasure, not my pride, that grants it.
Nay, pray you, guardian and good sir, put on;
How ill it shews to have that reverend head
Uncover'd to a boy!
CHAROMONTE.   Your excellence
Must give me liberty, to observe the distance
And duty that I owe you.[2]

Take another instance, from *The Duke of Milan* :

SFORZA.   Excuse me, good Pescara.
Ere long I will wait on you.
PESCARA.   You speak, sir,
The language I should use.[3]

---

[1] *The Virgin Martyr,* IV., 3, 72-92. *Cf. Believe As You
List,* IV., 2, 183-204.

[2] I., 1, 103-114. The whole play exhibits this element of
grace more than any other of our author. It should be
acted by Lysis and Charicles, Glaucon and Adeimantus.

[3] IV., 3, 175. It is to be noted that great courtesy is
observed and expected in greetings and leave-takings in
Massinger's plays. Thus in *The Virgin Martyr,* II., 2,

And this, from *The Bashful Lover* :

FARNESE. Madam, I am bold
To trench so far upon your privacy
As to desire my friend (let not that wrong him,
For he's a worthy one) may have the honour
To kiss your hand.
MATILDA. His own worth challenges
A greater favour.
FARN. Your acknowledgment
Confirms it, madam.[1]

I have used the word "lucid" of Massinger's style; perhaps a more appropriate word would be dexterous; not that he is obscure like Chapman, or like Shakspere in his later manner, far less turgid, but he is not afraid of somewhat long sentences. What he is really afraid of, unlike Fletcher, is a full-stop at the end of the verse. There are two devices which the reader will notice, often in combination; in the first place, Massinger is very fond of the "absolute" construction, and loves to multiply parentheses. The following passages from *A New Way* will serve as illustrations :

FURNACE. She keeps her chamber, dines with a panada,
Or water gruel, my sweat never thought on.[2]
WOMAN. And the first command she gave, after she rose,
Was, her devotions done, to give her notice
When you approach'd here.[3]

Or again, from *The Emperor of the East* :

Astraea once more lives upon the earth,
Pulcheria's breast her temple.[4]

Or from *The Bondman :*

Macrinus gets into trouble for the curtness of his salutation; similarly, Wellborn in *A New Way*, V., 1, 114. Compare also *Roman Actor*, IV., 1, 67; *A Very Woman*, I., 1, 147.
[1] I., 1, 246. [2] I., 2, 36. [3] II., 2, 71. [4] I., 1, 77.

And, to those that stay,
A competence of land freely allotted
To each man's proper use, no lord acknowledged.[1]

We find the "absolute" construction occasionally in Shakspere, as in *The Merchant of Venice* :

So are those crisped snaky golden locks
Which make such wanton gambols with the wind,
Upon supposed fairness, often known
To be the dowry of a second head,
The skull that bred them in the sepulchre.[2]

Or in *Hamlet* :

Folded the writ up in form of the other,
Subscribed it, gav't th' impression, placed it safely,
The changeling never known.[3]

A passage from *The Fatal Dowry* will show an elaborate use of parenthesis:

What though my father
Writ man before he was so, and confirm'd it,
By numbering that day no part of his life
In which he did not service to his country;
Was he to be free therefore from the laws
And ceremonious form in your decrees ?
Or else because he did as much as man,
In those three memorable overthrows,
At Granson, Morat, Nancy, where his master,
The warlike Charalois, with whose misfortunes
I bear his name, lost treasure, men, and life,
To be excused from payment of those sums
Which (his own patrimony spent) his zeal
To serve his country forced him to take up ![4]

Compare also these lines from *The Guardian* :

And if you shew not
An appetite, and a strong one, I'll not say
To eat it, but devour it, without grace too,

---

[1] IV., 2, 96.   [2] III., 2, 92.   [3] V., 2, 51.   [4] I., 2, 162-175.

For it will not stay a preface, I am shamed,
And all my past provocatives will be jeer'd at.[1]

From *The Picture* :

HONORIA. That you please, sir,
With such assurances of love and favour,
To grace your handmaid, but in being yours, sir,
A matchless queen, and one that knows herself so,
Binds me in retribution to deserve
The grace conferr'd upon me.[2]

From *A Very Woman* :

PAULO. This friend was plighted to a beauteous woman,
(Nature proud of her workmanship) mutual love
Possess'd them both, her heart in his heart lodged
And his in hers.[3]

From *The Bashful Lover* :

ALONZO. By me, his nephew,
He does salute you fairly, and entreats
(A word not suitable to his power and greatness)
You would consent to tender that, which he
Unwillingly must force, if contradicted.[4]

From *The Parliament of Love* :

What coy she, then,
Though great in birth, not to be parallel'd
For nature's liberal bounties, (both set off
With fortune's trappings, wealth); but, with delight,
Gladly acknowledged such a man her servant ?[5]

It has been pointed out by Zielinski that " the perfection of language in regard to the formation of periods
depends upon the presence and prevalence of abbreviated

---

[1] II., 3, 28-32.   [2] I., 2, 136-141.   [3] IV., 2, 46.
[4] I., 2, 17.
[5] I., 5, 44. The longest series of parentheses in Massinger
is to be found in Cardenes' speech in *A Very Woman* (I., 1,
240-256). For clumsy periods see *Fatal Dowry*, IV., 2, 99-
104; V., 2, 23-34; *Roman Actor*, IV., 2, 123-128.

not show
ve already
from time
ie Duke of

ime;
s,
pire.[1]

1

2

od laid by,

ill.[4]

est single

hose dis-
s lavished
he second
dent will
able that
rked him

ven from

V., 2, 22.
ugh I do
e pleased
d so much
assinger.

xpression he describes "abso-

an expedient which the poems
made familiar to this generation,
the relative pronoun.[2] And so
th a seemingly negligent grace
sion. It is clear that such a
repays a careful study of the

this combination the words of
of the East. He is talking of the
ne Minister Pulcheria:

> She indeed is
nd disdains a rival.
you know, promised much,
ss she transcends, and makes
r. I will tell you
o entertain the time
happiness to see her,
ce she hath borne herself,
le brevity; though the subject
field, as would require
purest eloquence
most famous orators
ing, Athens, shew'd the world)
should undertake to be
.[3]

r is not only lucid and dexterous;
use of its ease, and more mature
of many of his contemporaries.
ve gained much in directness if he

/, Eng. trans. by Strong and Stewart,

how common this idiom is in Shaks-
and other authors of the period. I
it lends itself in a peculiar way to the
s style.

had studied Massinger. This strength does
itself so much in isolated fine lines, for, as we h
seen, epigram was foreign to his nature, thoug
to time we get such lines, as, for example, in *1*
Milan :

> One smile of hers would make a savage
> One accent of that tongue would calm the se
> *Though all the winds at once strove there for en*

Or, again, in the same play:

> How coldly you receive it !   I expect
> The mere relation of so great a blessing,
> *Borne proudly on the wings of sweet reveng*
> Would have call'd on a sacrifice of thanks

Or, again, in *A New Way :*

> OVERREACH. The garments of her widowho
> *She now appears as glorious as the spring.*[3]

Or in *The Roman Actor :*

> Could I imp feathers to the wings of tim
> Or with as little ease command the sun
> *To scourge his coursers up heaven's eastern*

We may remark in passing that Massinger's
lines are usually decasyllabic.

It has been remarked by Mr. Swinburne, v
cerning judgment of the Jacobean dramatists ha
just praise on Massinger's art and style, that in
act of *Sir John Van Olden Barnavelt,* " the st
say, ' This tune goes manly,' " and it is remar
our poet had formed in 1619 the style which m
to the end of his life.[5]

An instance of this simple strength may be g

---

[1] I., 3, 339.   [2] V., 1, 25.   [3] III., 3, 4.
[5] *Contemporaries of Shakespeare,* p. 183.   The
not accept all Mr. Swinburne's estimates, I am at on
and humiliated at the thought that he has expresse
better than myself many of my conclusions about M

The City Madam, where Luke debates whether he shall agree to the proposition of the pretended Indians:

> LUKE.   Give me leave—(*walks aside*)
> I would not lose this purchase.   A grave matron !
> And two pure virgins !   Umph, I think my sister,
> Though proud, was ever honest, and my nieces
> Untainted yet.   Why should not they be shipp'd
> For this employment ?   They are burthensome to me,
> *And eat too much.*[1]

When rudeness is necessary it is uttered with some vigour, as in *The Fatal Dowry*, where this is what Romont gets for his well-meant pains:

> ROCHFORT.   Sir, if you please
> To bear yourself as fits a gentleman,
> The house is at your service; but if not,
> Though you seek company elsewhere, your absence
> Will not be much lamented.[2]

The rejected lover in such a scene as the following has no illusions left him:

> MUSTAPHA.   All happiness——
> DONUSA.   Be sudden.
> 'Twas saucy rudeness in you, sir, to press
> On my retirements; but ridiculous folly
> To waste the time that might be better spent,
> In complimental wishes.
> CORISCA.   There's a cooling
> For his hot encounter !   (*aside*)
> DONUSA.   Come you here to stare ?
> If you have lost your tongue and use of speech,
> Resign your government; there's a mute's place void
> In my uncle's court, I hear; and you may want me
> To write for your preferment.[3]

Two minor features of Massinger's style may be mentioned here:

---

[1] V., 1, 51.   [2] III., 1, 302.
[3] *The Renegado*, III., 1, 30-39.

1. The catalogue line, so familiar to the student of Lucretius—*e.g.* :

Believe as You List, I., 2, 85. The sapphire, ruby, jacinth,
amber, coral.
,,   II, 2, 312. All circumstances,
Answers, despatches, doubts, and difficulties.
Picture, V., 1, 59. The comfortable names of breakfasts,
dinners,
Collations, supper, beverage.
Emperor of East, 2 Prol., 8. With his best of fancy, judgment,
language, art.
I., 2, 194. To his merchant, mercer, draper,
His linen-man, and tailor.
V., 2, 88. As sacred, glorious, high, invincible.
City Madam, II., 1, 72. Tissue, gold, silver, velvets, satins,
taffetas.
IV., 3, 69. Entreaties, curses, prayers, or im-
precations.
Unnatural Combat, II., 1, 128. All respect,
Love, fear, and reverence cast
off.
Great Duke of Florence, II., 1, 7. We of necessity must be
chaste, wise, fair.

2. A more marked feature is the repetition of words or short phrases in various parts of the line.[1] The following instances may be given from (*a*) *The Great Duke of Florence* :

I., 1, 154. It is the duke !
The duke.
I., 2, 41. Our duchess; such a duchess.
I., 2, 95. See, signiors, see our care.
I., 2, 131. Take up, take up.
II., 1, 71. Fie ! fie ! the princess.
III., 1, 102. Tells
His son, this is the prince, the hopeful prince.

---

[1] Oliphant (*Englische Studien*, xiv., 60) notes this feature as Fletcherian

(b) *The City Madam* :

> II., 1, 58. I blush for you,
> > Blush at your poverty of spirit.
>
> III., 1, 11. I am starv'd,
> > Starv'd in my pleasures.
>
> V., 1, 12. Far, far above your hopes.
>
> V., 1, 81. The height
> > Of honour, principal honour.
>
> V., 2, 67. A manor pawn'd,
> > Pawn'd, my good lord.

And, thirdly, the versification of Massinger is musical and melodious. Boyle says that Milton's blank verse owes much to the study of it. " In the indefinable touches which make up the music of a verse, in the artistic distribution of pauses, and in the unerring choice and grouping of just those words which strike the ear as the perfection of harmony, there are, if we leave Cyril Tourneur's *Atheist's Tragedy* out of the question, only two masters in the drama, Shakspere in his latest period and Massinger."[1] Coleridge says that it is " an excellent metre, a better model for dramatists in general to imitate than Shakspere's. Read Massinger aright, and measure by time, not syllables, and no lines can be more legitimate, none in which the substitution of equipollent feet, and the modifications by emphasis, are managed with such exquisite judgment."[2] Be it noted that this praise comes from a master of his art, for no one who has once appreciated Coleridge's command of vowel-syzygy and the velvet-like texture of his blank verse can refuse him that title.

Massinger's blank verse is equal to all the emotions which the author can express and kindle. It never fails him, nor, on the other hand, does it obtrude itself unduly on the sense conveyed. Only after reading a considerable passage of our poet do we understand how much the

---

[1] Boyle, *N. S. S.*, Trans., p. 378.   [2] *Op. cit.*, p. 403.

versification contributes to his lifelike and dignified atmosphere.

Moreover, the metre of Massinger is admirably suited to his style. There seems a hidden but real harmony between them. Some might call his metre at times slipshod and undignified, from the fact that, except in elevated passages, the characters speak in rhythmical sentences which approximate to prose. Boyle, who declares that " Marlowe and Massinger are the two extremes of the metrical movement in the dramatists,"[1] has pointed out that "Massinger's blank verse shows a larger proportion of run-on lines and double endings in harmonious union than any of his contemporaries.[2] Cart-

---

[1] *E. S.*, vii. 70.

[2] *N. S. S.*, xxvi. 584. The "run-on" line ends with a preposition or other word which syntactically requires the next line. Take as an example *Fatal Dowry*, V., 2, 255:

> For the fact, as of
> The former, I confess it; but with what
> Base wrongs I was unwillingly drawn to it,
> To my few words there are some other proofs
> To witness this for truth.

The "double" or "feminine" ending is the outstanding feature of Fletcher's verse. *Cf. Fatal Dowry*, V., 2, 137:

> ROCHFORT. You say you are sorry for him;
> A grief in which I must not have a partner.
> 'Tis I alone am sorry, that when * I raised
> The building of my life, for seventy years,
> Upon so sure a ground, that all the vices
> Practised to ruin man, though brought against me,
> Could never undermine, and no way left
> To send these grey hairs to the grave with sorrow,
> Virtue, that was my patroness, betrayed me.

Five instances in nine lines. Fleay (*Shakespeare Manual*, p. 171) points out that in Shakspere's part of *Henry VIII* the proportion of double endings to blank verse is 1 to 3; in Fletcher's, 1 to 1·7. The weak and sugary effect of double endings is very apparent in Rowe's *Fair Penitent*, the eighteenth-century play, based on *The Fatal Dowry*.

---

* Gifford inserts " when."

wright and Tourneur have more run-on lines, but not so many double endings. Fletcher has more double endings, but very few run-on lines. Shakspere and Beaumont alone exhibit a somewhat similar metrical style."[1] This is interesting, because we shall see later on that Massinger was a devoted admirer and imitator of Shakspere in thought, device, and expression. It is not strange, there- fore, that he should also copy his metre, or rather, develop his own on the same lines. To show how flexible and dexterous the metre of Massinger is, I will give two in- stances from *The Bashful Lover*. In the first Uberti encourages Gonzaga to persevere with the contest:

> UBERTI. Sir, these tears
> Do well become a father, and my eyes
> Would keep you company as a forlorn lover,
> But that the burning fire of my revenge
> Dries up those drops of sorrow. We, once more,
> Our broken forces rallied up, and with
> Full numbers strengthen'd, stand prepared t' endure
> A second trial; nor let it dismay us
> That we are once again t' affront the fury
> Of a victorious army; their abuse
> Of conquest hath disarm'd them, and call'd down

Boyle (*E. S.*, v. 74) takes six of Massinger's plays: *The Unnatural Combat, The Duke of Milan, The Bondman, The City Madam, The Bashful Lover,* and *The Guardian*. These are his conclusions: "The plays show in general a high per- centage of double endings, generally 40 per cent. or more. The percentage of run-on lines is a little lower, but seldom sinks for more than a scene below 30 per cent. The light and weak endings together make 5 to 7 per cent. The versifica- tion is exquisitely musical. There are very few rhymes." The corresponding figures for Fletcher are: double endings, over 50 per cent.; run-on lines, under 20 per cent.; and light and weak endings almost negligible; rhyme, rare. Shakspere in his later manner (e.g., *The Tempest*) has 33 per cent. double endings. (*E. S.*, vi. 71.)

[1] Fleay (*Shakespeare Manual*, p. 123) takes a piece of Dryden's *All for Love*, and rewrites it, as far as metre (and metre only) is concerned, in the styles of Fletcher, Beaumont, Massinger, Greene, and Rowley.

The Powers above to aid us.   I have read
Some piece of story, yet ne'er found but that
The general, that gave way to cruelty,
The profanation of things sacred, rapes
Of virgins, butchery of infants, and
The massacre in cold blood of reverend age,
Against the discipline and law of arms,
Did feel the hand of heaven lie heavy on him
When most secure.[1]

In the second Gonzaga refuses the hand of his daughter
Matilda to Lorenzo:

GONZAGA.   Two main reasons
(Seconding those you have already heard)
Give us encouragement; the duty that
I owe my mother country, and the love
Descending to my daughter.   For the first,
Should I betray her liberty, I deserv'd
To have my name with infamy razed from
The catalogue of good princes; and I should
Unnaturally forget I am a father,
If, like a Tartar, or for fear or profit,
I should consign her, as a bondwoman,
To be disposed of at another's pleasure;
Her own consent or favour never sued for,
And mine by force exacted.   No, Alonzo,
She is my only child, my heir; and if
A father's eyes deceive me not, the hand
Of prodigal nature hath given so much to her,
As, in the former ages, kings would rise up
In her defence and make her cause their quarrel;
Nor can she, if that any spark remain
To kindle a desire to be possess'd
Of such a beauty, in our time, want swords
To guard it safe from violence.[2]

Anyone who compares the metre of Massinger with that
of Fletcher will find that our author observes far stricter

---

[1] IV., 3, 5-24.   [2] I., 2, 49-71.

laws than his friend. The plays of Massinger abound in lines divided between two speakers, or even three, which, nevertheless, observe the strict rule of the metre.[1]

The way in which Massinger's style and metre suit one another can best be illustrated by a passage or two from *The Parliament of Love*; the first is where Bellisant speaks about the decay of chivalry.

BELLISANT.   Ere they durst
Presume to offer service to a lady,
In person they perform'd some gallant acts
The fame of which prepar'd them gracious hearing,
Ere they made their approaches; what coy she, then,[2]
Though great in birth, not to be parallel'd   ̃
For nature's liberal beauties (both set off
With fortune's trappings, wealth); but with delight,
Gladly acknowledg'd such a man her servant,
To whose heroic courage and deep wisdom,
The flourishing commonwealth, and thankful king,
Confess'd themselves for debtors ? Whereas, now,
If you have travelled Italy, and brought home
Some remnants of the language, and can set
Your faces in some strange and ne'er-seen posture,
Dance a lavolta, and be rude and saucy,

---

[1] In this respect Massinger resembles Beaumont and Ford, whose metre in divided lines, unlike Webster's and Fletcher's, is very regular. For strict division cf. *City Madam*, I., 3, 44; II., 1, 109; V., 1, 4 and 70; V., 2, 66; V., 3, 126; *Guardian*, I., 1, 80, 221, 308; II., 3, 116; III., 2, 61; IV., 3, 16; *New Way*, I., 2, 48 and 63; II., 2, 151; III., 2, 241; V., 1, 233; *Very Woman*, I., 1, 26 and 147; V., 6, 31; *Bashful Lover*, I., 1, 114, 163, and 207; II., 2, 36, 37; II., 3, 9; II., 4, 42; III., 1, 99; III., 3, 71 and 80; V., 1, 39, 40, 48, 50, 176; *Roman Actor*, I., 3, 32. Instances can be given of lines divided between four speakers —e.g., *Very Woman*, V., 3, 23; V., 4, 167; *Bashful Lover*, II., 7, 20; *Roman Actor*, I., 4, 50; IV., 1, 83; *Guardian*, V., 4, 209. The carelessness of the metre in *The Old Law* is in itself proof that Massinger had little to do with it.

[2] An instance of "emphatic" double-ending (*Oliphant, E. S.*, xiv., 71), common in Fletcher, rare in Massinger.

Protest and swear and damn (for these are acts
That most think grace them), and then view yourselves
In the deceiving mirror of self-love,
You do conclude there hardly is a woman
That can be worthy of you.[1]

The second is a speech of Leonora exposing Cleremond's
baseness:

I, burning then with a most virtuous anger,
Razed from my heart the memory of his name,
Railed and spit at him; and knew 'twas justice
That I should take those deities he scorn'd,
Hymen and Cupid, into my protection,
And be the instrument of their revenge;
And so I cast him off, scorn'd his submission,
His poor and childish whinings, will'd my servants
To shut my gates against him; but, when neither
Disdain, hate, or contempt could free me from
His loathsome importunities, and fired too
To wreak mine injur'd honour, I took gladly
Advantage of his execrable oaths,
To undergo what penance I enjoin'd him;
Then, to the terror of all future ribalds,
That make no difference between love and lust,
Imposed this task upon him. I have said, too;
Now, when you please, a censure.[2]

The critics may differ in their estimate of Massinger's
style and metre; but it is simple truth to say that they
are unique in our literature, in their correctness, dignity,
ease, and classical frugality.

Let us now turn to the poet's faults. It is said that
his range of thought is limited, and this may be at once
conceded. It might also be said that Greek tragedy is
limited, and the statement is true of all our Elizabethan
playwrights; yet we return to them again and again, for
they have something to give us which we cannot do without. It is idle to depreciate one period of our literature

---

[1] I., 5, 38.   [2] V., 1, 226.

at the expense of another. Are not the old madrigal writers limited, and Farrant and Byrd, Orlando Gibbons and Blow ? and yet we enjoy them; nay, to take even Purcell himself, when we confess that the pleasure he gives us is due to the fact that he is more daring, less shackled than his generation, " so modern " as we say, are we not in the end forced to confess that he too is unmistakably limited, " bewrayed " by his quaint and stately rhythms to be one of the seventeenth century ?

Our age has a wider and subtler range of psychology; to revert from " The Georgian Poets " of 1911 to Massinger is like going back from the films of a cinema palace to a tondo of Luca Signorelli. Both films and tondo have their uses. We may take a single illustration of this point from *The Brothers Karamazov*. The great Russian novelist, among other problems, deals in that book with the case of the young man who is in love with two women at once. That is the sort of complicated interest which we do not expect our Elizabethan writers to cope with, in as great detail as a modern writer uses. The problem occurs in *The Bondman*, where the heroine, Cleora, is distracted between her plighted love to Leosthenes and her warm sense of obligation to Marullo;[1] it is interesting and instructive to see how simply the whole thing is touched upon, and how soon the doubt is solved by the discovery of Leosthenes' former intrigue with Statilia. May we not say, with Aristophanes, in comparing Massinger and Dostoevsky:

Τὸν μὲν γὰρ ἡγοῦμαι σοφόν, τῷ δ'ἥδομαι.[2]

Then it is said that Massinger's work is not free from coarseness. The answer to this accusation may be made in more ways than one. I might with confidence reply to such critics: If you wish for real vulgarity of diction,

---

[1] *Cf.* also Matilda in *The Bashful Lover* (IV., 3, 170), and Olinda in *The Lovers' Progress*.

[2] *Frogs*, l. 1413.

read Marston; if you wish for real vulgarity of mind, read Middleton; if you wish for poisoned morals, read Ford and Tourneur; and then revise your judgment of Massinger. It is notorious that all the stage writers of the Elizabethan age are tarred with the same brush; there is much in Shakspere himself that we wish he had not written; still more is this true of Ben Jonson. In *The Virgin Martyr*, where we have the odious servants, Hircius and Spungius, it is generally believed that the parts of the play in which they appear are due to Dekker, not to Massinger, whose other works present nothing so disgusting. There are, at any rate, no lapses of taste in Massinger like those which we find in Fletcher; nothing like the fate of Rutilio in *The Custom of the Country*, or of Merione in *The Queen of Corinth*, or of the Father in *The Captain*. It must be confessed that Massinger's conception of love is apt to be earthly, physical, sensuous; there is but little in his plays about the marriage of true minds,[1] too much about "Hymen's taper" and "virgin forts." Captivated by the charms of female beauty, his intellect is too concrete in its ideals to rise above mere morality to the mysteries of the diviner love. So far it must be allowed that his art interests and stimulates the passions of his audience without elevating them. But if at times we feel a monotonous limitation in his outlook in these matters, if we miss the healthy breezes of bracing commonsense and cheerful self-restraint, we are never pained by the triumph of what is low, corrupt, or morbid.

When it is said that his women are impure it is necessary to enter a clear protest.[2] There are offensive and

---

[1] *Cf.* the dialogue in *A Very Woman*, I., 1, 1-24. "Heaven's greatest blessings" (line 21) is a very characteristic phrase. *Cf.* also *Emperor of the East*, II., 1, 216.

[2] Boyle (*N. S. S.*, 385-88) is severe but not, to my mind, convincing. Reading between the lines, one arrives at the conclusion that Boyle admired Massinger enormously, and would have allowed none else to abuse him except himself. *Cf.* his spirited attack on Charles Lamb's "unfair judgment" (pp. 371-2).

heartless women in Massinger, such as Domitia in *The Roman Actor*, and Beaumelle in *The Fatal Dowry* ;[1] there are odious old women, like Borachia and Corisca. There are pert and vulgar ladies' maids; but you have only to read *The Bondman*, *The Bashful Lover*, *A Very Woman*, *The Maid of Honour*, *The Great Duke of Florence*, *The Emperor of the East*, *The Picture*, to see that his world includes some charming female characters—not, indeed, so lovely as those of Shakspere, but still, types which show that he had not lost his faith in human nature, as, when we read Fielding, we feel regretfully almost obliged to allow, in spite of Sophia Western and Amelia, is the case with our great novelist.

It is true that there are ladies in Massinger's plays who offer their hands in marriage to the men they love, and very charmingly the thing is done, though there is nothing equal to the scene between the Duchess and Antonio in Webster's masterpiece; as, for example, Artemia in *The Virgin Martyr*, the Duchess of Urbin in *The Great Duke*, Calista in *The Guardian*.[2] This feature is not confined to Massinger among the writers of his age; to mention no other instances, what about Arethusa in *Philaster*, Bianca in *The Fair Maid of the Inn*, Beliza and the Queen in *The Queen of Corinth*,[3] Frank in *The Captain*, Clara in *Love's Cure* (IV., 2), Martia in *The Double Marriage* (II., 3), Lamira in *The Honest Man's Fortune* (V., 3), Erota in *The Laws of Candy* ? Or, what about Desdemona in *Othello*,[4] or Olivia in *Twelfth Night* ?[5] What about the

---

[1] Rubens took his wives as models for his art; let us hope that Massinger's portrait of the imperious woman was not drawn from his wife. We happen to know that he was married.

[2] I., 1. *Cf.* also Matilda in *The Bashful Lover* (III., 3, 147), and Donusa in *The Renegado* (II., 4).

[3] IV., 1; V., 4. *Cf.* also Thamasta in Ford's *Lover's Melancholy* (III., 2), Calantha's request to her father in *The Broken Heart* (IV., 3), Fiormonda in *Love's Sacrifice* (I., 2), Hidaspes in *Cupid's Revenge* (I., 3).

[4] Act I., 3.

[5] III., 1, 161. *Cf.* also *Romeo and Juliet*, I., 5, 95.

plot of *All's Well that Ends Well?* To the vulgar mind all things are vulgar. *Honi soit qui mal y pense.*[1] It may certainly be conceded that in some of Massinger's plays, as, for instance, *The Unnatural Combat* and *Believe as You List*, the feminine interest is comparatively slight. Brander Matthews tells us that Massinger's women " are all painted from the outside only ";[2] " they are not convincing; they lack essential womanliness." This may be due to the fault which the same critic points out in our author, that " he is heavy-handed and coarse-fibred ethically as well as æsthetically." One may reply that if the theatre be the mirror of life Massinger had an undoubted right to bring bad women on the stage; there are good and noble women also among his characters, and if they are not " convincing," perhaps we may quote Coleridge's remark about Shakspere, that " he saw it was the perfection of women to be characterless." However far our author may fall short of his great model in grace, charm, and delicacy, he at any rate deserves credit for having imagined female characters who are full of passions and made of " flesh and blood." [3]

Massinger resembles other dramatists of his age; at times we feel that they talk like the little boys on the links in Stevenson's *Lantern-Bearers*. But Massinger is a robuster mind than Fletcher, for example; if he brings vice upon the stage, and if he speaks too freely about things which we prefer not to have mentioned, if " like Hogarth, he enjoys his own portrayal of degrading vice and its appalling consequences,"[4] we must, to do him

---

[1] The situation is not unknown in modern fiction; take, for example, *Dr. Breen's Practice* and *The House of Lynch*. *Cf.* Jebb's *Bentley*, p. 197.

[2] *Op. cit.*, p. 317.

[3] A favourite phrase of Massinger's—e.g., *Emperor of the East*, II., 1, 345; V., 2, 83; *Great Duke of Florence*, II., 3, 112; *Unnatural Combat*, I., 1, 312; IV., 1, 110; *Parliament of Love*, II., 3, 77.

[4] B. Matthews, p. 318.

justice, take his work as a whole. Indeed, most of the critics have singled out as one of his special claims to praise his sturdy morality,[1] and the general effect on any fair mind of a perusal of his plays is a conviction that he loved virtue. Vitelli[2] may make the best of both worlds, but he converts Donusa, and faces death and torture with fortitude. Goodness emerges from Massinger's plays, sometimes compromised for the moment, but always triumphant in the end. There is considerable outspokenness, but not much lubricity, and no perverted morality. Passages which offend can nearly always, as in Shakspere, be omitted without damaging the course of the plot. Moreover, as has often been pointed out, the works of Massinger are almost wholly free from blasphemy and profanity, and attacks on the clergy, such as moved the wrath of Jeremy Collier in later times.

It may be a fanciful suggestion, but it is possible that the drama of that day suffered from the fact that boys took the female parts.[3] No one would deny the artistic

---

[1] Especially Sir A. W. Ward (*English Dramatic Literature*, iii., pp. 41-42). *Cf.* also G. C. Macaulay in *Cambridge History of English Literature*, vol. vi., p. 121, and Schelling's verdict.

[2] The Venetian in *The Renegado*.

[3] Dr. Bradley (*Oxford Lectures*, pp. 373-4) minimizes the objections to this custom, without, however, dwelling on the moral problem. *Cf.* also Mr. Percy Simpson's remarks in *Shakspere's England*, ii., p. 246. Prynne deals with it (*Histriomastix*, ed. 1633, pp. 214-216). He allows, reluctantly, that " men actors in women's attire are not altogether so bad, so discommendable as women stage-players," but goes on to say: "since both of them are evill, yea extremely vitious, neither of them necessary, both superfluous as all playes and players are; the superabundant sinfulnesse of the one, can neither justifie the lawfulnesse, nor extenuate the wickednesse of the other. . . . This should rather bee the conclusion, both of them are abominable, both intolerable, neither of them laudable or necessary; therefore both of them to bee abandoned, neither of them henceforth to be tollerated among Christians."

Ford, in *Love's Sacrifice* (III., 2), refers to the novelty of women-antics—*i.e.*, of women acting in masques. It is clear that Queen Henrietta Maria, with her passion for appearing

loss thereby involved, but there was a moral loss as well.
It made it possible for things to be said that would not
have been said by men to women, still less by women to
men.   It unconsciously invested the love-scenes with an
air of unreality and grossness.   It prevented the relation
of the sexes from being depicted with that union of passion
and purity which, though difficult, is possible.

It has been said that Massinger is hard and metallic,
and devoid of pathos.   This charge, again, is largely true.
You will not find in him scenes which clutch the heart
like those of *Dr. Faustus*, or *The Duchess of Malfi*, or *The
Broken Heart*, or *The Maid's Tragedy*, or *The Wife for a
Month ;* you will not find the sublimity of Ordella's self-
sacrifice in *Thierry and Theodoret*, or the chivalry of *A
Fair Quarrel ;* still less will you find anything so appalling
as the end of *King Lear*, or *Othello*, or *Romeo and Juliet*.
There is plenty of passion in Massinger; like the legendary
lion, he lashes with his tail, and you can almost see him in
the act; but his rhetoric does not entirely carry you away.
Let me recall the fine passage which was quoted just now
from *The Roman Actor*.[1] I hope everyone will allow
its eloquence; but the repetition of the commonplace
phrase, "we cannot help it,"[2] natural and forcible as it
is, falls short of the ideal grandeur at which the passage
aims.   We feel that Fletcher could have made a finer
thing of the prison-scene in *The Emperor of the East*.

---

on the stage in masques, however much she may have been
before the times, must have caused great scandal to the Puritan
party.   The complications which sometimes arise from the use
of men for female parts may be illustrated from Middleton's
amusing play, *The Widow*, where Martia is disguised as a man,
Ansaldo, and, to escape further complications, is subsequently
disguised as a woman, *being a boy all the time*.   We find the
same thing in the second Luce in *The Wise Woman of Hogsdon*.

[1] *Supra*, p. 38.

[2] Though Massinger does not owe much to Chapman, it is
to be noted that this trick of repeating a phrase occurs several
times in Chapman's popular play, *Bussy d'Ambois*.   *Cf.*
III., 1., "He shall confess all, and you then may hang him,"
and towards the end of the same Act, "Ay, anything but

It is significant that the most tender passage in Massinger,[1] where Leonora bids Almira take consolation, has been assigned by some to Fletcher. In other words, Massinger is not in the front rank of genius, but no one would claim for him such a place.

Again, one might urge that his plays are not stores of worldly wisdom, like Shakspere's; his aphorisms are not deep; they do not bite.[2] Consequently he does not lend

---

killing of the King ; " and in *The Conspiracy of Byron*, Act II., in La Fin's speech, " I can make good " four times at the end of the line. *Cf.* " Behold the Turk and his great Empress" in *Tamburlaine*, pt. I., V., 1; "I love my lord; let that suffice for me " in Greene's *Orlando Furioso*, I., 1.

[1] *A Very Woman*, III., 4.

[2] A few instances of γνῶμαι may be given from Massinger; his debt to Shakspere will be clear:

Fatal Dowry, I., 1, 20:
> There is a minute
> When a man's presence speaks in his own cause
> More than the tongues of twenty advocates.

Guardian, I., 1, 241:
> For a flying foe
> Discreet and provident conquerors build up
> A bridge of gold.

Guardian, IV., 1, 99:
> O dear madam,
> We are all the balls of time, toss'd to and fro,
> From the plough unto the throne, and back again;
> Under the swing of destiny mankind suffers.

(*Cf. Plautus' Captivi*, Prologue, 22, "Enimvero di nos quasi pilas homines habent;" *Pericles*, II., 1, 63; and *The Duchess of Malfi*, p. 99a; *Parliament of Bees*, char. vii.).

Bashful Lover, IV., 1, 69:
> Fortune rules all;
> We are her tennis-balls.

(*Cf.* also Greg's *Henslowe Papers*, p. 143.)

Bashful Lover, III., 2, 3:
> A diamond,
> Though set in horn, is still a diamond
> And sparkles, as in purest gold.

himself to quotation. Yet this does not of necessity detract from his greatness. No one would question the excellence of the *Waverley Novels*, but Leslie Stephen has pointed out that we only make one quotation from Scott's novels.[1] Aristotle has told us that " excessive brilliance of diction obscures characters and sentiments."[2] There

---

Very Woman, IV., 1, 90:

> Revenge, that thirsty dropsy of our souls,
> Which makes us covet that which hurts us most,
> Is not alone sweet, but partakes of tartness.

Duke of Milan, I., 1, 60:

> Dangers that we see
> To threaten ruin, are with ease prevented;
> But those strike deadly that come unexpected.

Great Duke of Florence, III., 1, 138:

> Love
> Steals sometimes through the ear into the heart,
> As well as by the eye.

Picture, II., 1, 79:

> Ill news, madam,
> Are swallow-wing'd, but what's good walks on crutches.

Virgin Martyr, IV., 1, 103:

> Pleasures forc'd
> Are unripe apples; sour, not worth the plucking.

A New Way, IV., 1, 187:

> Though I must grant
> Riches, well-got, to be a useful servant,
> But a bad master.

Bondman, I., 3, 100:

> He that would govern others, first should be
> The master of himself, richly endu'd
> With depth of understanding, height of courage,
> And those remarkable graces which I dare not
> Ascribe unto myself.

Bondman, III., 1, 6:

> But turbulent spirits, raised beyond themselves
> With ease, are not so soon laid; they oft prove
> Dangerous to him that call'd them up.

---

[1] *Hours in a Library*, i., p. 167.
[2] *Poetics*, 1460*b*, 4.

are few passages of high poetical emotion in Massinger; there is little magic in the rhythm of individual lines. Like most of his contemporaries he shows at times a strange insensibility to smooth rhythm in the heroic couplet. He has an anapæstic lilt in various parts of the line, inherited from Shakspere, and found in Milton's early poems, which is not ineffective in its way, and which seems to have aimed at varying the monotony of the ten-syllable line.[1] He has not much power of rhyme,[2] nor are his plays studded with such lyrics as Shakspere and Fletcher could write upon occasion.[3]

Again, the comic element in Massinger is at times dull, forced, and ordinary; it does not take us very far to label a foolish Florentine gentleman with the name of " Sylli ";[4] the hungry soldier is rather a time-worn type,[5] nor

---

[1] *Cf.* Appendix VI. and the discussion in Robert Bridges' *Milton*, Appendix D, pp. 56-57. The same thing is found again and again in Shirley's *Lady of Pleasure*.

[2] For a rhymed passage *cf. A Very Woman*, IV., 1, 141-152.

[3] We have a few unimportant poems in rhyme from his pen, which show the same characteristics of style as his blank verse, though fettered by the restraints of the couplet. Some of his songs are not at all bad; *cf.*, for example, *Emperor of the East*, V., 3: " Why art thou slow, thou rest of trouble, Death ?" *Guardian*, IV., 2, The songs of Juno and Hymen; V., 1, the " entertainment of the Forest's Queen." *Picture*, II., 2, the song of Pallas; III., 5, song beginning, " The blushing rose and purple flower." It must, however, be conceded that these songs are commonplace.

[4] *Maid of Honour.* The same name is found in Ben Jonson's unfortunate *New Inn*, produced in 1629. *Cf.* also *City Madam*, II., 2, 182:
MARY. Whose sheep are these, whose oxen ? The Lady Plenty's.
PLENTY. A plentiful pox upon you.
New Way, IV., 2, 2:
Did not Master Marrall
(He has marr'd all I am sure) strictly command us ?
New Way, IV., 2, 68:
No, though the great Turk came, instead of turkies
To beg any favour, I am inexorable.

[5] Belgrade in *The Unnatural Combat.*

can Greedy compare with Lazarillo. Though the situations are humorous, we do not split with laughter over Massinger, as we do in reading Aristophanes, or Shakspere, or Molière.[1] We do not find in him the mercurial lightness of *A Trick to Catch the Old One*, or the invincible absurdity of "The Roarers" in *The Fair Quarrel*. But it is necessary to remember that the comic business is of the kind which gains by acting, or indeed requires it, and to allow that towards the end of his life Massinger came forward as a grave and powerful satirist of contemporary men, reminding us of Ben Jonson, but, to my mind, excelling him; for he shows less asperity with greater lucidity and ease.[2] He is not unduly morose or bitter, yet he wins conviction with an admirable sanity and sobriety. The plays will repay good acting, and, after all, plays are meant to be acted; it is significant that the last of Massinger's plays to hold the stage was his comedy, *The New Way to pay Old Debts*, and it is very much to be wished that it should be revived in England.[3]

Some critics have accused Massinger of redundancy in style, a characteristic which clearly will strike different people in different ways. Thus, Hallam regards this feature as on the whole meritorious, giving "fulness, or what the painters would call impasto, to his style, and if it might not always conduce to effect on the stage, suitable on the whole to the character of his composition." Mr. Bullen,[4] after an eloquent tribute to "Massinger's admirable ease and dignity," and to "his rare command of an excellent work-a-day dramatic style, clear, vigorous, and

---

[1] Boyle (*N. S. S.*, pp. 588-9) points out that Massinger "succeeds admirably in depicting the witty pertness of a saucy page." It does not, therefore, follow that he had been one himself, as has been supposed by some.

[2] In *The New Way* and *City Madam*.

[3] Mr. Ben Greet's Company has from time to time given a charming alfresco performance of *The Great Duke of Florence*.

[4] Preface to Sir John V. O. Barnavelt (*Old Plays*, vol. ii., p. 204).

free from conceit and affectation," proceeds to allow that
" he is apt to grow didactic and tax the reader's patience;
and there is often a want of coherence in his sentences,
which amble down the page in a series of loosely linked
clauses." I do not myself feel that this charge comes
to very much.

The real fault of Massinger lies in an imperfect presenta-
tion of character. This point has been felt by many
writers, and put in various ways. Coleridge bluntly says:
" Massinger's characters have no character." [1] Brander
Matthews puts it in another way when he observes that
" the plots are not the result of the characters, but the work
of the playwright," [2] a criticism we may remark in passing
eminently applicable to Fletcher. It has been said that the
characters are conventional, like those in the Italian or
Spanish sources from which they are derived; the violent
tyrant and the arrogant queen are the most familiar of
these types. I do not think this statement arrives at the
root of the matter. Characters may be conventional and
yet interesting and lifelike. A great many of the personages in Massinger's plays, important and unimportant
alike, act reasonably; he takes great pains to discriminate
them, and the effect is successful and consistent. Let us
recall the great characters in Massinger; they are Paris,
Luke, Sir Giles Overreach, Durazzo, Marullo, Malefort,
Charalois, Antiochus, Camiola, Dorothea, Donusa, Almira.
In the second rank we may put Timoleon, Romont, Bertoldo, John Antonio, Mathias, Wellborn, Athenais, Marcelia, Sophia, Cleora. Of these persons, the two that I
think most men would like to have known best are Paris
and Camiola. Notice, by the way, that there is seldom
more than one great character in a play. Now, in
Henry VIII there are three, the King, Catherine, and
Wolsey. The question arises whether Massinger, even
with Fletcher's help, could have worked on this scale. If

---

[1] *Op. cit.*, p. 405.
[2] *Op cit.*, p. 312.

Massinger wrote *Henry VIII* it is certainly, with all its faults, his most remarkable achievement.

The point which I wish to emphasize is that there are many characters in Massinger drawn with care and ability. Think, for example, of the skilful contrast between Pulcheria and Athenais in *The Emperor of the East*, showing how easy it is for two good women to quarrel. Further, it is clear that the attempt to produce composite and developing characters is praiseworthy, even if it be not always successful, because it is more true to life than Ben Jonson's brilliant but illusory delineation of " humours." Human beings are too complex to be labelled in this slapdash way, however amusing it may be on the stage.

And yet we must allow that a certain number of the more important characters act outrageously; the explanation being that the faults which Massinger loves to portray and censure are such as show themselves in outrageous ways—such as anger, pride, impotence in the Latin sense, uxoriousness, and above all jealousy.[1] Take the case of Theophilus in *The Virgin Martyr*, who kills his daughters because they have been reconverted to Christianity; or of Domitian in *The Roman Actor*, who goes through life killing people as he would kill flies. It is not enough to say that there are such people in the world; the point is, that in Massinger they shock us without appalling us. Sforza behaves to Marcelia much as Othello behaves to Desdemona; we feel at once a difference of power in the two plays.[2] Massinger has many villains, but Shakspere manages better with Richard III and Iago. Think again of the uxoriousness of Ladislas, Theodosius, Domitian, which some have held to be a covert satire on Charles I. We despise these weak and servile husbands.

---

[1] *Cf.* Sforza in *The Duke of Milan;* Theodosius in *The Emperor of the East;* and especially, Leosthenes in *The Bondman.*

[2] The first quarto of *Othello* appeared in 1622, *The Duke* in 1623.

Now, is there anything we can urge in Massinger's justification ? I think there is. We read his plays nowadays, we do not see them acted. We are therefore apt to forget how impressive and vigorous good acting is. The display of passion on the stage with gesture, attitude, frown, and scorn, would render more tolerable some of these scenes which offend us in the study by their crudeness. Such a part, for instance, as Leosthenes in *The Bondman*, the jealous and yet guilty lover, has great opportunities for the actor. It might even be urged that Massinger wrote thus because he knew the capabilities of the actors who were going to perform his plays.

The same consideration applies to a feature in Massinger which will strike every reader. He sets himself at times to represent growth, or, at any rate, change, of character. Even Shakspere seldom tries to do this,[1] and it was too hard a task for his pupil. His most ambitious venture in this direction is in *The Picture*. In that play Mathias has a magic portrait, which shows him whether his wife is faithful to him or not in his absence; and the alternations of the mind in husband and wife alike are drawn with considerable power. Luke in *The City Madam* is perhaps the most skilfully drawn example of a development of character. The hypocrite is quite carried away by the riches to which he unexpectedly succeeds.[2] Another successful conversion is that of Theophilus at the end of *The Virgin Martyr*. It is due partly to his eating the heavenly fruit, for which he had asked Dorothea at her death, partly to the effect which the

---

[1] Perhaps Macbeth and Lady Macbeth are the only instances. Notice in *Henry VIII* various rapid changes of mind—*e.g.*, III., 2, 336: SURREY. "I forgive him "; V., 2, 172: GARDINER. "With a true heart and brother love I do it." Henry V and Antony are other instances which will occur to everyone. In the case of the former, at any rate, I for one feel that Shakspere cuts the Gordian knot.

[2] The soliloquy of Luke over his brother's wealth is one of the most splendid efforts of eloquence in English. (*City Madam*, III., 3.)

grace and beauty of Angelo produce on his mind. The gradual growth of his new belief, in spite of all that Harpax can do, is managed with much skill, and it is in itself true to nature that the man who had been violent in one direction should ultimately be violent in another. Moreover, we are bound to remember that when people are soon persuaded, the play gets on. Indeed, I think we have in this consideration the clue to the whole matter; " the Stage Poet " had a practical mind.

Change of mood and vacillation of purpose, under the stress of temptation, or due to the conflict of contrary impulses, are features of some of Massinger's best scenes. The wavering of the love-sick Caldoro while Durazzo is abusing him is very true to life.[1] The skill with which the " melancholy " Vitelli's changes of mood are depicted in *The Renegado*[2] suggests the theory that Massinger is drawing his own portrait. The alternation of pride and humility in Honoria in *The Picture*[3] is forcibly shown. The just anger of Sophia at the end of the same play yields skilfully to a combined intercession.

As a rule, however, the changes are too rapid. Thus, in *The Maid of Honour*, Aurelia, when she hears that Camiola has ransomed Bertoldo and bound him with a promise to marry her, suddenly changes her mind; she has been on the point of marrying the faithless soldier, but, as she says:

On the sudden
I feel all fires of love quench'd in the water
Of my compassion.[4]

Though the change is natural, it is inartistically effected; it comes too suddenly. Think, however, what an opportunity this would be for a great actress. If we were in the audience, we should see the gradual development reflected in her expression and bearing long before she utters the words which embody her thought.

---

[1] *Guardian*, I.,   [2] I., 1.   [3] I., 2.   [4] V., 2, 129.

Other instances of the same thing are to be found in Donusa's conversion to Christianity in *The Renegado*,[1] in the change of faith effected in Calista and Christeta by Dorothea's story of the King of Egypt and Osiris' image,[2] and in the indecision of Lorenzo about matrimony in *The Bashful Lover*.[3]

Change of mind is an ungrateful and inartistic experience. It has landed many honest politicians in bitter and undeserved reproaches. From Aristotle's time onwards Euripides has been blamed for his Iphigenia at Aulis, who first feared to die, and then offered herself for her country.[4] We certainly feel that in Massinger there are occasionally instances of cheap repentance which do not seem real. Take the case of Corisca in *The Bondman ;* a bad woman repents, but though convinced we are not pleased at the spectacle.[5] If Massinger had ever read the *Poetics* of Aristotle, he forgot or ignored the precept that a character should be ὁμαλόν, or " consistent."[6] If this is not the case there is a danger that

---

[1] IV., 3, 133:

VITELLI. Your intent to win me
To be of your belief, proceeded from
Your fear to die. Can there be strength in that
Religion, that suffers us to tremble
At that which every day, nay hour, we haste to ?
DONUSA. This is unanswerable, and there's something tells
me
I err in my opinion.

[2] *Virgin Martyr*, III., 1, 186.

[3] IV., V. *Cf.* especially IV., 1, 138:

LORENZO. Stay, I feel
A sudden alteration.
MARTINO. Here are fine whimsies.

[4] *Poetics*, 1454a, 33.

[5] III., 3; V., 3, 33. After all, Corisca does not repent of her worst faults, only of her luxury and cruelty to her slaves. *Cf.* also The Projector in *The Emperor of the East*, I., 2, 257. On the other hand, the conversion of the courtiers in the same play (II., 1, 154) is according to character.

[6] *Poetics*, 1454a, 26.

the effect will be μιαρόν, or "odious," to use a word
of which Aristotle is fond. I think, then, that this charge
is proven. Massinger saw how effective on the stage a
sudden change of character might be, but lacked the necessary art to make it convincing. Hence some of his characters are not even ὁμαλῶς ἀνώμαλοι.[1] Perhaps the
explanation is this, that, being a master of language,
he overvalued the persuasiveness of rhetoric.[2] It is not
enough to portray the varying emotions which sway the
mind at a particular moment; to produce a satisfactory
whole they have to be fused together. The reader should
not feel that the characters are at the mercy of the situations in which they are placed, or they will appear to be
lay-figures or puppets, rather than live flesh and blood.

Yet even here a defence of some sort can be set up for
our poet. I will endeavour to make my meaning clear by
an analogy from music. It may have occurred to someone to ask what the music of Mozart would have been
like if he had lived after Beethoven. Would it have been
more serious and sublime than it is ? The question is
worth asking, even if the only answer to it be this, that
without Mozart Beethoven would never have existed.
I think it is fair to argue that Massinger, in his constant
effort after the representation of change of character,
was before his time; he was seeking after a complex but
possible effect, which the novelist can undertake but which
the limitations of the stage render almost impossible.[3]

---

[1] *Poetics*, 1454a, 28.

[2] Leslie Stephen has anticipated me here. "The truth
seems to be that Massinger is subject to an illusion natural
enough to a man who is more of the rhetorician than the seer.
He fancies that eloquence must be irresistible. He takes the
change of mood produced by an elevated appeal to the feelings
for a change of character " (*Hours in a Library*, ii., p. 164).

[3] Here again I find myself in agreement with Leslie Stephen.
"Massinger's plays are a gradual unravelling of a series of
incidents, each following intelligibly from the preceding situation, and suggestive of many eloquent observations, though not
developments of one master thought. We often feel, that if

Is it fanciful to say that if he had lived in the eighteenth century, if he had had before his eyes the work of Fielding, Richardson, and Smollett, he would have been a good novelist, less cynical than Fielding, more concise than Richardson, more ideal than Smollett ? There are authors like Euripides and Virgil whose very failures by a strange paradox seem part of their greatness; and we may perhaps say that Massinger, by pointing the way somewhat tentatively and blindly to subtle psychological studies, has helped to build up the noble fabric of the English novel.

Let us now turn to some miscellaneous points of interest in Massinger; and first, let us note his imitation of Shakspere. It is tempting to suppose that as he was at one time a dependent of a family which was intimate with Shakspere he may have come across the man himself;[1] it is, at any rate, simpler to remember that as he was thirty-two years of age when Shakspere died, he can hardly have failed to meet him in his professional relations. But we have no evidence of the fact. All we can say is that his plays, like those of Fletcher, Webster, Tourneur, and others,[2] show a constant study of Shakspere.[3]

---

external circumstances had been propitious, he would have expressed himself more naturally, in the form of a prose romance than in a drama " (*Op. cit.*, ii., p. 157). *Cf.* also Coleridge's remark that Massinger's plays are " as interesting as novels." How much character-drawing is there in Boccaccio or Paynter ?

[1] Mr. Nichol Smith (*Shakspere's England*, ii., p. 202) doubts the " association of Pembroke with Shakspere."

[2] Sir Sidney Lee (*Life of W. Shakespeare*, 1915, p. 441) notes " the almost magical success " with which Massinger echoes Shakspere's tones.

[3] In a " mock " romance published at London in 1656, *Wit and Fancy in a Maze* (Book 2, chapter iv.), the Enchantress Lamia and the hero Don Zara del Fogo go to Elysium and find everything in an uproar. Ajax and Ulysses are quarrelling; Homer and Hesiod; Statius and Virgil. Last of all Ben Jonson "had openly vaunted himself the first and best of English poets." This is much resented by Chaucer, Chapman, and Spenser; last of all Shakspere and Fletcher appear " with a strong party " to claim the first place. Among " their life

First let me give a few examples of the imitation of incidents. In *The Roman Actor*,[1] Paris refers to a tragedy " in which a murder was acted to the life," which forced a guilty hearer to make discovery of his secret; this recalls the play scene in Hamlet.[2] In *A Very Woman*[3] Almira makes Antonio tell her his history. The hint of this is taken from *Othello*.[4] In *The Fatal Dowry*[5] Beaumelle and her maid arrange to be overheard, like Hero and Ursula in *Much Ado about Nothing*.[6] The device by which Beaupré recovers her husband in *The Parliament of Love* is imitated from *All's Well that Ends Well* and *Measure for Measure*. The banditti in *The Guardian*[7] respect the poor like the outlaws in *The Two Gentlemen of Verona*.[8] The forest scenes in the same play recall *As You Like It* and *Midsummer-Night's Dream*.[9] In *The Bashful Lover*[10] the pretty tale of a sister which Ascanio tells is a reminiscence of *Twelfth Night*.[11] The incident in the same play of Hortensio with Ascanio in his arms[12] is modelled on *As You Like It*.[13] Malefort's behaviour to the tailor[14] is imitated from Petruchio's in *The Taming of the Shrew*.[15] ·The gibberish of the pretended Indians in *The City Madam*[16] reminds us of Parolles' adventure in *All's Well*.[17] The scene in *The Emperor of the East*[18] where Eudocia professes to have eaten the apple is modelled on *Othello*[19], where Desdemona asserts that the handkerchief is not lost. In *The Bondman*[20] Zanthia overhears Corisca's confession of love in her sleep, as Iago

---

guard " are mentioned Goffe, Massinger, Dekker, Webster, Suckling, Cartwright, Carew. Did Ben Jonson dislike Massinger as Mr. Phelan conjectures ?

[1] II., 1, 100.   [2] IV., 2.   [3] IV., 3.
[4] I., 3.   [5] III., 1, 261.   [6] III.,1.
[7] II., 4. The good brigand goes back beyond Robin Hood to Herodotus, VI. 16.   [8] IV., 1.
[9] Compare especially V., 2, 104 with *Midsummer Night's Dream*, II., 2, 145.
[10] II., 1, 22.   [11] II., 4.   [12] III., 1, 24
[13] II., 7.   [14] *Unnatural Combat*, III., 2, 13.
[15] IV., 3.   [16] III., 3, 91-2.   [17] IV., 1.
[18] IV., 5.   [19] III., 4.   [20] II., 2, 93.

does Cassio's.[1] In *A New Way to pay Old Debts*[2] Sir Giles Overreach is carried off for treatment to a dark room like Malvolio in *Twelfth Night*.[3] Almira in *A Very Woman*[4] reminds us of the sleep-walking scene in *Macbeth*. The ghosts in *The Unnatural Combat*[5] and *The Roman Actor*[6] are used like those in the finale of *Richard III*. Parallels in thought and diction are also numerous. Take *The Roman Actor*[7]:

> ARETINUS. Are you on the stage,
> You talk so boldly ?
> PARIS. The whole world being one,
> This place is not exempted.

This goes back to Jaques in *As You Like It*.[8] In *The Maid of Honour*[9] Jacomo talks of " trailing the puissant pike ;" the phrase of Pistol in *Henry V*. [10] In *The Emperor of the East*[11] Athenais makes use of the phrase " prophetic

---

[1] *Othello*, III., 3.

[2] V., 1, 376. *Cf.* also Security in prison in *Eastward Ho* (Act V.); Grimaldi in *The Renegado* (IV., 1, 4).

[3] III., 4, 148. On the other hand, Paulo in *A Very Woman* (III., 3, 5) observes:

> To choke up his spirits in a dark room,
> Is far more dangerous.

[4] II., 3.   [5] V., 2.   [6] V., 1.

[7] I., 3, 49. Rowley uses the metaphor in the dedication of *A Fair Quarrel*.   [8] II., 7.   [9] III., 1, 49.

[10] IV., 1. The language of Ding'em in *The City Madam* (IV., 1, 15) takes us back to Pistol:

> Thy word's a law,
> And I obey. Live, scrape-shoe, and be thankful,
> Thou man of muck and money, for as such
> I now salute thee; the suburbian gamesters
> Have heard thy fortunes, and I am, in person,
> Sent to congratulate.

Cf. also *A New Way*, I., 2, 59:

FURNACE. " I am appeased, and Furnace now grows cool."

[11] I., 2, 318. *Cf. Prophetess*, I., 2, 31:

> I presently, inspired with holy fire,
> And my prophetic spirit burning in me,
> Gave answer from the gods.

soul," which we remember in *Hamlet*.[1] Leosthenes uses
the same phrase in *The Bondman*[2] when the mutinous slave
Cimbrio boasts of the excesses of his friends. The pun
which Hircius makes on the cobbler's awl[3] occurs in the
first scene of *Julius Cæsar*. The madness of the English
slave in *A Very Woman*[4] comes from the grave-diggers'
scene in *Hamlet*.[5] The " many-headed monster, multi-
tude " of Theodosius in *The Emperor of the East*[6] takes us
back to Coriolanus' " beast with many heads ";[7] while the
reference in the same play[8] to the "stomach " reminds us
of the fable of Menenius.[9] In *The Bashful Lover*[10] Uberti
discourses thus :

> I look on your dimensions, and find not
> Mine own of lesser size; the blood that fills
> My veins, as hot as yours, my sword as sharp,
> My nerves of equal strength, my heart as good.

This reminds us of Shylock in *The Merchant of Venice*[11]
and the King in *Henry V*.[12] Clarindore's language in
The Parliament of Love[13] is modelled on Malvolio in *Twelfth
Night*.[14] The same is true of Sir Giles Overreach in *A New
Way*.[15] Shakspere's dislike of spaniels reappears in the
same play.[16]

No doubt we must make deductions for the common

Double Marriage, II., 4, 30 :
     Who stole her ?   Oh ! my prophetic soul !
[1] I., 5, 40.   [2] IV., 2, 39.
[3] *Virgin Martyr*, III., 3, 46
[4] III., 1, 118.   [5] V., 1, 170.
[6] II., 1, 99.   *Cf.* also *Roman Actor*, III., 2, 35.
[7] IV., 1, 1.   [8] III., 2, 18.   [9] *Coriolanus*, I., 1, 99.
[10] I., 2, 40.   *Cf.* also *A New Way*, I., 3, 88, and *Emperor of
the East*, V., 2, 83 :
     I am flesh and blood, as you are, sensible
     Of heat and cold, as much a slave unto
     The tyranny of my passions as the meanest
     Of my poor subjects.
[11] III., 1.   [12] IV., 1, 103.   [13] II., 1, 54.
[14] II., 5.   [15] IV., 3, 131-137.
[16] II., 1, 38.   *Cf.* Bradley, *Shakspearean Tragedy*, p. 268.

idioms of the day,[1] but the cumulative evidence of these parallels with the elder dramatist is overwhelming.[2]

Massinger is very fond of introducing doctors in his plays; so no doubt are the other dramatists of this period. It is interesting to compare Paulo in *A Very Woman* with Corax in *The Lover's Melancholy* of Ford, who deals successfully with two cases of mental derangement. Ford is more subtle, Massinger more dignified. Thus we find in *The Virgin Martyr*[3] a consultation about Antoninus' health. Sapritius, the afflicted father, hails the doctors thus:

> O you that are half gods, lengthen that life
> Their deities lend us; turn o'er all the volumes
> Of your mysterious Æsculapian science
> T' increase the number of this young man's days.[4]

Compare with this another passage in *The Duke of Milan:*

> SFORZA.   O you earthly gods,
> You second natures, that from your great master,
> Who join'd the limbs of torn Hippolytus,
> And drew upon himself the Thunderer's envy,
> Are taught those hidden secrets that restore
> To life death-wounded men![5]

In *A Very Woman*[6] Paulo, on entering with two surgeons, is thus addressed:

> DUKE. My hand! You rather
> Deserve my knee, and it shall bend as to
> A second father, if your saving aids
> Restore my son.

---

[1] Thus, to take an instance at random, the madness of the Englishman is referred to in Webster's *Malcontent* (III. 1).
[2] *Cf.* also Appendix IV.   [3] IV., 1.
[4] IV., 1, 1. The last line shows how prosaic Massinger could on occasion be. In judging our older writers, however, it is important to remember that words change their poetical value with time; it is clear, for example, that in James I.'s age, "undertaker," "proceedings," "punctually," "aunt," were regarded as legitimate in poetry.
[5] V., 2, 49-54.   [6] II., 2, 23.

VICEROY. Rise, thou bright star of knowledge,
Thou honour of thy art, thou help of nature.
Thou glory of our academies !

The old saying, " Ubi tres medici ibi duo athei," referred
to by Sir T. Browne in *Religio Medici* is recalled to us by
these lines :

VICEROY. Observe his piety; I have heard, how true
I know not, most physicians, as they grow
Greater in skill, grow less in their religion;
Attributing so much to natural causes,
That they have little faith in that they cannot
Deliver reason for; this doctor steers
Another course.[1]

We find them again in *The Emperor of the East*,[2] where
a surgeon is contrasted with an empiric who vends his
wares and talks much Latin, like the quack in Ben Jonson's
Alchemist, while Paulinus complains of the many medical
impostors who prey upon the rich. The crisis of *The Duke
of Milan*[3] owes much to the action of doctors. The plot
of *A Very Woman* hinges largely on the skill of the doctor
Paulo, to whom we have referred above. In this play
we have two victims of melancholy, Almira and Cardenes;
the former is cured by falling in love with the disguised
John Antonio; the latter is Paulo's patient. The recovery
of the avaricious father in *The Roman Actor*[4] is due to Paris
acting in the part of a doctor. The physician Dinant in
The Parliament of Love gives the gallants a good lesson
(IV., 5). And in *The Picture*[5] we find an elaborate
simile, in which soldiers are said to be the surgeons of
the State. In the same play Hilario,[6] when on starvation

---

[1] *A Very Woman*, II., 2, 96.   [2] IV., 4.
[3] V., 2.   [4] II., 1.
[5] II., 2, 84-98; cf. also *A Very Woman*, II., 2, 2; *Bondman*,
I., 3, 216; *Emperor of the East*, III., 2, 54; *Guardian*, III., 1,
23; *Parliament of Love*, I., 4, 23; *Believe as You List*, V., 1, 69;
Unnatural Combat, IV., 1, 131 and 231.
[6] III., 1, 12-16.

fare, is accosted by a surgeon, who invites him to sell himself for "a living anatomy to be set up in the surgeons' hall." Such passages,[1] and the zest with which Massinger refers to potatoes, eringos, and the like,[2] together with the rather wearisome allusions which he makes to "caudles" and "cullises,"[3] lead us to wonder whether at one time of his life he may have seriously studied medicine. There is a significant passage in *The Parliament of Love*,[4] where Chamont says to the doctor Dinant,

Good master doctor, when your leisure serves,
Visit my house; when we least need their art,
Physicians look most lovely.

And close intercourse with doctors may have suggested the lines immediately below:

NOVALL. The knave is jealous.
PERIGOT. 'Tis a disease few doctors cure themselves of.

At the same time, let us not forget the passages where he shows a knowledge of the law;[5] nor the fact that books have been written to prove that Shakspere must have had a training in this or that profession.[6] The really interesting point about the doctors in Massinger is that they are so often praised as the healers of the mind; the dramatist who delights in drawing gloomy, passionate characters seems to have a high opinion for the profession which

---

[1] *Cf.* also *Bondman*, II., 2, 36; IV., 4, 22; *Bashful Lover*, V., 1, 72-156; *Emperor of the East*, IV., 3, 39; *Duke of Milan*, IV., 3, 97; *Unnatural Combat*, IV., 1, 199; *Parliament of Love*, V., 1, 526-7; *Guardian*, I., 1, 13; II., 5, 56; *Picture*, III., 4, 21.

[2] *New Way*, II., 2, 17-22; *Picture*, IV., 2, 26-33.

[3] *Picture*, I., 2, 30; IV., 2, 79; *Bondman*, I., 2, 36; IV., 2, 44; IV., 4, 21; *A New Way*, II., 2, 20; IV., 2, 99; *Emperor of the East*, I., 2, 223; *Parliament of Love*, IV., 1, 49; *Guardian*, I., 1, 297.

[4] III., 1, 26; III., 1, 32.

[5] *Cf. New Way* and *City Madam*, *passim*.

[6] *Cf.* Churton Collins' *Studies in Shakspere: No. V.*, "Was Shakspere a lawyer?" Mr. Arthur Underhill, in *Shakspere's England*, Vol. i., No. xiii., decides that Shakspere's "knowledge of law was neither profound nor accurate."

undertook to cure "melancholy."[1] In *A Very Woman* he takes care to praise and reward the doctor more highly than the surgeons. On the other hand, like most of his contemporaries, he naturally makes the physician a part of the machinery rather than an individual character. Even the doctor in *A Fair Quarrel*, who takes an unusually large part in the plot, can hardly be said to be more than a carefully drawn lay figure. The same remark applies to the friars of Shakspere.

The chief question about Massinger which interests the student of English is the authorship of *Henry VIII*. Did he take part in writing that play with Fletcher? There is a great mass of literature on this subject. As one who has read the undoubted plays of Massinger many times, I am bound to say that while there is much in the play which reminds one of Shakspere and Fletcher, I find little trace of Massinger's style. I do not deny that there are one or two slight reminiscences; thus the word "file"[2] is a favourite one with Massinger. We find blushing in the play once or twice,[3] but then we find it elsewhere in Shakspere. Anne's remark to the old lady, "Come, you are pleasant,"[4] is in Massinger's manner, but he may have taken the turn from Shakspere. The strict metre of such a line as this is like Massinger;[5] the same remark applies again:

---

[1] *A Very Woman*, II., 2, 60-64. It is to be noted that doctors are common also in Fletcher, the reason being that there are so many duels, and unexpected recoveries, in that author. Thus, the surgeon diets the Duke of Sesse in *The Double Marriage* (II., 4); and in the same play the doctor plays tricks on Castruccio's food (V., 1). In *The Sea Voyage* (III., 1) the surgeon is introduced merely to make fun of his apparatus. Doctors, chirurgeons, and apothecaries appear in fifteen of the plays of Beaumont and Fletcher. The same remark applies to Webster; *cf. The Duchess of Malfi, The White Devil*, and especially *The Devil's Law-case*.

[2] *Henry VIII*, I., 1, 75; I., 2, 42; III., 2, 171.

[3] II., 3, 42 and 72; III., 2, 305, 307, 353.   [4] II., 3, 93.

[5] III., 2, 37; *cf.* III., 4, 69. Beaumont observes a similar strictness.

SURREY. Has the King this ?
SUFFOLK.   Believe it.
SURREY.   Will this work ?

The fourth scene of the second act is a great law-court scene, and Massinger has several such, in which he may be copying Shakspere. The combination of courtiers in dialogue which we get in various parts of *Henry VIII* is like Massinger;[1] but, to my mind, the scenes are more clumsy than their parallels in Massinger. Sudden changes of mind are found in *Henry VIII*;[2] and this is probably the strongest bit of evidence in favour of Massinger's authorship. The characters are not harmoniously rounded off: Buckingham's prayers for the King[3] do not please us; the King's scruples of conscience are not convincing;[4] Wolsey's meekness[5] and piety[6] do not ring true, though they anticipate the picture of his last year which we get in Cavendish's Life—but all these blemishes may be due to hasty work or dual authorship. Failure in representing vacillation and complexity of character is, as we have seen above, a note of Massinger, but the failures of this kind in *Henry VIII* are marked by a sentimentality which reminds us of Fletcher.

Let us see now what there is in the play unlike Massinger. To begin with, there are many passages in Shakspere's difficult later style,[7] and there is a complete absence of Massinger's sinuous sentences and frequent parentheses, as also of his peculiar vocabulary; there are many flights of high and tender poetry which are beyond his compass; there are brilliant γνῶμαι, such as—

GRIFFITH. Noble madam,
Men's evil manners live in brass, their virtues
We write in water,[8]

---

[1] *E.g.*, I., 1; III., 2.   [2] *E.g.*, III., 2, 336; IV., 2, 73; V., 4, 172.
[3] II., 1, 88-94.   [4] II., 2, 143.   [5] III., 2, 297-8
[6] III., 2, 365.
[7] *E.g.*, I., 1, 39-44; II., 3, 13-16, 18-22, 32; II., 4, 70-73, 78, 79, 129, 130; IV., 1, 56-59; V., 1, 2-5, 11-16, 36; V., 3, 10-12, 20-31, 43-45.   [8] IV., 2, 45.

or,

> CHANCELLOR. But we are all men,
> In our own natures frail, and capable
> Of our flesh; few are angels,[1]

which are quite out of his range of power.

Again, there is a curious series of links in the play, by which characters who are to come on later are introduced; it seems to be an attempt to give unity to a disconnected work. Thus, the King's belief in Cranmer is early indicated;[2] Cromwell's future success is foreshadowed by Wolsey;[3] Gardiner's dislike of Cranmer is brought before us.[4] This is a method of which I can recall no instance in Massinger's undoubted plays.

In spite of his roughness and ferocity, Henry is more of a man than any of Massinger's tyrants; there is no parallel in Massinger to Anne Boleyn, slight as her portrait is; while Katherine and Wolsey are alike far superior to anything of his. Lastly, the pageantry and processions of the play do not appear in Massinger's simple designs.

The authors of *Henry VIII* were essaying an impossible task. They were trying to construct an historical play out of materials which were too various to make artistic unity feasible, and they had to make an unattractive character the centre of the piece. Consequently, they decided to end the play at the christening of Elizabeth, and to cover their retreat with gorgeous rhetoric about the Virgin Queen[5] and her Stuart successor. It would have been quite impossible to introduce the death of Anne Boleyn, or any further incident of the reign, without harrowing the feelings of the spectator and losing all sense of proportion. But they do make a desperate effort to centre our attention on the King as a commanding figure; he comes before us as " the first gentleman in

---

[1] V., 3, 10. [2] II., 4, 238.
[3] III., 2, 447. [4] IV., 1, 103.
[5] *Cf.* II., 3, 77; III., 2, 50—both instances of the method of anticipation referred to above.

Europe," and as the anxious lover of his people; he is represented as torn by conflicting emotions about the divorce, and as badly treated by Rome; all we can say is, these facts are true, however unskilfully the play brings them before us. Whatever the King does, we are meant to like him. His victims all conspire to invoke the blessings of Heaven on his head; Buckingham,[1] Wolsey,[2] Katherine,[3] all agree in this, reminding us of John Stubbs the Puritan, who, when his right hand was cut off for writing a book against Elizabeth's proposed marriage, put off his hat with his left, and said with a loud voice, " God save the Queen." The christening scene in Act V. is skilfully constructed so as to concentrate our interest on Henry; we feel that he is a royal and heroic figure, whose faults may in the last resort be palliated by the consideration that he is the father of Elizabeth.

I agree with the critics who regard the play as a failure from the artistic point of view; it lacks unity, and it moves awkwardly. It might even be called a spectacular experiment. But I rate it higher than they seem to do; its faults are largely due to the subject; it has much of Shakspere in it, as for example, the conscientious way in which the historical details are introduced.[4] It is full of superb and moving passages, and it uses the eleven-syllable line with skill and tenderness. If some of its defects remind us faintly of Massinger, its excellences are altogether beyond his abilities. Doubtless, it is natural to wish that each play of Shakspere should excel its predecessor, and to be unwilling to confess that he ended his career with something that was not supremely excellent. In the same way we may be sorry that one

---

[1] II., 1, 88. [2] III., 2, 393. [3] IV., 2, 125.

[4] Thus Gardiner's dislike of Anne Boleyn (V., 1, 22) is true to history, though artistically a blemish on the play, because redundant.

The way in which in IV., 1, and elsewhere, historical details are dragged in is quite unlike Massinger, and very like Shakspere. Cf. lines 17-19, 24-29, 38-42, 47-49, 51, 52, 101-103.

of Mozart's last works, *Titus*, was a failure. But it is better to take things as we find them than to seek to twist them into something else on inadequate grounds.

Boyle's attribution of *Henry VIII* to Fletcher and Massinger[1] was coldly received by the New Shakspere Society.[2] Let us look at his arguments. I trust that condensation will do them no injustice.

1. There is a change in the conception of the character of Buckingham. Such changes constantly occur in the plays which Fletcher and Massinger wrote together, notably in the character of Sir John Van Olden Barnavelt. Therefore Massinger wrote part of *Henry VIII*. This line of argument, even if valid, would only prove collaboration by Fletcher with someone else.

2. The Shakspere play *All is True* may have perished in the "Globe" fire of 1613. *Henry VIII* was written to take its place, but not produced before 1616. The evidence quoted for the date 1616-17 is very weak, and does nothing to prove Massinger's co-operation.

3. If it be urged that the reputed authors of the play were alive in 1623, when it was published as Shakspere's work in the Folio, Boyle replies,[3] "that, with the exception perhaps of Ben Jonson, it would never have occurred to a dramatist of that age to claim as his property what was published under another's name." This is a bold statement. Can an instance of such indifference be quoted ? Or are we merely bidden to remember that Massinger was poor ?

4. Boyle then works through the scenes which he ascribes to Massinger.

I., 1.—The opening is like *The Emperor of the East*, III., 1. "An untimely ague" corresponds to "a sudden fever." The resemblance of the scenes is undoubted, and the parallel phrases are remarkable. Note, however,

---

[1] *New Shakspere Society's Transactions*, 1880-86, xxi.
[2] See Discussion on January 16th, 1885.
[3] *Ibid.*, p. 447.

that the writer says the same thing twice (lines 4 and 13),
while lines 9-12 are not like Massinger.

I., 4.—Lines 1-18, and 60 to the end. I find no trace
of Massinger's style in these passages. He never wrote
lines 75-6:

> The fairest hand I ever touch'd !   O beauty,
> Till now I never knew thee !

or such a phrase as " let the music knock it " *ad finem.*

II., 1.—Lines 1-54, and 136 to the end. I find no trace
of Massinger's style in these passages. Boyle has to
allow that Fletcher altered several lines in 1-54; this is
precarious and subjective reasoning.

II., 3.—Lines 1-11 are in the parenthetic manner, but
quite unlike Massinger's. " Soft cheveril conscience " in
line 31, and " you'd venture an emballing " in line 47,
are instances of the strong vocabulary which marks the
play.[1] Picturesque phrases of this kind are not characteristic of Massinger's style.

Nor did Massinger ever sink so low as line 64:

> A thousand pound a year, annual support.[2]

II., 4.—No doubt Massinger loves a forensic scene, but
this one leads to nothing and leaves the mind in confusion.
Now, Massinger was too good an artist to do that. The
things the people say in this scene must have passed through
their minds in real life, but they are combined in such
a way as to be true to history rather than to dramatic
propriety. The author aims at telling what happened,
and what happened does not always make a good play.
It might even be urged from what we know of Massinger
that he was too good a " stage-poet " to undertake an
English historical play with its necessary limitations.

III., 2, 1-203.—The scene, like so much else in the play,
lacks the refinement and courtliness which Massinger

---

[1] For other instances see II., 4, 208; III., 2, 39-42, 55-56,
96, 159; V., 1, 22-3, 36, 109-11; V., 3, 43-45.

[2] The same remark applies to V., 3, 8.

always has at his command. It may be noted that the bluff, coarse atmosphere of the " Shaksperian " scenes is very suitable to the central figure of the play.[1] Henry VIII infects his surroundings with himself, and this might be quoted as an indication of Shaksperian skill.

IV., 1.—The prosaic details of this scene are unlike anything in Massinger.[2]

V., 1.—The point of this scene is to concentrate our attention on Elizabeth's birth. The scene " sprawls " sadly, to use Boyle's description of Fletcher's method. First we have Gardiner and Lovell, then Henry and Suffolk, then Henry and Cranmer, then Henry and the old lady. Massinger constructed better than this.

V., 3, 1-113.—Such a speech as Cranmer makes (lines 58-69) is too short for Massinger's ample method, and its terse, broken style is singularly unlike his.

5. The few parallels of diction which Boyle brings forward are either from plays which are not certainly by Massinger, or may be explained as due to reminiscence or common phraseology.

6. Boyle has much of value to say in his criticisms of the characters. But again and again he seems to forget that the author is hampered by the story. He could not treat Henry VIII as Schiller treated Mary Stuart; to idealize the events would have been an act of *lèse-majesté*.

It is true that Anne Boleyn is not a creation of the same order as Shakspere's later heroines—Imogen, Miranda, Marina, Perdita. Though beautiful and charming, she is shallow and commonplace. Is not this, however, the Anne Boleyn of real life ?

" Katherine is inferior to Hermione in *The Winter's Tale*." But why should not her portrait be drawn on different lines ? Is she not a proud Spanish princess ? She is certainly one of the great figures of English Tragedy.

Wolsey is meant to be great but is really vulgar, while

---

[1] Compare such a line as V., 3, 94.   [2] See p. 87, n. 4.

" his utter collapse after disgrace is unnatural." The reply
is that Wolsey is a mixed character, and none the worse
dramatically for that; very able, very unscrupulous in his
use of the courtier's tricks, very fond of power; but not
wholly bad. His repentance is true at once to human
nature and to history.

" The king is unintelligible." The fact is, it was impossible to make a hero of Henry VIII; it does not, therefore, follow that Massinger helped to write the play !
Boyle is correct when he says that it is with Henry as it is
with Wolsey: " we receive our impressions of the characters from the opinions formed of them by others."
In other words, the characterization of the play is faulty.
Some critics have supposed that this fact is due to loss
of mental power by Shakspere; it is simpler to hold the
collaboration with Fletcher as responsible for the jolts
and jars which the play gives the reader. If anyone still
holds that Shakspere wrote the whole play, he might
plausibly take the line that Shakspere was experimenting
in the new style and metre of his popular young rival
Fletcher. If, however, Shakspere in his retreat at Strat-
ford, in days when posts were infrequent and locomotion
slow, forwarded scenes and suggestions for Fletcher to
work up at his own sweet will, something like what we
have would be the result. Fletcher was evidently on his
mettle on this occasion. I cannot prove that Fletcher
did not invite Massinger to help him in such an enterprise, and I know how fond Massinger was of studying
Shakspere. The latter argument, however, cuts both
ways. Again, Massinger may have had an earlier Shaksperian style, very unlike his mature style; but this is
pure hypothesis. The evidence which we have does not
justify us in saying more than this, that he knew the play
of *Henry VIII* well.[1]

---

[1] For " catalogue lines," *cf.* I., 2, 33; II., 1, 116; II., 3, 29;
III., 2, 342; V., 5, 48. For assonances, *cf.* I., 3, 25, 27, 31,
35, 41; II., 1, 126; II., 2, 28, 48; II., 3, 86; II., 4, 92;

It would take me too far from my purpose to discuss the authorship of *The Two Noble Kinsmen* in detail, interesting as the problem is, but as many critics have assigned the " un-Fletcherian " parts of the play to Massinger, I have, as in duty bound, read the play carefully several times. There is very little trace of his style, or method, or metre. The only passage which reads to me like Massinger is assigned by Boyle to Fletcher.[1] Mr. Dugdale Sykes, in an acute article,[2] has produced some parallels between Massinger and *The Two Noble Kinsmen ;* but though one or two of them are striking, they do not prove his case when they are looked at in connexion with the context.

Take, for example:

3RD QUEEN. He that will all the treasure know o' th' earth
Must know the centre too.[3]

Mr. Sykes compares these lines in *The Parliament of Love :*

CLEREMOND. And I should gild my misery with false
comforts,
If I compared it with an Indian slave's,
That with incessant labour to search out
Some unknown mine, dives almost to the centre.[4]

On this passage I make two remarks: first, such similarity of thought as is found here may be due to imitation or unconscious reminiscence of *The Two Noble Kinsmen.* A man who constantly repeats himself is surely the sort of person who would delight to borrow thoughts and phrases from other writers, and to imitate whole scenes and in-

III., 2, 125, 129, 213, 214, 236, 255, 259; V., 2, 32; V., 3, 23, 60, 72, 103; V., 4, 94; V., 5, 30. For repetitions of words, *cf.* III., 1, 110; III., 2, 29; V., 1, 98, 138. Passages which remind us of Massinger are I., 4, 101; II., 3, 93; V., 1, 62, 70, and 71; Epilogue, 5.   [1] V., 1, 1-7.

[2] *Modern Language Review*, April, 1916.

[3] I., 1, 124. My numeration in *The Two Noble Kinsmen* is Mr. Tucker Brooke's.   [4] III., 2, 14.

cidents. Are we to suppose that Massinger confined his studies to Shakspere ?

Secondly, let us judge the passage as a whole; it runs thus:

> He that will all the treasure know o' th' earth
> Must know the centre too; he that will fish
> For my least minnow, let him lead his line
> To catch one at my heart.

Anything more unlike Massinger than this fishing for minnows cannot be imagined.

Take again the parallel,[1] " which alone should be conclusive of Massinger's authorship ":

> PIRITHOUS. Though I know
> His ocean needs not my poor drops, yet they
> Must yield their tribute there. My precious maid,
> Those best affections, that the heavens infuse
> In their best temper'd pieces, keep enthroned
> In your dear heart.[2]

In *Believe as You List* we have:
> Though I know
> The ocean of your apprehensions needs not
> The rivulet of my poor cautions, yet,
> Bold from my long experience, I presume, etc.[3]

Though the similarity of thought and expression in the first three lines is manifest, the archaic simplicity of the first passage differs greatly from the mature flow of the second.

What is Mr. Sykes' theory ? " If we admit Massinger's collaboration in this play, at the very outset of his literary career, before his style was definitely formed, and when the influence of the foremost dramatist of the age was strongest upon him, the apparently ' Shaksperian ' quality of its verse can readily be explained." On this proposition I make two remarks;

---

[1] *Op. cit.*, p. 143. [2] *The Two Noble Kinsmen*, I., 3, 8.
[3] V., 1, 161.

first, that as we have none of Massinger's early works, I cannot prove that he never wrote in the style of *The Two Noble Kinsmen ;* I can only assert with absolute certainty that none of his extant works has the least resemblance to it. Secondly, as to the supposed " Shaksperian " colour of the play, this is a point on which one's judgment varies each time one reads it. There is a great deal in the " un-Fletcherian " parts which reminds one of Shakspere; some of it is so like his later style that it is not surprising to find that many great critics have assigned it to him; many other passages, however, seem just not to ring true; they are obscure because they have little meaning. For let not the fact be disguised, in spite of one great lyric, several splendid scenes, and some fine speeches, there is much poor stuff in *The Two Noble Kinsmen.*

The simplest explanation of the double ascription in the quarto of 1634 is to suppose that Shakspere helped Fletcher in some way. He may even have written the un-Fletcherian parts,[1] though, personally, I find traces of Fletcher in them also; he may have left material which Fletcher worked up; he may have merely suggested the construction of the plot, a department in which Fletcher is weak.

If, however, the " Shaksperian " parts be deemed unworthy of Shakspere, why assign them to Massinger, whose work they do not resemble ? Could no one else have imitated Shakspere except Massinger ? Why should not Fletcher himself for once have caught the Shaksperian manner ? Why should he not have confided the execution of a part to someone else who was soaked in Shakspere's style ? Why should not Beaumont have helped him here as elsewhere,[2] or possibly Heywood ?

The archaic flavour of the play is to me the outstanding fact about it; we know that plays on this subject were acted

---

[1] II., 1 reads to me like Shakspere.
[2] A Danish scholar, Dr. Bierfreund, maintains this thesis (Tucker Brooke, Introd., p. xlv).

in 1566 and 1594. The archaic flavour may be due to the influence of Chaucer on the writers; it is more likely to be due to an earlier play having been taken and altered. It might also be due to the collaboration of someone like Heywood, who, though late in time, is surprisingly simple and early in style. The rustic scenes are an instance of this very early manner.[1] If Shakspere and Fletcher took an old play, and the former contributed a few turns to the revised edition, then everything would be accounted for.[2] It will be said that there are scenes which remind us of Lady Macbeth and Ophelia; why should not an already existing play have suggested to Shakspere something which he worked up in those two characters into a far finer result ? We know for a fact that much of his best work is based on older plays. This random hypothesis is quite as probable as the supposition that Massinger had anything to do with *The Two Noble Kinsmen.*

Let us next consider Mr. Tucker Brooke's position.[3] After a searching and masterly analysis of the merits and defects of the play, he ends with a guarded tendency towards assigning the " un-Fletcherian " parts to Massinger on the following grounds: " The metrical tests give him an even better title than his master [*i.e.*, Shakspere] to the doubtful parts of our play." To this I reply that style is a more important test than metre. There are, secondly, " the structural and psychological imperfections of the work "; thirdly, " the tendency to unnecessary coarseness of language "; fourthly, " the feeble imitation of Shakspere "; fifthly, " the frequent similarity to Massinger's acknowledged writings." The only serious argument against the assumption is that there is nothing in Massinger to compare with " the magnificent poetry of the un-Fletcherian part."

Let us briefly look at these arguments. The work

---

[1] II., 3; III., 5.
[2] This is perhaps what Mr. Bullen believes about the play.
[3] *The Shakespeare Apocrypha.*

is " structurally and psychologically imperfect." True, and this point might be quoted to support the theory that the play is based on an old and immature tragedy. As far as concerns structure, Massinger's plays are always strong; so that part of the argument falls to the ground. No doubt his psychology is his weak point, but its weakness is of a different kind from that which we find in *The Two Noble Kinsmen*. There are no violent emotions of the sort in which he rejoices in it. There are no characters in Massinger resembling Palamon and Arcite. Mr. Brooke refers to their " spinelessness," and it is true that they are not much differentiated. I suppose, however, that he would allow that they start by being a romantic pair of friends, that their quarrel when they first see Emilia is lifelike, and that their subsequent behaviour is chivalrous. When he refers to " the really revolting wishy-washiness and ingrained sensuality of Emilia " he uses exaggerated language. The fact is, that Emilia is in a very difficult position, and if her character is ambiguous it is the fault of the story rather than of the author.

" The tendency to unnecessary coarseness of language." This is based in the main on Hippolyta's language,[1] with which Mr. Sykes compares a passage in *The Unnatural Combat*.[2] I have discussed the supposed coarseness of Massinger's heroines elsewhere. In spite of everything that Boyle can say, with his catalogue of twenty-two passages, I wonder who is right about Massinger's women, Boyle or Courthope, who says that " his portraits of women show more delicacy of feeling and imagination than those of any English dramatist with the exception of Shakspere."[3] I, at any rate, feel that Courthope is nearer the truth than Boyle and his followers.

" Feeble imitation of Shakspere." That there is imitation of Shakspere in Massinger we all know; but I deny that it is feeble, and we know that others of the same age,

---

[1] I., 1, 209. [2] III., 1, 74. [3] *H. E. L.*, iv., p. 361.

like Fletcher, Webster, and Tourneur, have delighted to imitate him.

" The frequent similarity to Massinger's writings." In the first place, I do not feel that the similarity is frequent; and secondly, as has already been pointed out, what similarity there is may be due to imitation of *The Two Noble Kinsmen* by Massinger. Are we to suppose that the only author he imitated or borrowed from was Shakspere ?

The final reservation raises mixed feelings. I am tired of those writers who grudgingly attribute to Massinger the leavings of other playwrights, making him the whipping boy of his age, and who proceed to qualify their theories by doubts as to his ability to attain to the excellences which they perforce discover in them. I will be, so far generous to Mr. Brooke as to allow that " the magnificent poetry of the un-Fletcherian parts " is unlike Massinger, because there is no reason for supposing that he wrote any of these parts. Massinger's fame can stand on its own merits without these churlishly conceded ascriptions of doubtful work.

And now let us pass to Boyle's notable article on this subject.[1] Much as I admire his learning and zeal, I am amazed at the perversity of his judgment and the thinness of his arguments. Let us take them in order. " There is a want of development in the dramatic character "[2] of *The Two Noble Kinsmen*. This Boyle ascribes to the fact that, as elsewhere, Massinger's conceptions were blurred by Fletcher's co-operation in other parts of the play. As this argument begs the question it has no weight. " Allusions to Shakspere are characteristic both of Massinger and *The Two Noble Kinsmen*."[3] Are we to suppose that no one imitated Shakspere except Massinger ? " The metrical structure of the play corresponds closely with Massinger's general style."[4] Here, however, Boyle

---

[1] *New Shakspere Society's Transactions*, 1880-5, pt. 2, xviii.
[2] Page 372   [3] Page 373.   [4] Pages 375-6.

has to allow that the percentages for double endings are not what you would expect. And I look with suspicion on a writer who professes to be so certain of these tests that he can assign I., 1-40, and V., 1-19, to Fletcher. "Massinger is fond of classical allusions, as is the author of *The Two Noble Kinsmen*."[1] This argument deserves no consideration when we remember that the fact is true of other Elizabethan writers. For example, we find "the helmeted Bellona,"[2] and Massinger is fond of the sonorous word.[3] Yes, but Bellona is not unknown in Shakspere. M. Arnold has pointed out that she occurs in a weak passage of Macbeth.[4] "Medical and surgical similes occur in both."[5] When we come to investigate these we find that the remarks in question are of a commonplace kind. "The characters of *The Two Noble Kinsmen* resemble those of Massinger."[6] Theseus, for example, resembles Lorenzo in *The Bashful Lover*. I see no resemblance. "Palamon and Arcite may be met with in many of Massinger's plays."[7] I fail to find them anywhere. "The three ladies are grossly sensual in their remarks."[8] I have dealt with this point before, and it really amounts to a mischievous obsession in Boyle's mind. Let us take the passages seriatim; Emilia is talking privately to Hippolyta[9] about a dead girl friend to whom she was devoted when young. In the course of this beautiful passage she says:

> The flower that I would pluck
> And put between my breasts, then but beginning
> To swell about the blossom, oh! she would long
> Till she had such another, and commit it
> To the like innocent cradle, where phœnix-like
> They died in perfume.

---

[1] Page 381. [2] I., 1, 76.

[3] *E.g., Roman Actor*, I., 4, 41; *Picture*, II., 2, 112; *Bondman*, I., 1, 13. Cf. *Tamburlaine*, pt. II., III., 2; *Orlando Furioso*, V., 2.

[4] *Macbeth*, I., 1, 54. [5] Page 387. [6] Page 393.

[7] Page 393. [8] Page 394. [9] I., 3, 76.

I am ashamed to waste words in vindicating this passage, which Boyle sets by the language of Iachimo in Cymbeline in describing the mole on Imogen's breast[1] to a company of gentlemen.

The next one is " decisive of the question of the authorship of our play."

> 1ST QUEEN. When her arms,
> Able to lock Jove from a synod, shall
> By warranting moonlight corslet thee, O when
> Her twinning cherries shall their sweetness fall[2]
> Upon thy tasteful lips, what wilt thou think
> Of rotten kings and blubbered queens ? What care
> For what thou feel'st not, what thou feel'st being able
> To make Mars spurn his drum ? O, if thou covet
> But one night with her, every hour in't will
> Take hostage of thee for a hundred, and
> Thou shalt remember nothing more than what
> That banquet bids thee to.[3]

Though there are passages in Massinger of which the thought is similar to that presented here, I do not judge it or them as severely as Boyle. The point, however, which I wish to make is this: these lines are typical of what I have called the archaic flavour of the play. Where in Massinger's works will you find " warranting moonlight," " tasteful lips," " twinning cherries," " rotten kings and blubbered queens," or " Mars' drum "? The idea that Massinger wrote this passage is quite preposterous; the only thing in it which reminds one of him is the " and " at the end of line 204.

Lastly, we have Hippolyta's words in the same scene:

> Yet I think
> Did I not by the abstaining of my joy,
> Which breeds a deeper longing, cure their surfeit

---

[1] II., 4, 134.

[2] Notice in passing that Beaumont is fond of using intransitive verbs transitively. He also has the phrase " twinning cherries." [3] I., 1, 195-206.

That craves a present medicine, I should pluck
All ladies' scandal on me.[1]

Hippolyta agrees in these lines to postpone her wedding
in order that the Queens should be avenged on Creon.
No doubt the lines are crude, but Boyle goes too far with
his " cloven hoof," his " effluvia of social corruption," his
" thick miasma."

" There is a close parallel between *The Two Noble
Kinsmen* and *A Very Woman* in the treatment of madness."[2] I do not see much similarity between the prose
of the one play and the poetry of the other, but so far
as any exists it is due to the common ideas of the age
as to the way in which to treat the mad. " The reflec-
tions in the dialogue of Palamon and Arcite,[3] on the
corruptions of Thebes, the neglect of soldiers, the ex-
travagance of fashion, are allusions such as Massinger
makes to contemporary English life."[4] The allusions
are such as any moralist might make, and if the rough
and immature style in which they are expressed is not
like Massinger's the argument falls to the ground.

" There are a good many expressions in common between *The Two Noble Kinsmen* and Massinger."[5] This is
the really serious argument; but let me repeat that similarity of thought and expression in isolated phrases does
not prove unity of authorship. Let us, however, look at
some of these parallels.

Reference is twice made in *The Two Noble Kinsmen* to
" the wheaten garland" of brides.[6] Massinger refers to
" the garland " of a bridegroom in three passages.[7] I
fail to see the connexion. Notice also that Massinger
does not use the epithet " wheaten " in these passages.

---

[1] I., 1, 209-213.   [2] Page 395.   [3] I., 2.
[4] Page 397.   [5] Pages 380-391.
[6] I., 1, 165; V., 1, 160. Shakspere has " the wheaten
garland " of peace in *Hamlet*, V., 2, 41.
[7] *Bashful Lover*, I., 1, 279; IV., 3, 164; *Maid of Honour*, I.,
2, 116.

Theseus says, "Troubled I am," and turns away.[1] It was quite natural that he should think twice before postponing his wedding. Boyle compares a passage where Ladislas is in uncertainty[2]:

> I am much troubled,
> And do begin to stagger.

People in Massinger's plays are often perplexed, and so they are in real life. Note that Theseus ends his remark with these words at the beginning of a line. When Massinger's characters are in perplexity their way of expressing themselves is quite different; it is more full and rounded off.

Theseus says: " Forward to the temple,"[3] being anxious to be married. "Similar words in similar situations occur in Massinger."[4] In neither case, however, is it a bridegroom who speaks.

The Two Noble Kinsmen, I., 165, 166:

> 1ST QUEEN. And that work presents itself to th' doing;
> Now 'twill take form, the heats are gone to-morrow.

Boyle says this is obscure, but can be explained by *Empress of the East*:

> That resolution which grows cold to-day
> Will freeze to-morrow.[5]

The thought is a familiar one; and can anyone suppose that Massinger wrote line 165 ?

The expression " our undertaker "[6] recalls a word used by Shakspere.[7] Massinger also has it twice;[8] the parallel is interesting, but the word was a cant political term of Jacobean times.

---

[1] I., 1, 82. [2] *Picture*, III., 4, 61.
[3] I., 1, 141. The exact phrase occurs in *Merchant of Venice*, II., 1, 44. "The temple" is part of Fletcher's stock-in-trade.
[4] *Maid of Honour*, V., 2, 45; *Picture*, I., 2, 306.
[5] II., 1, 3. [6] I., 1, 77.
[7] *Twelfth Night*, III., 4, 349.
[8] *Renegado*, III., 3, 78; *New Way*, V., 1, 27.

The fact that apes imitate is referred to in these lines:[1]

'Tis in our own power—
Unless we fear that apes can tutor's—to
Be masters of our manners.

In *The Emperor of the East* we find:

You are master of the manners and the habit,
Rather the scorn of such as would live men,
And not, like apes, with servile imitation
Study prodigious fashions.[2]

Surely there is no need to assume common authorship here. The imitative ape has been common property for a long time.

A peculiarity of a sick man is referred to thus:

I must no more believe thee in this point
Than I will trust a sickly appetite,
That loathes even as it longs.[3]

Massinger in *A Very Woman* has:

No more of Love, good father,
It was my surfeit, and I loathe it now,
As men in fevers meat they fall sick on.[4]

The simile is a part of ordinary experience and literary convention. You might as well argue that Massinger wrote *Euphues*.

The jailer's daughter leaves the scene with this remark:

It is a holiday to look on them; Lord, the difference of men.[5]

Lidia, in *The Great Duke of Florence*, when Sanazarro seems to be treating her rudely, exclaims:

Oh, the difference of natures![6]

But she does not leave the stage.

---

[1] I., 2, 47, 48.
[3] I., 3, 91.
[5] II., 1, 66. *Cf.* Margaret in *Friar Bacon and Friar Bungay*, I., 3, *ad finem*.
[2] I., 2, 275-278.
[4] IV., 2, 50.
[6] II., 3, 151.

We might say: Oh, the difference of styles ! In the one case we have a rustic maiden of low birth; in the other, a lady justly offended.

I do not deny that some of the parallels are remarkable, but they may be due to imitation or reminiscence. Take the words:

> Thou, O jewel,
> O' th' wood, o' th' world, hast likewise blest a place
> With thy sole presence.[1]

In *The Great Duke of Florence* we find:

> And what place
> Does he now bless with his presence ?[2]

The phrase is one which Massinger's courtly mind would treasure and delight to use.

Theseus, addressing Artesius, says:

> Forth and levy
> Our worthiest instruments, whilst we despatch
> This grand act of our life, this daring deed
> Of fate in wedlock.[3]

Phrases like this are found in Massinger; thus in *The Maid of Honour*, Roberto says of the wedding of Bertoldo and Aurelia:

> And rest assur'd that, this great work despatch'd,
> You shall have audience.[4]

They may be due to reminiscence, though it is simpler to regard them as the current English of the day.

The strongest evidence for Boyle's theory is contained in Palamon's invocation to Venus:[5]

---

[1] III., 1, 10.

[2] I., 1, 49. *Cf. Bashful Lover*, I., 1, 54; III., 3, 132.

[3] I., 1, 178-181.

[4] V., 2, 51. *Cf.* also *Unnatural Combat*, III., 2, 157; *Duke of Milan*, V., 2, 82; *Bondman*, IV., 2, 75; *City Madam*, V., 3, 108; *Guardian*, I., 1, 191. In these last instances marriage is not referred to, nor is the word " despatched " used.

[5] V., 1, 106.

I never practised
Upon man's wife, nor would the libels read
Of liberal wits; I never at great feasts
Sought to betray a beauty.

These words certainly remind us of Leosthenes in *The Bondman*, both in thought and style:

Nor endeavour'd
To make your blood run high at solemn feasts,
With viands that provoke; the speeding philtres;
I worked no bawds to tempt you; never practised
The cunning and corrupting arts they study
That wander in the wild maze of desire.[1]

I think, however, that reminiscence will suffice to account for the parallel. The man who could write the last line of this passage has no need to buttress up his fame with *The Two Noble Kinsmen*, though it is of course conceivable that he edited it for publication in 1634.

Lastly, the method of Massinger calls for a few words. It has been noticed by all the critics that he often repeats himself. As is the case with Plautus the same metaphors, thoughts, and words recur from time to time in similar situations. It is clear that this characteristic might help us to trace those parts of Fletcher's plays in which Massinger collaborated.

One or two simple instances of this fact may be quoted: the characters in Massinger are very fond of blushing;[2]

---

[1] II., 1, 128.

[2] *Picture*, II., 2, 159, 163; *Unnatural Combat*, I., 1, 4; III., 2, 70; IV., 1, 103; *Great Duke of Florence*, I., 2, 75 and 155; II., 1, 186; IV., 2, 88; V., 3, 40; *Guardian*, I., 2, 142; II., 3, 47; III., 5, 34; IV., 1, 86; *Maid of Honour*, I., 1, 175; III., 3, 214, 221 and 234; *Duke of Milan*, I., 3, 30; *Parliament of Love*, II., 2, 23; III., 3, 150; *A Very Woman*, II., 2, 28; IV., 3, 99; *Bashful Lover*, III., 3, 68; *New Way*, I., 1, 31; III., 1, 17; III., 2, 49; *Virgin Martyr*, I., 1, 321; *Fatal Dowry*, I., 1, 85; II., 2, 107 and 313; *Emperor of the East*, Prol., 2, 14; II., 1, 324; *Bondman*, I., 3, 290; *Renegado*, II., 1, 66. It is true that blushing plays a great part in all our old dramatists. Compare in Fletcher, *False One*, II., 3, *ad finem ;* II., 6,

references to the talkativeness of women are frequent;[1]
metaphors from the sea and sailing are very common;[2]
people are fond of saying that they mean to do something
but they do not know what;[3] the exact courtier kneels
and kisses the robe of a lady or her foot, and is sometimes
rebuked for doing so.[4]

22; Leandro, in *The Spanish Curate*, I., 1; and in Shakspere,
Henry V, V., 2, 253; *Much Ado*, IV., 1, 35, 160-163; *Antony
and Cleopatra*, I., 1, 29; V., 2, 149. *Cf.* also *Eastward Ho*, I., 1.
"Give me a little box on the ear, that I may seem to blush";
II., 1. "As I am a lady, if he did not make me blush so that
mine eyes stood awater." *Every Man in his Humour*, V., 1.
"Nay, Mistress Bridget, blush not." *The Devil is an Ass*, I., 3;
Friar Bacon and Friar Bungay, I., 2; *James IV.*, III., 3.

[1] *Guardian*, III., 6, 55; IV., 2, 52; *Old Law*, III., 1, 272;
Emperor of the East, IV., 5, 202.

[2] *Picture*, I., 1, 43; II., 1, 71-75; *Maid of Honour*, I., 1,
157; II., 2, 119; V., 2, 267-270; *Unnatural Combat*, II., 1, 135
and 220; II., 3, 29; *Bondman*, III., 3, 98-102; III., 4, 65; *Renegado*, II., 1, 31-34; IV., 1, 147; V., 3, 76-81; *Guardian*, III., 1,
8-10 and 42; III., 6, 6; IV., 1, 13 and 21; *Emperor of the East*,
IV., 1, 59; IV., 3, 22; V., 3, 137; *New Way*, III., 2, 220; IV.,
3, 4; *A Very Woman*, V., 3, 21; *Bashful Lover*, V., 2, 12; V., 3,
146; *Duke of Milan*, II., 1, 420; *Believe as You List*, I., 1, 117;
IV., 3, 27.

[3] *Picture*, II., 2, 336:

> HONORIA. I am full of thoughts,
> And something there is here I must give form to,
> Though yet an embryon.

Bondman, I., 3, 315; II., 1, 74-77; V., 2, 103; *Renegado*, III.,
3, 97; *The Virgin Martyr*, III., 2, 98; *Guardian*, II., 3, 140;
Emperor of the East, V., 1, 129; *Bashful Lover*, IV., 1, 200;
Roman Actor, IV., 2, 105. *Cf.* also *Emperor of the East*, III.,
3, 13; *Thierry and Theodoret*, I., 2.
It is a touch which goes back to Ovid's *Metamorphoses*, vi.
619: "Magnum quodcumque paravi: quid sit, adhuc dubito."

[4] *Believe as You List*, V., 1, 129; V., 2, 143; *Picture*, I., 2,
127-129 and 152-153; III., 6, 34; IV., 1, 104; IV., 4, 16; V.,
3, 48; *Maid of Honour*, V., 1, 20; *Roman Actor*, I., 2, 14;
Great Duke of Florence, II., 1, 44; IV., 1, 38; *Bondman*, III.,
2, 59; III., 3, 26; *Parliament of Love*, II., 3, 82; *Emperor of the
East*, I., 1, 95; I., 2, 148; II., 1, 158 and 334; *New Way*, II.,
2, 84; *Bashful Lover*, V., 1, 39; *City Madam*, III., 1, 67. *Cf.*
also *Duke of Milan*, IV., 1, 46; *Renegado*, III., 3, 79; IV., 2,
104. Hortensio "kisses the ground" in *Bashful Lover*, III.,

As a good moralist, Massinger dislikes suicide[1] and duelling.[2] The latter practice is referred to in his plays as a new-fangled importation from abroad.

Let us now quote some of his favourite words: references need not be given for " honour "; wherever we find "atheist" for a bad man,[3] or "magnificent" for munificent,[4]

3, 124. This may merely mean to kneel (*cf. ibid.*, IV., 1, 168, and *Thierry and Theodoret*, II., 3); but *cf. Roman Actor*, III., 2, 193.

[1] *Old Law*, I., 1, 565; *Believe as You List*, IV., 2, 58-60, 90-92; *Guardian*, II., 4, 11-13; *Bashful Lover*, II., 6, 13; *Maid of Honour*, II., 4, 18; IV., 3, 127; *A Very Woman*, II., 1, 71; IV., 2, 151. Donusa, the Turkish princess, recommends it in *The Renegado*, III., 2, 83. *Cf.* also *Duke of Milan*, I., 3, 210-212.

[2] *Guardian*, II., 1, 79-85; *A Very Woman*, V., 6, 40-54. Fletcher is full of duels; thus the plot of *The Little French Lawyer* is largely concerned with a duel. In *Love's Progress* we have a duel in which the seconds fight; they want to do so in *The Honest Man's Fortune*. In *Love's Cure*, V., 3, a duel with seconds is commanded by the State. The illegality of duels is referred to in *The Maid's Tragedy*, V., 4.

[3] It is true that this use is not confined to Massinger, being a common idiom of the day. I quote the passages where the word is not used in a religious sense: *Maid of Honour*, IV., 3, 81; *Unnatural Combat*, I., 1, 356; *City Madam*, I., 3, 126; V., 3, 135; *Guardian*, I., 1, 176; *New Way*, IV., 1, 154. For Webster's similar use of the word *cf. The Duchess of Malfi*, p. 61a; *The White Devil*, pp. 29b and 47a.

[4] *Maid of Honour*, III., 3, 142; *Roman Actor*, I., 1, 87; II., 1, 186; IV., 2, 85; *Great Duke of Florence*, I., 1, 135; III., 1, 14; V., 3, 10; *Fatal Dowry*, V., 2, 187; *Parliament of Love*, IV., 1, 8; IV., 4, 18; *Guardian*, II., 1, 53; III., 4, 6; *A Very Woman*, II., 2, 60; *Picture*, I., 3, 176; II., 2, 158, 307; V., 3, 47; *Duke of Milan*, I., 1, 74; III., 1, 221; V., 4, 18; *Emperor of the East*, II., 1, 73, 147; III., 1, 28; III., 2, 82; V., 3, 189; *Renegado*, I., 2, 78; II., 4, 95. *Cf.* also *Beggar's Bush*, V., 2. Ford uses "royal magnificence" in the same way in *Perkin Warbeck* (II., 1). In Ben Jonson's *Staple of News* (IV., 1) we find " very communicative and liberal, and began to be magnificent." In Greene's *James IV*, I., 1:

Your mightiness is so magnificent,
You cannot choose but cast some gift apart.

The word " munificent " occurs in *New Way*, IV., 2, 109.

or the Latin phrase " nil ultra,"[1] or the Greek words
" apostata "[2] and " embryon ";[3] wherever we find
"frontless"[4] impudence and "sail-stretched" wings[5] and
" libidinous "[6] Caesars; wherever the moisture of the
lips is compared to nectar,[7] wherever we read of
" the centre "[8] or of " horror,"[9] or of washing an

---

[1] *Maid of Honour*, IV., 3, 100; *Unnatural Combat*, II., 3,
49; *Renegado*, IV., 3, 42; *Parliament of Love*, II., 3, 70;
Guardian, V., 4, 231; *New Way*, IV., 1, 103; *Bashful Lover*, I.,
1, 217; cf. *Prophetess*, IV., 6, 57.

[2] *Unnatural Combat*, I., 1, 251, 393; *Virgin Martyr*, III., 1,
28; IV., 3, 62; V., 2, 52; *Renegado*, I., 1, 138; IV., 3, 159;
Believe as You List, II., 2, 107 and 325; V., 1, 8.

[3] *Great Duke of Florence*, III., 1, 358; *Guardian*, II., 3, 141;
Bashful Lover, IV., 1, 200; *Picture*, II., 2, 337; *Believe as You
List*, I., 2, 44. Cf. *Thierry and Theodoret*, II., 3.

[4] *Unnatural Combat*, V., 1, 37; *Parliament of Love*, V., 1,
115; *Guardian*, IV., 1, 77; *Duke of Milan*, II., 1, 138; *Believe
as You List*, IV., 4, 30. Cf. *Cupid's Revenge*, II., 2, ad finem.

[5] *Unnatural Combat*, I., 1, 283; *Bondman*, I., 3, 23. Cf.
Prophetess, II., 3, 1.

[6] *Unnatural Combat*, V., 2, 234; *Bondman*, III., 2, 17; IV.,
3, 34; *Parliament of Love*, V., 1, 221; *Guardian*, I., 1, 192;
III., 6, 17; V., 2, 132; *Bashful Lover*, III., 3, 88; *Picture*, III.,
4, 46; *Duke of Milan*, II., 1, 288.

[7] *Maid of Honour*, IV., 4, 93-95; V., 1, 14; *Roman Actor*,
I., 2, 64; II., 1, 198; *Duke of Milan*, I., 3, 206; V., 2, 212;
Parliament of Love, II., 3, 94; *Guardian*, II., 5, 59; V., 2, 52;
Emperor of the East, II., 1, 355; IV., 5, 106; *New Way*, III.,
1, 75; *Bashful Lover*, III., 3, 33; *Picture*, I., 3, 128; III., 5,
71. Cf. *Love's Cure*, I., 3.

[8] *Maid of Honour*, IV., 4, 107; *Roman Actor*, IV., 1, 121;
Parliament of Love, III., 2, 17; *Guardian*, III., 6, 29; *Virgin
Martyr*, V., 2, 238; *Emperor of the East*, V., 3, 109; *Renegado*,
II., 5, 159; *Unnatural Combat*, V., 2, 266. Cf. *Hamlet*, II., 2,
159; *Troilus and Cressida*, I., 3, 85. Cf. also *Prophetess*, II., 1;
V., 2; *Spanish Curate*, I., 2; *Atheist's Tragedy*, IV., 4; *Honest
Whore*, IV., 1; *Parliament of Bees*, char. vii.

[9] *City Madam*, I., 2, 75; *Unnatural Combat*, I., 1, 223; II.,
1, 145; V., 2, 293; *Great Duke of Florence*, II., 1, 142; III., 1,
13; V., 3, 113; *Parliament of Love*, V., 1, 102; *Believe as You
List*, I., 1, 73; I., 2, 147; II., 1, 65; III., 3, 143; *Bondman*,
III., 2, 1; III., 3, 162; IV., 3, 6; V., 3, 156; *Renegado*, III.,
5, 44; *Picture*, I., 1, 79; II., 2, 130 and 155; IV., 1, 65; *Guardian*,
(III., 6, 31; *Emperor of the East*, III., 4, 55; V., 3, 105; *A Very*

Ethiop,[1] there we are on familiar ground. Again, it is a characteristic of Massinger, which offends some of his readers more than others, that he is always ready with the obvious remark. Thus, when Marrall, after a career of tergiversation is finally kicked off the stage, he says:

This is the haven
False servants still arrive at.[2]

In *The Emperor of the East*, when the complications about Paulinus' apple are getting rather serious, the Princess Flaccilla makes the remark, which is certainly in the mind of the reader:

All this pother for an apple ![3]

When Leosthenes allows himself to be intolerably coarse in his language to Cleora, we read these words:

CLEORA. You are foul-mouth'd.
ARCHIDAMUS. Ill-manner'd, too.[4]

When Hilario seeks to amuse his mistress with an absurd message from the front, and she observes, " This is ridiculous,"[5] we feel inclined to say, " Not only ridiculous, but not worth writing." When Cardenes, after lying as dead

---

Woman, IV., 3, 210; *Bashful Lover*, II., 6, 19, and 50; IV., 2, 58; *Roman Actor*, II., 1, 178; III., 2, 116; V., 2, 67; *Duke of Milan*, I., 1, 49; I., 3, 374; II., 1, 411; V., 2, 117.

[1] *Roman Actor*, III., 2, 94; *Bondman*, V., 3, 144; *Parliament of Love*, II., 2, 70. Bunyan has the phrase in *The Pilgrim's Progress*, pt. ii.: "They saw one Fool and one Want-Wit washing of an Ethiopian with intention to make him white, but the more they washed him, the blacker he was." Warner, in his translation of *The Menaechmi* (1595), line 247, has "This is the washing of a Blackamore." The expression goes back to Lucian *adv. Indoct.*, 28, Αἰθίοπα σμήχειν. It occurs in *Love's Cure*, II., 2.

[2] *New Way*, V., 1, 349.

[3] *Emperor of the East*, IV., 5, 213.

[4] *Bondman*, V., 3, 95. *Cf. Maid of Honour*, II., 2, 180.; *The Bashful Lover*, IV., 1, 138; V., 1, 56; *A New Way*, I., 1, 52; III., 1, 81; *Emperor of the East*, III., 3, 25.

[5] *The Picture*, II., 1, 123.

for some time, gives signs of life, the Viceroy very justly observes:

> This care of his recovery, timely practis'd,
> Would have expressed more of a father in you,
> Than your impetuous clamours for revenge.[1]

It will be remembered that Shakspere had used this device in his day. Compare *Richard II:* "Can sick men play so nicely with their names ?"[2] *Midsummer-Night's Dream:* "Lord, what fools these mortals be !"[3] 1 *Henry VI :* " Here is a silly stately style indeed !"[4]

What impression do we get of Massinger from his writings ? He was the intimate friend and associate of Fletcher; how far was he a man of the same stamp ? Both as a poet and a stylist Fletcher is his superior; he is more tender and more varied; in isolated scenes he attains a high degree of pathos. From time to time the bursts of lovely poetry which illustrate his plays make us bow the head as though in the presence of an enchanter. The fifty plays which are currently associated with his name, with all their faults, are a veritable fairyland. Again, there is a terse piquancy about him, which expresses itself in clear-cut, vigorous lines, such as we find rarely in our poet. And he has a real vein of humour, which makes one laugh heartily.[5] Nor is his direct and lucid prose style to be despised. On the other hand, he was not a great artist; his plots, though usually bustling, are often improbable; his character-drawing is constantly fickle and inconsequent. Thus, according to Boyle,[6] in *The Honest Man's Fortune*, Tourneur and Massinger make Montague a gentleman; in Act V. Fletcher destroys all that was good in Massinger, but makes good sport for

---

[1] *A Very Woman*, I., 1, 404. *Cf.* also *Parliament of Love*, V., 1, 149. We cannot but remember poor Valentine's prolonged but vocal agony in Gounod's opera.

[2] II., 1, 84.   [3] III., 2, 115.   [4] IV., 7, 72.

[5] Take as an example the death-bed scene in *The Spanish Curate*, IV., 5.

[6] *E. S.*, VIII., 2.

the groundlings." He maintains that the same thing happens to Buckingham in *Henry VIII* and to Barnavelt. Though there are many life-like characters in his works, to whom we feel attracted, such as Leon in *Rule a Wife and have a Wife* and Valerio in *The Wife for a Month*, they are too often made to do improbable things. Again, as a moralist Fletcher falls far behind Massinger. He shows from time to time a high-flown and tainted sentimentality which is far removed from real life. Indeed, the bad use to which he puts his great talent is often enough to make angels weep. He more than anyone is responsible for the Puritan reaction; he more than anyone is responsible for most of what was bad in the Restoration drama, and he has had his reward. Except by the student, his work is forgotten. It can hardly be doubted that the death of Fletcher was a gain to Massinger in emancipating him from the co-operation of a fascinating but unsafe guide.[1] In standing alone he learnt to perfect all that was best in his own gifts.

It is difficult to form a clear judgment of Beaumont. The more I read what scholars attribute to him, the more I feel disposed to agree with Sir A. Ward that Beaumont and Fletcher were men of the same mind and tastes. It is plain that the author of *Philaster, The Maid's Tragedy,* and *A King and No King* had a range of passion and pathos beyond Massinger. *Philaster* is incomparable, and as we

---

[1] Some idea of the way in which the two poets collaborated may be obtained from the facts collected in Appendix III. Diderot, in a passage quoted by Twining, in his edition of Aristotle's *Poetics* (p. 253), recommends collaboration: " On seroit tenté de croire qu'un drame devrait être l'ouvrage de deux hommes de génie, l'un qui arrangeât, et l'autre qui fît parler" (*De la Poés. Dram.*, p. 288). What Euripides thought of the arrangement will be seen in *The Andromache*, lines 476-77:

πόνων θ᾽ ὕμνου συνεργάταιν δυοῖν
ἔριν Μοῦσαι φιλοῦσι κραίνειν.

It is clear that the early death of Beaumont was a disaster to Fletcher.

read the other two plays we hurry on from scene to scene; when we put the book down we are perturbed. They have carried us away in spite of their grave faults. The glorious nonsense of *The Knight of the Burning Pestle* is equally beyond Massinger. On the other hand, such disagreeable plays as *The Coxcomb* and *Cupid's Revenge* do not invite a second perusal. I do not feel that Beaumont was cleaner in mind than Fletcher, or more balanced in judgment. When we come to the department of metre we seem to be on surer ground; the metre of Beaumont has high qualities, and his decasyllabic verse reminds me of the cold purity of a waterfall. In style his lines constantly have a marked simplicity and directness which anticipate Wordsworth. He can write a line in which the words run in the order which they would have in prose, and hence his great strength. On the other hand, he is often careless about the length of his lines, possibly from a love of variety. He is fond of rhyme, and introduces prose freely into his scenes. His models appear to have been Marlowe for metre and Ben Jonson for treatment. He has a liking for burlesque, as witness *The Knight of the Burning Pestle, The Woman-Hater,* and Arbaces in *A King and No King.*[1] All this is very unlike Massinger.

It may be asked, how does Massinger compare with Webster ? This question naturally rises in the mind at a moment when a gifted writer, snatched from us before his time, has left us an interesting and scholarly study of Webster. Mr. Rupert Brooke makes no secret of his contempt for Fletcher, and " the second-rate magic " of Massinger; he regards Webster as the last of the strong school of Elizabethan dramatists.

Are we to compare *Westward Ho!, Northward Ho!,* and *The Cure for a Cuckold* with *A New Way to pay Old Debts* and *The City Madam ?* They are less refined, less

---

[1] Massinger's only attempt at burlesque—Hilario in *The Picture*—though ludicrous, is dramatically impossible.

skilfully constructed. The stage is more crowded, and the characters are worse drawn. The same considerations apply to the *Malcontent*[1] and *The Devil's Law-case*. Mr. Brooke practically allows that he means by Webster, *The White Devil* and *The Duchess of Malfi*, and these plays alone. Let it be said at once that it is an ungrateful task to magnify one poet at the expense of another. We allow that in these two plays Webster comes nearer to Shakspere than any of his compeers. He has a great, a subtle, a well-stored mind; he produces isolated tragic effects of the most poignant kind; he is a master of atmosphere; he plays with the feelings of his auditors; he can dazzle them by " his miraculous touches of poetic beauty."

On the other hand, he is not a clear thinker, nor are his plays skilfully planned. I should imagine that they read better than they act. For instance, the scene in *The Duchess of Malfi*, where Ferdinand gives the heroine the dead hand, fills us with horror. I doubt if it would be effective on the stage. Webster's rhymes are poor, and his prose worse than Massinger's. Sir Sidney Lee[2] says his blank verse is " vigorous and musical "; to me it seems too often ragged and halting. But the chief objection to Webster is that he lives in " a world of repulsive themes and fantastic crimes." He revels in the sinister suggestions aroused by skulls, dead hands, ghosts, echoes, and madmen. His mind was morbid, and his successes are like lightning flashes of splendid power piercing a gloomy and sullen background.

The fact that he was not a productive writer may weigh less with some critics than with others; more important is it to remember that Massinger's plays held the stage much longer than Webster's. This fact may fairly be taken to prove the appeal which the former has success-

---

[1] It is generally believed now that Marston wrote this play. He was an author of surprising vigour, and a master of strong English, but his taste is bad, and all his work lacks finish.　　　　　[2] *D. N. B., s.v.*

fully made to the human heart. Webster, in short, compared with Shakspere, reminds us somewhat of the contrast between Mantegna and Raphael.

In one or two respects Webster has affinities with Massinger. Both frequently imitate Shakspere; and both repeat themselves continually, though in different ways. Whereas Massinger used the same vocabulary and terms of thought again and again, Webster quotes whole sentences from one of his plays in another, as if he felt, like some of the Greek writers of antiquity, that when he had said a thing as it should be said, he had the right to use it again.[1]

It is difficult to compare Massinger with Ben Jonson: both wrote Roman plays and domestic comedies; but Ben Jonson has at once a greater mind and a wider range of experiment. He was a learned man, a great figure in society, the dictator of a circle of wits, the centre of many friendships and enmities. He would probably regard Massinger as a pale-featured, gentle hack. We know more about his full-blooded personality than about any other writer of the period, and while there is much in him to offend, there is more to inspire our respect.

Our immediate object is to compare the two writers as dramatists. It is at once clear that they work on different lines. Massinger is a follower of Shakspere and Fletcher, though we can trace in some of his tragedies the influence of Webster and Tourneur. In his comedies, we see some approximation to Ben Jonson; it is instructive to compare *Eastward Ho!* with *The City Madam*. A fundamental difference of method is at once seen; Massinger deliberately eschews the use of prose. It must at once be conceded that he has left nothing on so colossal a scale as *Every Man in his Humour, Volpone, Epicoene, The Alchemist*, and *Bartholomew Fair*. Here we find skilful plot, masterly characterization, and ludicrous com-

---

[1] Dorothea's story of the King of Egypt (*Virgin Martyr*, III., 1, 163-182) reminds us of an expedient familiar in Webster.

binations. How heartily we laugh over the Plautine scene before Cob's house in *Every Man in his Humour*,[1] or at the intrusion of unbidden guests at Morose's wedding, or at the deception practised on the two knights in the gallery.[2] How dazzled we are with the kaleidoscopic "vapours" of the great Fair. On the other hand, in what Dryden calls the "dotages," we find a great falling off. Ben Jonson can be very dull. Still even in *The Devil is an Ass* and *The Staple of News* there is a vein of original fancy, which reminds us that we are dealing with no imitator, but with an original and poetical mind. Nor must we forget the splendid series of Masques, into which Ben Jonson put some of his best work; to this Massinger has but little to oppose. And then, as we all know, Ben Jonson bursts out from time to time with a great lyric, whereas Massinger's songs are commonplace. Lastly, in *The Case is Altered*, we have a plot in the manner of Fletcher which is so successful as to make us regret that Jonson did not try this type of play again. Though it has not the atmosphere of Massinger, it has something of the mellow graciousness at which he, like Fletcher, aimed.

It would be silly to deny Jonson's superiority of intellect, and of attainment when at his best. His faults are, however, very serious. Though he can draw a man of good breeding, his women are very ordinary. He is too fond of incorporating long passages from the classical authors whom he knew so well; he would have been more attractive if he had used Aristophanes and Plautus, Ovid and Libanius, as inspirations rather than as materials. The notes on Sejanus are a liberal education, but after all, "the play's the thing." The use of "humour" and "vapours," though at first brilliant and captivating, even becomes artificial and tedious; no one is the embodiment of one passion or weakness. Let us be thankful that human nature is not so simple or consistent, for in that case it would cease to interest. More serious still, Jonson

---

[1] IV., 8.   [2] *Epicoene*, IV., 2.

has no sense of proportion; we read Knowell's soliloquy in *Every Man in his Humour*,[1] and we say, "Fine! but too long"; and we say this again and again as we read his works. The great length of the fifth act of Sejanus is a good instance of this fault. Indeed, it is impossible that the play was acted in the form which we now have—it would have emptied the house, like Burke's speeches. When Jonson gets on to some subject of which he knows the technical terms, such as "fucuses"[2] or "alchemy," he is almost as tedious as Kipling's Macandrew. His plots are at times too skilful; thus, even Brainworm in time gets on our nerves. His coarseness is that of a common soldier, and his puns are bad.

Are there any points of contact between the two authors? I do not wish to suggest that Massinger owed nothing to the older writer, though parallels of diction may mean little but the simultaneous use of the idioms of the day. Thus in *The Staple of News* we find, "I do write man,"[3] "blacks,"[4] "kiss close,"[5] "nectar,"[6] "magnificent"[7]; tossing in a blanket is referred to,[8] and the saints[9] at Amsterdam, while the cook's fortifications[10] remind us of a passage in *A New Way to pay Old Debts*. In Sejanus we find "passive fortitude" commended.[11] "He puts them to their whisper,"[12] reminds us

---

[1] II., 3.
[2] *The Devil is an Ass*, IV., 1. *Cf.* the light touch of Massinger when dealing with the toilet of a lady in *A Very Woman*, I.. 1, 30-59.
[3] *Staple of News*, I., 1; III., 1—*Emperor of the East*, I., 1, 118; III., 2, 58. [4] *Ibid.*, I., 2—*Fatal Dowry*, II., 1, 51.
[5] *Ibid.*, II., 1—*Roman Actor*, IV., 2, 103. *Cf. The Alchemist*, IV., 2.
[6] *Ibid.*, IV., 1—*passim* in Massinger.
[7] *Ibid.*, IV., 1—*passim* in Massinger.
[8] *Ibid.*, IV., 1—*Parliament of Love*, IV., 5, 12.
[9] *Ibid.*, IV., 1—*Renegado*, I., 1, 31.
[10] *Ibid.*, IV., 1—*New Way*, I., 2, 25. (*Cf.* also Prologue to *A Wife for a Month*.)
[11] IV., 5—*A Very Woman*, IV., 1, 155; *Believe as You List*, V., 2, 17. [12] III, 2—*Roman Actor*, I., 3, 95.

of *The Roman Actor*. Sejanus' change of temper to his satellites[1] when he fancies danger is past resembles that of Domitian in the same play. *The City Madam* has touches of plot and style which recall Volpone.

There is, however, little contact between Ben Jonson and Massinger. Their births were separated by only ten years, but a much longer period than that seems to divide them. Friend of the great as he was, Ben Jonson was yet an Aristophanic, nay, a Rabelaisian democrat; Massinger is a gentleman and a courtier. The one has the vigour and immaturity of the Elizabethan age, and in him we feel in contact with the obsolete Mystery and Morality plays;[2] the other has the refinement and romance of the Caroline era. The one is a powerful satirist and a pugnacious fighter; the other lives in an ideal world. On the one side is *vis consili expers ;* on the other, a more limited intellect with a surer artistic sense. If I may venture to say so, they differ from one another as an apple from a pear. I do not deny that Ben Jonson was the greater man, but I find him more archaic and more difficult to read than Massinger. Much of the interest of his plays is dead for us, his local colour and topical allusions, which require so many notes, are more tedious; his personal likes and dislikes, his egotism, his vanity, are wearisome; and though his blank verse is strong and manly, it is not so melodious as Massinger's. The older man stands foursquare and solitary; the younger man reaches forward to posterity, and we feel him to be linked by his art and grace to ourselves. Though Dryden never mentions Massinger, there is a dignified capacity which is common to the two authors.

Massinger's chief rival in the latter part of his life was Shirley. Shirley's plays are full of interest; his graceful

---

[1] *Sejanus*, V., 7—*Roman Actor*, V., 2, 61.
[2] Courthope lays far too much stress on Massinger's imitation of the Morality (*History of English Poetry*, vol. iv., p. 352). It only appears in *The Virgin Martyr*.

style rises occasionally into poetry, at which the author himself seems to smile; his plots are full of ingenious turns; his female characters are more confidently developed than Massinger's, nor is he unable to draw a lifelike man, as we see from Lorenzo in *The Traitor* and Columbo in *The Cardinal.* He excels in the battledore and shuttlecock of love-making; he tells us far more of the manner of well-bred contemporary society than Massinger. Indeed, it is probable that he had a greater success in his day than his rival, and was more in touch with Court circles, though even the loyal Shirley discreetly satirizes from time to time the government of Charles I. He is not devoid of humour and epigram; his dialogue is light and sprightly. He reaches back to Fletcher and forward to Dryden; we seem, as we read his plays, to be a long way removed from the labour of Jonson, the pomp of Chapman, the vernal simplicity of Heywood. On the other hand, we miss in him the breadth and strength, the dignity, the nobility, and the fire of Massinger. He is more of a photographer than a painter. Though his style has eloquence, the thought is often far from clear, and the long sentences are clumsy. There is something slight and unsubstantial about the whole thing, while the metre is continually careless and lame.

In assigning Massinger's place in the drama of his age, we have to remember that the period falls into two well-defined parts. He has very little in common with Marlowe, Greene, and Peele, and still less with the charming Dresden china of Lyly. Marlowe's generation breathes the freshness and vehemence of the spring, while Massinger reflects the silver lights of September. So rapid was the development of fifty years, that to pass from the one to the other is like going from the lancet windows of Salisbury Cathedral to the tracery of William of Wykeham. While we miss the purity and simplicity of Early English, it would be foolish to ignore the strength of design and proportion that maturity and experience brought. The towers and battlements, the lierne vaulting, the large windows, and generous clerestories of Perpendicular do much to atone for the spiritless detail and mechanical wall-panelling. A similar consideration applies to the Jacobean dramatists when compared with their Elizabethan predecessors.

Shall I be thought presumptuous in setting Massinger against Shakspere ? The attempt may, at any rate, help to elicit a true estimate; the suggestion has often been made before. Shakspere seems to have been from his writings a man of great receptivity, unerring knowledge of human nature, profound wisdom, and infinite sweetness, the master of all the arts which we associate with a good poet. Massinger reminds us of Ben Jonson, though he is less consciously clever, less cumbered with learning, less combative.[1] He is modest,[2] manly, lucid, sane, and

---

[1] There are no signs in Massinger of literary or other private quarrels. One or two passages seem to be inspired by sarcasm directed on the gossip of the day—*e.g.*, *Duke of Milan*, III., 2, 18-55.

[2] Stress is laid more than once on Massinger's modesty in the commendatory verses from his friends. *Cf.* Sir Thomas Jay's verses prefixed to *A New Way*, and Prologue to *A Very Woman*, lines 5, 6; Prologue to *The Bashful Lover*, line 4. This feature may account for a lack of worldly wisdom and self-assertion, which prevented him from reaping the full fruits of the fame which he deserved as Fletcher's collaborator in so many plays. Gerard Langbaine, in his *Account of the English Dramatic Poets* (Oxford, 1691), pp. 353-60, deals thus with Massinger: " He was extremely beloved by the poets of that age, and there were few but what took it as an honour to club with him in a play—witness Middleton, Rowley, Field, and Dekker, all which join'd with him in several labours. Nay further, to shew his excellency, the ingenious Fletcher took him in as a partner in several plays. He was a man of much modesty and extraordinary parts." In *The New Year's Gift* to his patroness, to be found in MS. in the library of Trinity College, Dublin, we have an indication that Massinger was ashamed of the profession of author; we read (lines 19-21):

> Nor slight it, Madam, since what some in me
> Esteem a blemish, is a gift as free
> As their best fortunes.

sensible, capable of just indignation, one who respects himself, a faithful friend,[1] and a wide reader; he knows a gentleman when he sees him; he can pay compliments with good breeding; he has had his ups and downs in life;[2] he is one who understood men better than women, and who, like Sir Thomas Browne, "loved a soldier";[3] a vigorous and business-like artist, he is never worsted by his theme, but makes it lifelike and interesting, with an unerring instinct for what is effective on the stage, his very faults being largely due to this useful knowledge. That there was a strain of noble melancholy in his mind can hardly be denied.[4] The character which seems to me to embody Massinger himself is Charalois in *The Fatal*

The last lines of the poem (43-46) show the familiar combination of modesty and independence:

> What I give I am rich in, and can spare;
> Nor part for hope with aught deserves my care;
> He that hath little and gives nought at all
> To them that have, is truly liberal.

[1] There are some fine friendships in Massinger—*e.g.*, Charalois and Romont in *The Fatal Dowry ;* Farnese and Uberti in *The Bashful Lover ;* Cleremond and Montrose in *The Parliament of Love ;* Antoninus and Macrinus in *The Virgin Martyr;* Pedro and Antonio in *A Very Woman*.

[2] *Cf.* the Prologues to *The Guardian* and *The Emperor of the East*. He speaks with feeling of the ungratefulness of courtiers. (*Bashful Lover*, V., 1, 52; *Maid of Honour*, II., 2, 110.)

[3] *Cf. Picture*, II., 2, 255; *Bondman*, I., 3, 300; *Unnatural Combat*, I., 1, 404; *Bashful Lover*, I., 1, 34; *Great Duke of Florence*, II., 1, 138; *Sir J. V. O. Barnavelt*, I., 1 (p. 215, Bullen's Old Plays); also the character of the Captain in *A Very Woman*. *Cf. Knight of Malta*, III., 2.

[4] Very significant are the words of Paulo in *A Very Woman* (IV., 1, 153):

> Who fights
> With passions, and o'ercomes them is endued
> With the best virtue, passive fortitude.

Cf. Roman Actor, I., 1, 118; III., 1, 113; *Duke of Milan*, III., 1, 73; and *Renegado*, I., 1, 79:

> All that I challenge
> Is manly patience.

Dowry. Whether he was musical I should doubt after the perfunctory reference to the art in *The Fatal Dowry.*[1] We find nothing in his plays like the famous idyllic description in Ford's *Lover's Melancholy.*[2] On the other hand, he knew that vocal and instrumental music were effective in a play; we need go no farther than the end of Act IV. in *The Virgin Martyr* for proof of this.[3] And Cario uses the terms of music with great precision in *The Guardian.*[4] On the whole we get the impression that he was an example of a rare combination, modesty with independence of mind, a fact which, considering what the circumstances of the literary life then were, is quite enough to explain the hard struggle he seems to have undergone.

It may be said that I am comparing a mighty genius with a second-rate intellect. Are there any points in which Massinger can hold his own against Shakspere? Granted that he falls short in passion, imagination,[5] wit, diction, rhythm, lyric rapture, where does he shine?

Cf. Sejanus, quoted above, p. 115, n. 11. *Queen of Corinth*, III, 2:

>   EUPHANES. To shew the passive fortitude the best.

And *Lover's Progress*, IV., 4:

>   ALCIDON. With all care put on
>   The surest armour, anvil'd in the shop
>   Of passive fortitude.

This point is emphasized in Swinburne's excellent sonnet on Massinger.

[1] IV., 2, 17-31, where Charalois declares, "I never was an enemy to 't [*i.e.*, music], Beaumont," and ends by saying: "I love it to the worth of 't and no further."

[2] I., 1.   [3] *Cf.* also V., 2, 130-37.   [4] IV., 2, 1-14.

[5] Massinger has some notable compound epithets from time to time; take as examples, "pale-cheek'd stars" in *Parliament of Love*, IV., 2, 61; "on black-sail'd wings of loose and base desires," *Parliament of Love*, V., 1, 215; "Such is my full-sail'd confidence in her virtue," *Picture*, II., 2, 318; "the brass-leaved book of fate," *Believe as You List*, I., 2, 136.

>   "Your must and will
>   Shall in your full-sailed confidence deceive you,"

A Very Woman, II., 2, 21.

It may at first hearing sound snobbish to point out that he was a University man, but a good deal of truth lies hidden in that simple phrase. Shakspere's plays are marked by many faults of construction, taste, and detail; he who never blotted a line should certainly, as Ben Jonson remarked, have blotted a good many. It always seems to me that this is a line of thought which is too much ignored by those who believe that Shakspere wrote his own plays, and that Bacon had nothing to do with them. The Baco-Shaksperians point, and very justly, to the surprising knowledge and culture shown in the plays; they refuse to believe that all this can have come from the brain of a Warwickshire rustic, forgetting the faults which are so glaring, faults which are precisely those which a learned and accurate scholar like Bacon would have avoided.

Now Massinger is a correct and artistic writer. The little tricks of style which were so dear to his mighty predecessor, the pun, the alliteration,[1] the conceit, the verbal quibble,[2] are far less obtrusive; he is free from

---

[1] We find not a few assonances and alliterations in Massinger, generally contained in two words: *Emperor of the East*, I., 2, 16, " gallows and galleys "; (*Cf. Renegado*, V., 2, 162, "the gallies or the gallows," and Webster's *White Devil*, p. 11*a*); *Believe as You List*, Prologue 14, " toss'd and turned "; *A New Way*, I., 1, 109, " sue and send "; *Emperor of the East*, IV., 1, 37, " sway and swing " (so in *Great Duke of Florence*, II., 2, 46); *Fatal Dowry*, IV., 1, 193, " confessor and confounder "; *Old Law*, III., 2, 45, " die and dye "; *ibid.*, 157, " venues in Venice glasses "; IV., 1, 61, " Siren and Hiren "; *City Madam*, I., 1, 36, " hole and hell "; V., 2, 77, " lords or lowns "; *Guardian*, I., 1, 60, " house and home "; II., 2, 23, " board and bed "; II., 5, 46, " fair and free "; III., 5, 76, " page or porter "; *Picture*, IV., 1, 65, " horns and horror "; *Bondman*, II., 1, 119, " hell and horror "; *Roman Actor*, I., 4, 63, " graced and greased "; II., 1, 376, " carke and caring "; *Renegado*, III., 4, 54, " toss and touse "; *Parliament of Love*, II., 1, 8, " tractable and tactable "; *Duke of Milan*, III., 1, 199, " palm or privilege "; III., 2, 46, " curvet or caper."

[2] *Cf.* Johnson's Preface to Shakspere (p. 19), " A quibble

that affectation and precious obscurity which are so marked in Shakspere's later style. And one small point may be noticed in passing here, as an indication of good breeding: the characters in Massinger very seldom address one another by name. It is significant that Greedy and Overreach both offend in this way.[1]

Though it is true that these faults were common to the age, they are so marked in Shakspere that it is impossible to ignore them in any estimate of the man. In the details of style, then, Massinger can claim credit for being more correct. In a word, what he lacks in genius and poetry he supplies to a certain extent by good taste and education. He shares this advantage with his age, which was learning to correct the errors of the past; the English language was advancing rapidly to more maturity and balance than it had in the previous generation.

I have already pointed out the careful study of Shakspere which we find in Massinger, and the copious use of his imperial vocabulary. When we take into account all the elements of the problem, when we make allowance for quantity of work done, as well as for quality, would it be too much to say that Massinger is as the pupil to the master, and that, though separated by " a long interval," he comes second ?[2] This may seem a hard saying,

is to Shakspere what luminous vapours are to the traveller; he follows it at all adventures; it is sure to lead him out of his way, and sure to engulf him in the mire." The whole paragraph is worth reading.

[1] *A New Way*, I., 3, 22; II., 1, 31, etc. The repetition of Graccho's name in *Duke of Milan*, V., 1, is intentional and effective. *Cf.* Kitely's repetition of "Thomas" in *Every Man in His Humour*, III., 2; "Sir Michael" in *1 Henry IV*, IV., 4, and " Sir Thomas " in *Henry VIII*, V., 1.

[2] Boyle (*N. S. S.*, 371-372), severe as he is on Massinger's characters, both male and female, agrees with this verdict. He traces the unjust depreciation of Massinger in part to Charles Lamb's ' unfair judgment." "The hard fate that accompanied the ' stage poet ' through life has clung to him up to the present time, and in spite of warm advocates, like Gifford and Cunningham, prevented him from occupying his legitimate position as a dramatist immediately after Shakspere."

unless it is explained. I allow that Ben Jonson had
a greater intellect; that Beaumont and Fletcher had
more genius, more pathos, more humour; that Marlowe,
Webster, and Ford, each in his own way, were greater
poets. I put Massinger next to Shakspere as a dramatist
pure and simple, because his best work is well-constructed
and interesting, his style and metre entrancing, his atmosphere charming and easy, yet ideal, his morality mature
and sane. And in praising his morality, I do not lay
stress on the benefits to be derived from the use of his plays
as a school-book, though that consideration is not to be
despised but rather maintain that in avoiding abnormal,
tainted, and morbid themes he is in advance of his age;
consequently he is easier for us to read and understand
than other writers whose gifts were greater than his;
he makes a successful and enduring appeal to the *communis
sensus* of mankind.

I now proceed to a short critical estimate of Massinger's plays. The most famous are *The Virgin Martyr*
in tragedy, and *A New Way to pay Old Debts* in comedy.
Opinions have differed strangely about *The Virgin Martyr*.
It went through four editions in quarto in the seventeenth
century, a fact which testifies to its immediate popu-
larity. Davies[1] considered it far inferior to any of his
other productions, and Mason was equally severe. Even
Hallam confessed that parts of it were far from pleasing.
There can be no doubt that these parts of the play, which
the critics now unanimously ascribe to Dekker, are re -
sponsible for giving Massinger a bad name for coarseness.
It is hard to carry supernatural machinery through, as
Fletcher's *Prophetess* shows, and we have here an Angel,
and a Devil, but they are on the whole managed successfully. The first act is admirably proportioned; the fourth
and fifth also are masterly. There are a thrill and a
glamour in the style of this play unlike anything else in
Massinger, due perhaps to the religious problem dealt

---

[1] Preface, p. lvii. of Monck Mason's edition.

with.[1]   The only fault of Dorothea is that, like other good people, she is a bad judge of character. It gives us a shock to find Spungius and Hircius members of her household, and at least we feel she should not have put her charities in their hands, but should have attended to the poor herself.[2]   The Princess Artemia is a type common in Massinger.[3]

In *A New Way to pay Old Debts* we have an ingenious plot which never flags, adequate comedy, and characters which are appropriately, if not very carefully, drawn. The style is strong and natural; it is not far from this play to Goldsmith, and indeed the eighteenth century must have owed much to it.   In its atmosphere of ease and propriety there are no harsh lights or discordant tints.

The central idea of the plot was probably borrowed from a play of admirable vivacity and dexterity, Middleton's *Trick to catch the Old One*, which appeared in 1607. What has Massinger added to Middleton ?   He has made the plot more probable, refining the characters, and raising the whole thing from prose to poetry.   We laugh less, but we admire more, for we feel that we are seeing something transacted which might have happened.

Sir Giles Overreach is Massinger's masterpiece, a superman of colossal wickedness, with no belief in the honour or virtue of men or women.[4]   Though fond of

---

[1] For another explanation, see Appendix X.

[2] Alinda, the heroine of Fletcher's *Pilgrim*, is equally indiscriminate in her bounty (Act I., 1, 2).   We may compare J. Taylor's *Holy Living*, Sec. VIII., Alms: "Trust not your alms to intermedial uncertain and under-dispensers."

[3] Where did he get her name from ?   A lady of the name is a subordinate character in Hroswitha's *Gallicanus*. The plays of Hroswitha have obvious affinities with *The Virgin Martyr*, but I cannot trace any other indications of borrowing.

[4] Brander Matthews, as a fellow-countryman of Jay Gould and Rockefeller, is well qualified to estimate Sir Giles Overreach; he points out that he is an instance of what the French call, "l'homme fort."   The part has been taken by many of our great actors, notably Garrick, who revived it in 1745.   *Cf.*

money, he is not a miser, but loves to lavish his gains; power is rather his foible; repeated success has made him reckless; his aim is to increase his estates by bullying his poorer neighbours, and by employing the sharp practices of the law. But he has yet one other ambition, to see his only daughter married to a lord and to hear her styled " Right Honourable." His unscrupulousness is expressed in often-quoted passages of great power; his frantic anger in the fifth act is depicted with a skill which leaves no sympathy in our minds for a father whose only daughter has treated him badly. Here Massinger is more successful than his great model in the case of Shylock and Jessica. I cannot agree that it is inconsistent with the character of Sir Giles that he should be anxious for his daughter to marry a lord—there are several passages in the earlier part of the play which show that he is not only a bully but a base-born snob.[1]

Where so much is admirable it is difficult to make selection, but we may point out that Wellborn's character is a fine piece of work; we pity his disgrace, we rejoice in his success, we believe in his desire to do better in the future. The grief of Lady Allworth for her husband and the jealous fears of young Allworth when Lord Lovell is to meet Margaret are excellently drawn. There are, moreover, touches of poetry in the play of a high order, as, for instance:

ALLWORTH.   If ever
The queen of flowers, the glory of the spring,
The sweetest comfort to our smell, the rose,
Sprang from an envious briar, I may infer,
There's such disparity in their conditions,
Between the goodness of my soul, the daughter,
And the base churl, her father.[2]

W. Hazlitt's *Dramatic Essays* for the performances of Kean and Kemble in 1816 (pp. 78-80, 91-92, 97-100). The two great actors had a different conception of Sir Giles; and Hazlitt is very severe upon Kemble. Kean was at Drury Lane, Kemble at Covent Garden.   [1] *Cf.* II., 1, 81 and 88.   [2] I., 1, 146.

Or in Allworth's speech about his love:

> Add this too; when you feel her touch, and breath
> Like a soft western wind, when it glides o'er
> Arabia, creating gums and spices;
> And in the van, the nectar of her lips,
> Which you must taste, bring the battalia on,
> Well-arm'd, and strongly lined with her discourse,
> And knowing manners, to give entertainment;
> Hippolytus himself would leave Diana,
> To follow such a Venus.[1]

The play which Massinger himself at one time esteemed the most highly was *The Roman Actor*,[2] but we have to remember that much of his best work was done after 1626, the date of the play. *The Roman Actor*, though most admirable, is strong and hard rather than inspired. More than any other of his works it shows us an element of greatness in the author's mind, which reveals itself in many ways; in the attractive and noble character of Paris, in the mastery shown in dealing with a Roman theme, the local colour of which is put on with a light and yet sure hand, in the skill with which the story is invested with the atmosphere of tyranny, in the breathless interest with which we follow the last moments of Domitian in Act V., in the dexterity with which three smaller plays are introduced into the action without in the least confusing the construction. In making an actor the hero of the play, and in giving him so many opportunities of showing his art, Massinger no doubt felt every confidence in the genius of J. Taylor, but perhaps the chief charm of the play is due to the reflection which it inspires in the mind of the reader, that it expresses with fire and conviction the struggling author's high ideal for the theatre as a social institution, and his esteem for actors. On the other hand, there is little comic relief, and little female

---

[1] III., 1, 72.

[2] See the Dedication: "I ever held this the most perfect birth of my Minerva." It was printed in 1629. It is interesting to compare it with *The Cardinal*, for which Shirley had a similar affection.

interest beyond the infatuation of the Empress. Indeed, the women who take part in the play are one and all unattractive, and though it might be fairly urged that they are probably adequate portraits of the originals, we cannot help feeling that the author ought to have seen that they were timid sketches. In other words, we are face to face here with an acknowledged limitation of Massinger's art. Nor should it be forgotten that while the play is full of noble and even impassioned rhetoric,[1] there are one or two prosy passages[2] and several small improbabilities.[3] In the third of the inserted plays Domitian, taking the part of an actor, avenges himself on Paris. This device by which characters in a play avenge themselves by taking parts in a subordinate play, occurs in the famous *Spanish Tragedy* of Kyd, and in Middleton's *Women, beware Women.* Most successful of all is the splendid climax of Act IV., where we have the clash of interest required by the highest form of tragedy; we sympathize with Paris, and yet we feel that the Emperor, who has been wronged, must avenge himself signally and at once.

It is the tragi-comedies which give me the most pleasure, the romantic plays with a happy ending, such as *The Great Duke of Florence, The Emperor of the East, The Bashful Lover* (the last of Massinger's plays which we possess), *A Very Woman ;* closely allied with these is *The Maid of Honour. The Great Duke of Florence* is full of

---

[1] *Cf.* Domitian's speech in II., 1, 160-168; and that of Rusticus in III., 2, 59-68.

[2] As, for instance, Paris' speech in I., 1, 21-26, and Stephanos' words in V., 1, 99-101.

[3] I., 4, where the Imperial princesses push one another about in seeking for a front place in the street as Domitian passes, is an example of this fault. We have already referred to the difficulties which are involved in the infliction of torture on the stage, as in III., 2. Again, it is improbable that the actors should have been waiting, as in IV., 1, outside the private gardens, ready to perform the very play which suited Domitian's purpose. We are also disconcerted to find the ghosts in Act V., 1, stealing the bust of Minerva. (*Cf.*, however, Virgil, *Æneid*, II., 294.)

courtesy and grace; there are some charming passages
of poetry, and the metre is liquid and easy. The whole
play is bathed in the sunshine of youth, and while there
is some good comedy in it, there is little for the expurgator
to do. The characters are all drawn with skill and propriety, especially the Duke, the Duchess of Urbin, and
Lidia. Petronella in disguise is Massinger's best comic
creation.

In *The Emperor of the East*, with a trivial plot and some
improbability in details, there is much admirable work,
especially at the beginning. The two courtiers get to the
point at once, mentioning Pulcheria in I., 1, 10. It was
a play at which the author worked hard, and of which he
thought highly.[1] The two good women, the sister and the
wife, are well drawn, and we understand how natural it
is that they should be antipathetic; we welcome the allowance they make for one another,[2] we sympathize with the
humiliation of each in her turn, and we rejoice in their
reconciliation. Especially pleasing are the gentle dignity
of Eudocia in III., 4, and her slowness to take up Chrysapius' suggestion in IV., 1. The Emperor is not an attractive character, as he is at once weak and violent; but we
have to remember that he is very young, and also that he
has been kept in leading-strings all the earlier part of his
life. I should like to believe, with many critics, that the
prose scene, in which the Empiric figures, is not due to
Massinger. It is a study in the manner of Ben Jonson.
Another touch of the older master is "The Projector,"[3] who
is, however, on very much fainter lines than Meercroft in
The Devil is an Ass. Imitation of Shakspere is prominent
in *The Emperor of the East*. Scenes I., 1, and III., 1, remind
us of Henry VIII's courtiers. The pictures in Act II.

---

[1] Prologue 2, 7:

> In each part,
> With his best of fancy, judgment, language, art,
> Fashion'd and form'd so, as might well, and may
> Deserve a welcome, and no vulgar way.

[2] *Cf.* IV., 1, 28, and IV., 5, 216.   [3] I., 2.

seem to be suggested by a similar scene in *The Merchant of Venice*. Act IV., 5 recalls *Othello*, III., 4; Act V., 2, 105-8 is modelled on *Othello* III., 3, 330-3.[1]

A Very Woman or *The Prince of Tarent* is based, as the Prologue tells us, on an old play; the author's modesty cannot forbear saying that, good as it was before, it is " much better'd now." By this he probably means that substantial additions have been made, that the plot has been put into better shape,[2] and that perhaps the comic element is cut down. Boyle assigns about two-fifths of the play to Massinger, including the quarrel between Cardenes and Antonio, and the great love scene between Antonio and Almira, but excluding the careful treatment of Cardenes' melancholy by Paulo the doctor.[3] I should myself unhesitatingly assign the latter scene to Massinger. The only scenes which can be safely attributed to Fletcher are those of the slave-market,[4] and that where Leonora seeks to console Almira.[5] The sprightly vivacity of the former and the tenderness of the latter are good evidence for this assignation. A perusal of this admirable masterpiece leads us to the conclusion that if Massinger, instead of collaborating with Fletcher, had rewritten the plays of the latter, our literature would have been greatly enriched.

I would not deny that a man may have several styles, and may write in the manner of another; especially is this possible when the other has been his bosom friend. Still there are a grace and delicacy about *A Very Woman* which seem to suggest the hand of Fletcher. The characters are drawn with great refinement and vividness. There is a pair of devoted friends, Antonio and Pedro, and over against them two charming ladies, Leonora and Almira,

---

[1] The way in which the apple circulates reminds us of the Umbrana in Beaumont's amusing *Woman-Hater*.

[2] The reference to an architect in IV., 2, 178, suggests that in the first draft of the play Paulo had appeared in that character.   [3] IV., 2.   [4] III., 1.   [5] III., 4.

the former at once sensible and kind, the latter almost
worthy of a place beside Shakspere's heroines.   The great
love scene, though suggested by Desdemona and Othello,
is not unworthy of Shakspere himself.[1]   Cuculo is an
amusing study of the old courtier, such as we get elsewhere
in Massinger.   Borachia, the lady who loves wine, is
drawn with a lighter hand than Massinger's; yet I feel
that Fletcher, unassisted or unpruned, would have made
the scenes in which she appears grosser than they are.
Antonio, the Prince of Tarent, reminds us of a clean-
limbed, honest English public-school boy; he is slow to
take offence, but brave when provoked, sorry for the mis-
chance of which he is the innocent cause, courteous, and
ready on all occasions.

The plot has been shaped with great attention to detail.
Thus, when Antonio, disguised as a slave, first meets his
friend Pedro, his master Cuculo does not allow him to
speak,[2] so that Pedro has no chance of identifying him
by his voice.   Later on, however, Pedro has an intuition
that the slave is other than he seems to be:

> " I do see something in this fellow's face still
> That ties my heart fast to him."[3]

He treats him as a friend, as though his intuition pierced
through the external disguise,[4] and when the recognition
takes place he naturally remarks:

> " Have I not just cause,
> When I consider how I could be so stupid,
> As not to see a friend through all disguises."[5]

Again, we have an indication at the end of the slave-
market scene that the slave who followed Paulo will be
an important link in the plot:

> PAULO.   Follow me, then ;
> The knave may teach me something.

---

[1] IV., 3.   [2] III., 2, 69.   [3] IV., 1, 17.
[4] IV., 3, 196; V., 3, 53.   [5] V., 5, 42.

SLAVE.   Something that
You dearly may repent; howe'er you scorn me,
The slave may prove your master.[1]

It is this slave who leads the pirates in their attempt to carry off Leonora and Almira. When Antonio appears in his former dress[2] we ask, how did he get it ? The answer is, from the Captain, his fellow-slave, whose life he had saved in the past by interceding with the Viceroy.[3]   Lastly, the Duke's reference (V., 2, 130) to the advice which the Viceroy had given him in II., 2, is one of those careful touches making for unity of design in which Massinger delights.[4]

No doubt the plot is not free from improbabilities; in real life Antonio would have revealed himself to Pedro, and Pedro and Almira would both have recognized him. We have already seen that Massinger is so fond of a story that he sometimes forgets to let his characters guide it. To round off the play harmoniously, Antonio should have had a soliloquy, to explain to the audience who he was, to lament over the change of his fortunes, to express a hope that all would come right in the end, to reassert his devotion to Pedro, and to protest his loyalty in spite of everything to Almira.   Perhaps something of the sort was cut out.

The Bashful Lover is the last play of " the strange old fellow "[5] that we possess; it reminds us in several respects of Fletcher; in the romantic atmosphere,[6] the over-wrought devotion of the hero, the bustling action and the complexity of the plot, and in a metrical detail.[7]   On the

---

[1] III., 1, 162.   [2] V., 5.   [3] II., 1, 35.
[4] *Cf. The Virgin Martyr*, I., 1, 405 and V., 2, 4.
[5] Epilogue, line 9.
[6] There is too much kneeling in this play; Hortensio kneels, I., 1, 200; Matilda, III., 3, 60 and 123; Lorenzo, IV., 1, 167; Matilda again, IV., 1, 184; Alonzo and Pisano, V., 1, 180; Matilda again, V., 3, 101; the Ambassador, V., 3, 169.
[7] *I.e.*, the " emphatic " double ending.   *Cf.* II., 4, 21; II., 6, 51; II., 7, 69; III., 1, 114; IV., 3, 81; IV, 3, 155.

other hand, the smooth and careful construction, the subordination of the comedy, the constant use of parentheses, and, above all, the vacillations of the violent Lorenzo, are characteristics of Massinger. There are many noble personages in the play, and considerable tenderness. Matilda's character is drawn well at the start; in the latter part she rather tends to become a lay figure. A princess with three aspirants to her hand, of whom two are princes, while the one she loves is to all appearance of lowly birth, is awkwardly placed. The same fault, as Boyle points out,[1] might be found with the hero, Hortensio; the fact is that the story rather carries the characters along in its sweep than is developed by them; moreover, Massinger seems in the last two acts to be more interested in the psychological study of Lorenzo's emotions than in his hero's fortunes. With all its beauties, the play betrays the advancing years of the author by a certain heaviness of touch, although the episode of Ascanio, the disguised page, is carried through with great delicacy and skill, and the varied incidents of Act II. make the battle one of the most lifelike in literature.

The Maid of Honour is well planned, and the characters well contrasted. Indeed, anyone who doubts Massinger's skill in this respect will be convinced by this play. Though the end is sombre, it is, as Leslie Stephen has pointed out, dignified and inevitable. As Bertoldo was sworn to celibacy, Camiola could not have married him, even if her self-respect had allowed it.[2] Here again we get an imperious lady, the Duchess Aurelia, who changes her mind too rapidly, but cannot be charged with viciousness. The comic touches, a foolish lover and a pair of effeminate courtiers, are quite good. The various moods of Adorni —his deepening devotion to Camiola, his humility at her rebuke, his fidelity in doing her commands, his tempta-

---

[1] *N. S. S.*, p. 393.
[2] The disappointment which we feel at Camiola's lot may be paralleled by Bellario in *Philaster*.

tion to commit suicide—are admirably portrayed. The King, too, is well drawn; he is a complex character, who is not wholly bad. The rough old soldier Gonzaga is a lifelike study, but the figure who dominates the play is the high-spirited and beautiful heroine. The careful skill of the author is shown in many details, among others, in the way in which Camiola, before taking the veil, persuades the King to forgive Fulgentio. For this to be possible the way is paved by the King's change of mind as to Camiola's character in IV., 5. The end of the play shows in what way Massinger is a greater artist than Fletcher. The latter would certainly have married off the Duchess Aurelia to the King or the Duke of Urbin, and provided Gonzaga with a wife.

No student of our comic drama can ignore the brilliant vigour of *The City Madam*.[1] The characters one and all contribute to an harmonious unity, the most lifelike perhaps being Sir John Frugal, the bluff, successful British merchant, tender-hearted, yet ashamed of being un-businesslike, and a good judge of men. The plot moves easily, not overloaded with satire. The women remind us of Ben Jonson's women, but with less strength there is a greater art shown here than Ben Jonson had at his command. The great triumph of the play is the hypocrite Luke, to whom some splendid rhetoric is assigned. He arrests our attention from the first; though not on the grand scale like Sir Giles Overreach, he is an innate villain, who only lacks opportunity to be capable of anything, a sordid soul, who does not know what goodness is. The

---

[1] *The City Madam* was printed in 1658. Perhaps this accounts for Colley Cibber's statement that Massinger died in 1659. The editor of the play, Andrew Pennycuicke, "one of the actors," being, as the name would seem to imply, a canny Scot, dedicated the first edition " to the truly noble John North Esquire," and the second, *totidem verbis*, "to the truly noble and virtuous Lady Anne, Countess of Oxford." I owe this fact to the kindness of Mr. P. Simpson. It is to be noted that both editions read " out-conquered," whereas Cunningham has printed " not-conquered."

two 'prentices are of the same kidney as Quicksilver in
Eastward Ho.

For sheer vitality and strength three of the plays stand
out conspicuously: *The Bondman, The Renegado,* and *The
Guardian.* Though they are disfigured by one or two
coarse scenes, one is carried along in reading them as if one
were in a sailing-boat, dancing along a fresh sea. Of *The
Bondman* Monck Mason says: " I don't recollect any play
whatsoever that begins or ends in a manner so pleasing,
uncommon, and striking." It contains four well-drawn
characters—Timoleon, Marullo, Leosthenes, and Cleora.
The plot is lively, though some critics, I think unjustly,
have accused the author of cutting the knot in the fifth
act. The disguised brother and sister who meet in Act
III., 1 should perhaps indicate their relationship. Timandra does not explicitly mention her brother till V., 1,
64. A reference earlier in the play to the wrong which
Leosthenes had done her would certainly make for clear-
ness. There is much fine eloquence in the play. The
one or two offensive comic scenes are not essential to
the plot.

The Renegado has an Oriental setting, which alone would
make it attractive on the stage. The character of Donusa
is on the grand scale, one of Massinger's successes; the
Merchant, the Jesuit, and Grimaldi are all well drawn.
There is some fine oratory and a good plot, which works
up to an exciting end. There is not much in the comic
line of value here.

The plot of *The Guardian* is more complicated than is
usual with Massinger. It contains some charming banditti scenes, while Alphonso's fictitious narrative in the
last act is one of the strongest pieces of writing in our
author. The guardian, Durazzo, the kind-hearted but
cynical and quick-tempered old man of the world, is one
of Massinger's most successful creations. On the other
hand, it will be allowed that there is too much concession
in *The Guardian* to a corrupt taste, due perhaps to poverty

and the depression of failure. The character of Iolante is unattractive; her intrigue with a man who turns out to be her brother is odious; her repentance is cheap and unconvincing. The earlier part of the play in its movement and morals alike reminds us of Fletcher.

The Picture is full of power, and enriched with some good strokes of satire; the alternations of mood in the chief characters are represented with skill, while the magic portrait on which the plot hinges seems to take a natural place in the story. There is, however, a crudeness and hardness of texture about the play, though Mathias and Sophia are well drawn, especially the latter. Everything comes right at the last, and true love is vindicated after the display of some proper pride; but one feels that the three venture their honour too far. " He comes too near who comes to be denied." The King's faults are overdrawn; the Queen very nearly spoils the play; the young courtiers, though realistic, are unpleasant; the comic element is poor and farcical.[1] In dealing with a psychological theme, Massinger was trying to adjust to the hard-and-fast concrete outlines of the drama a story which would have been easier to manage and more attractive to read if it had been cast in the form of a novel. There would then have been possible gradations of light and shade, which would have made the treatment less bald. It would have supplied Richardson with a problem worthy of his heart-breaking and long-drawn analysis.

The Duke of Milan is a gloomy play, with a somewhat intricate plot, presenting to us that strange " Italianate "[2] world of treachery and poison with which Webster, Ford, and Tourneur make us familiar. We must remember, on the other hand, that Italy gives an atmosphere which

---

[1] Hilario is Massinger's one attempt at the Shaksperian "fool"; but what a contrast there is between Hilario and Touchstone or Feste !
[2] Dekker's word.

domestic plays like *The Yorkshire Tragedy* and *Arden of Feversham* lack. As in *The Bondman* and *The Unnatural Combat*, the plot is developed late, though hints are given before. Thus, the ill-treated sister is early referred to,[1] while the last words of the same act prepare us for Francisco's villainy. The finest scene in the play is Act III., 1, which is bathed in the romantic atmosphere so congenial to our author. Sforza submits to his enemy, the Emperor Charles, without forfeiting our esteem, while the Emperor shows a noble magnanimity. There is a subdued comic element in the person of Graccho, the musician.

The Duke of Milan is carefully written[2] and skilfully constructed; the author has taken great pains to draw the characters of Sforza and Marcelia, though Francisco is perhaps more successful than either.[3] The Duke's last words are the clue to his character:

> I come: Death, I obey thee!
> Yet I will not die raging; for alas!
> My whole life was a frenzy: good Eugenia,
> In death forgive me.[4]

The chief " frenzy " of his life was his devotion to his wife Marcelia. This peerless beauty combines pride[5] with a kindly simplicity which is no match for Francisco; while she dearly loves her husband and forgives him in her last words, she is not altogether attractive. On the other hand, her anger with Sforza for leaving orders that she should be killed if he did not return safe from his

---

[1] II., 1, 20.

[2] Notice the skill with which Sforza, in I., 3, works up to his unexpected and terrible request.

[3] A clever passage is that where Francisco points out that nothing succeeds like success (IV., 1, 16-36).

[4] V., 2, 256. *Cf.* IV., 2, 75:

> Hold but thy nature, Duke, and be but rash,
> And violent enough.

Cf. also I., 2, 30; I., 3, 369; III., 3, 252.

[5] I., 1, 111-125.

hazardous enterprise is natural, and the scene in which she receives him coldly and provokes his violent anger would be effective when acted.[1] We are inevitably reminded of *Othello*, and the comparison is most instructive as revealing the great gap which separates the pupil from the master. Marcelia is not so gracious as Desdemona, nor Sforza so strong as Othello, nor Francisco so devilish as Iago. As is usually the case with Massinger, the fifth act carries along our interest to the end. We do not weep, but we are certainly moved by the horror of the Duke's death. The princesses of the Ducal House are responsible for an improbable scene[2] when they flout Marcelia in the absence of her lord. Their behaviour reminds us of the ladies in *The Roman Actor*. In style *The Duke of Milan* is marked by several passages of fine poetry and a comparative absence of the parenthetic construction.

The Fatal Dowry is a famous and much-admired play, adapted by Nicholas Rowe in the eighteenth century to form the basis of his *Fair Penitent*.[3] There are some fine scenes here, notably the funeral, which is as effective as anything our poet has written. On the other hand, the scene in which Rochfort is robed and blindfolded, and

---

[1] III., 3. [2] II., 1, 121.

[3] Though Rowe behaved badly in concealing his theft from Massinger, the critics have been unfair to his play. It is very instructive to compare the simple structure of *The Fair Penitent*, written on French lines, with the larger scheme and wealth of incident in *The Fatal Dowry*. We are reminded of the contrast between an English and a Dutch garden. After all, some people prefer their yew-trees cut into cocks and hens, while others do not. I can imagine a being who would prefer Gounod's *Romeo and Juliet* to Shakspere's. In *The Fair Penitent*, the law-court scene, the father's funeral, and the music-master disappear. We get the "gay Lothario" from this once popular play. Mr. Phelan (p. 60) has properly pointed out that "for Lothario we entertain a latent regard, for his elegant and gallant bearing," whereas Novall, junr., "is not calculated to gain love." In other words, while Massinger's moral is superior, Rowe is more true to life. *Cf.* some interesting remarks by Hazlitt (*Dramatic Essays*, pp. 93-95) on Rowe's play and Miss O'Neill as Calista.

assents to his daughter's death, recalls Fletcher in its improbability; nor is it likely that Beaumelle would marry Charalois at such short notice. All we can say about this is that hurried weddings are one of the presuppositions of the Jacobean drama.[1] There are an heroic atmosphere, a fine friendship, and much rhetoric of a high order in *The Fatal Dowry*. Moreover, as the moral lines at the end point out, there is the clash of law and natural vengeance in this play, which is a legitimate source of dramatic power. Charalois, Romont, Malotin, and Pontalier are all well drawn: the " sweet and gentle nature " of Charalois is particularly attractive, though he is not incapable of passionate anger,[2] which makes the punishment he inflicts on his guilty wife in IV., 4 more credible. On the other hand, a story is at a disadvantage in which the father, though generous and dignified, is impulsive and quixotic, the heroine is worthless, and her lover contemptible.[3] The style in places is less lucid than usual, which may be due to the co-operation of Field; moreover, the metre is more halting than Massinger's is wont to be, and I think it probable that the play has been carelessly printed. There is much spirited sarcasm in Act III., and some fun in Act IV.[4]

The Unnatural Combat is full of splendid rhetoric; indeed, there are perhaps too many soliloquies. This early work is grim as an iron-bound coast; yet the affairs of the honest, brave, and poverty-stricken captain, Belgarde, provide a lighter element, and the moralizing of the pert page in III., 2 is both sensible and light-handed in execution. The reason for the son's antipathy to his father is hinted at from time to time in the first act; its disclosure is postponed too late. We should

---

[1] *Cf. Unnatural Combat*, III., 2, 144, and Fletcher, *passim*.
[2] *Cf.* I., 1, 203.
[3] Novall never meant to marry Beaumelle. *Cf.* IV., 1, 100; V., 2, 264.
[4] For a discussion of the authorship of the play, see Appendix XI.

also have been prepared for the wrongs and treachery of Montreville, which burst upon us too suddenly in the last act. The evil passion of Malefort is powerfully depicted; here, again, we have a careful study of conflicting emotions. Though he struggles against his evil desires, we feel that a bad man must come to a bad end.[1] The play would have been better rounded off if in the initial part some indication had been given that he seemed to everyone a man whose mind, for some mysterious reason, was unbalanced and unhinged.[2] Once allow that such a theme can be tolerable as that which we have here, and the hints which Montreville drops from time to time are adequate to stir the suspicion of the spectator.

The style is more like rhythmical prose than that of any other of Massinger's plays. Here alone in our author do children occur, and that in an unpleasing context.[3] The ghosts of Malefort's victims, which appear in the last scene, seem to me a legitimate and powerful episode. It was natural to compare this violent play with Chapman's tragedies; Malefort reminding us of *Bussy d'Ambois* and Byron; but there is little in common between the two authors. In the first place, Massinger knows how to construct a play; in the second place, there is hardly a line in *The Unnatural Combat* which is obscure, whereas in the last act of *Bussy d'Ambois*, Chapman's masterpiece, there is hardly a line which is intelligible.

The *Parliament of Love* contains much fine poetry[4] and one great forensic scene, such as our author loves.[5] It is, however, in too fragmentary a state for us to judge

---

[1] There is much in Act III. of *A King and No King* which reminds us of Malefort's passion; but Massinger is a better moralist than the authors of that brilliant play.

[2] Beaufort senior's words in III., 2, 32-41, should, however, be carefully observed.

[3] IV., 2, 87. *Cf.*, however, Sir John Van Olden Barnavelt, III., 2.

[4] *E.g.*, Charles's speech about Cupid, V., 1, 33-60.

[5] Act V. We must allow that Cleremond and Leonora are too long-winded.

it fairly.[1]   The atmosphere is unreal, the interest flags,
the boisterous comedy is unattractive. There are more
women than is usual in Massinger, and duelling and friendship inspire two noble scenes (III., 2; IV., 2). Though
vice is humbled, we ask here, as in *The Picture*, does
virtue gain by the way in which its opposite is portrayed ?
And are not the characters, male and female alike, un-
discriminated ?   The interest, in other words, is concentrated in the triple story, and doubtless we feel some satisfaction in the punishment of Clarindore, the betrayer of
secrets.[2]   There are a good many half-lines in the manner
of Fletcher.

Though *Believe as You List*[3] is full of dignity and poetry,
it has a plot without much nexus, of the sort which
Aristotle would blame as ἐπεισοδιώδης.[4]   We are wafted
from Carthage to Bithynia, from Bithynia to Lusitania,
from Lusitania to Sicily. Though Antiochus is truly
a king even in his misfortunes, and excites our respect
and compassion, the play can hardly have been a success.
The melancholy tinge is too uniform; the improbabilities
of the recognitions are too glaring. The Courtesan and
Berecinthius cannot be said to have added to the gaiety
of nations; of the other characters Flaminius alone has
individuality. The peculiar circumstances under which
the play was written may help to explain the fiasco.

---

[1] We may conjecture that the missing part of Act I. contained (*a*) a scene in which "three citizens" described the
situation, and the absence of the King; (*b*) a scene of love-
making between Cleremond and Leonora, containing the incident referred to in II., 2, 93-100; (*c*) a scene in which Beaupré
obtained Chamont's protection, and asked for an introduction
to Bellisant (*cf*. V., 1, 470).   Bellisant may also have appeared
before I., 4, as her denunciations of the gallants are referred
to in II., 1, 23. And Bellisant knows in III., 3, 145, that Clarindore had " cast off " Beaupré. Clarindore is the sort of man
who might have boasted of this.
[2] V., 1, 520. Massinger did not like people who cannot keep
a secret. *Cf. A Very Woman*, IV., 2, 142.
[3] For a fuller discussion of this play and the MS., see
Appendixes VII. and VIII.   [4] *Poetics*, 1451*a*, 16, 1451*b*, 34.

The Old Law does not owe much to Massinger. As it was a favourite play, it may have owed its association with his name to revision on his part.[1] There is a charming tenderness in places and a rollicking improbability about the whole scheme, both alien to the staid Massinger. The humour is not his, but better; his phraseology is markedly absent;[2] the prose scenes show another concep-

---

[1] Touches which remind one of Massinger occur, but they are few and far between—*e.g.*:

I., 1, 30-70, reminds us of him here and there. (The same applies to Cleanthes' speech, I., 1, 323-345.)

I., 1, 248: "personal opposition." (*Cf. Believe as You List,* IV., 2, 98.)

I., 1, 362:

CLEANTHES. How do you fare, sir ?
LEONIDES. Cleanthes, never better.
(In the *Henry VIII* manner.)

II., 1, 41-61: The first courtier's speech.
II., 2, 73-94: Lysander's speech.
IV., 2, 1-130: see especially lines 3, 41, 72, 109
V., 1, 54-82.
V., 1, 119-132: Lysander's speech.
V., 1, 156-175.
V., 1, 232-250: Cleanthes' speech. (Notice the parenthesis in lines 246-7.)

The play is usually assigned to 1599, on the strength of the passage where Gnotho gets the clerk to alter the Parish Chronicle (III., 1). Gayley thinks the mention of 1599 "purely dramatic" (*R. E. C.,* III., p. lv). He says the style is not like that of Middleton in 1599, and points out that Rowley was only fourteen years of age in that year. "If Massinger had any share in the play, it was in revision, after Middleton's death in 1627." Gayley dates the play 1614-16. It must be pointed out, however, that it is not easy to alter 40 to 39. The author could have chosen a date whose figures were more easy to deal with. I therefore think the usually accepted date is right, though it does not, of course, settle the question of authorship.

Massinger was fond of scenes in courts of justice, and it is highly probable that he elaborated the details of Act V.

[2] We find "horror" in IV., 2, 72 and 160; a certain number of the alliterations referred to above (p. 121), I., 1, 66; II., 1, 210, 265; II., 2, 119; V., 1, 546, 550, 605, 650; and words doubled (I., 1, 67, 88, 206, 220, 268, 354, 389; II., 1, 154, 275; II., 2, 91; III., 1, 304, 363).

tion of art; the careless metre suggests Rowley. It is clear that whoever wrote the comic parts of *The Old Law* was responsible for Chough, Trimtram, and the Roarers in *A Fair Quarrel*. The scene is laid in " Epire," a region which seems to have been regarded by our ancestors as a place for strange things to happen, and a vague background like the city of Callipolis ;[1] it seems to have the same character in the present day. A King of " Epire " figures among Diocletian's court in *The Virgin Martyr*, and in *The Dumb Knight*[2] we find a Duke of Epire. The classical allusions and Latin phrases suggest that the author of *The Old Law* was a man of some culture.

My task is now ended. I shall consider myself happy if I persuade some of my readers to make the acquaintance of Massinger's plays.[3] We have lately been celebrating the tercentenary of Shakspere's death. The best way of honouring a great author is to read his writings; but to appreciate aright the greatness of Shakspere we should be wise to combine with our study a just estimate of his contemporaries and satellites; and, of the many dramatists of that century, none seem to me more worthy of affectionate consideration than Philip Massinger. It is especially instructive to return to his writings from the perusal of the masterpieces of his contemporaries; though from time to time they display rich gifts of pathos, poetry, and humour, they are too often marred by waywardness, unnaturalness, want of proportion, and grossness; it is a relief to resume the study of an author whose work is sober, well balanced, dignified, and lucid. While he shares with them the modern atmosphere of romance and adventure, he is the most Greek of his generation; and this is the real secret of his abiding charm. The

---

[1] *Believe as You List*, IV., 1; *Love's Triumph through Callipolis;* Peele's *Battle of Alcazar*.

[2] Dodsley's *Old Plays*, vol. x. (Hazlitt).

[3] There is a good edition of *A New Way to pay Old Debts* by K. Deighton (G. Bell, 1893). Brander Matthews has also edited the play, prefixing a valuable estimate of the poet.

passionate, the abnormal, the lurid, the farcical elements, in which his contemporaries revel, are not, indeed, entirely absent, but they are less conspicuous; the luxuriance of the thicket does not hinder the wayfarer from following the path; we pluck the roses without tearing our flesh on the thorns; and as we contemplate the marble splendour of his verse we almost forget that sculpture has its limitations.

APPENDIXES

I.—The Small Actor in Massinger's Plays.

II.—Massinger's Knowledge of Greek.

III.—The Collaborated Plays.

IV.—Influence of Shakspere on Massinger.

V.—Warburton's List.

VI.—A Metrical Peculiarity in Massinger.

VII.—"Believe as You List."

VIII.—Collation of "Believe as You List."

IX.—"The Parliament of Love."

X.—Authorship of "The Virgin Martyr."

XI.—Authorship of "The Fatal Dowry."

XII.—"Sir John Van Olden Barnavelt."

XIII.—"The Second Maiden's Tragedy."

XIV.—"The Powerful Favorite."

XV.—"The Double Falsehood."

XVI.—"A Trick to Catch the Old One."

XVII.—The Dublin MS.

XVIII.—Alliteration in Massinger.

XIX.—Mr. E. Gosse's First Quartos.

XX.—Bibliography.

APPENDIX I

THE SMALL ACTOR IN MASSINGER'S PLAYS

THERE are several passages in our author in which reference is made to the low stature of the actor of a female part.

Duke of Milan, II., 1, 108: Graccho, speaking of Mariana:
> Of a little thing,
> It is so full of gall !

II., 1, 156:
> MARCELIA. For you, puppet—
> MARIANA. What of me, pine-tree ?

„ 172:
> MARIANA. O that I could reach you,
> The little one you scorn so.

„ 177:
> GRACCHO.   Forty ducats
> Upon the little hen.

„ 181:
> MARCELIA. Where are you,
> You modicum, you dwarf ?
> MARIANA. Here, giantess, here.

„ 188:
> MARIANA. Or right me on this monster (she's
>   three foot
> Too high for a woman).

Bondman, I., 2, 3: Cleon, speaking to Corisca:
> Beauty invites temptations, and short heels
> Are soon tripp'd up.

(This passage may have another interpretation.)

Renegado, I., 2, 9: Manto, speaking of Paulina:
> And though low of stature,
> Her well-proportion'd limbs invite affection.

II., 5, 159: Asambeg, of Paulina:

Such a spirit,
In such a small proportion, I ne'er read of.

V., 2, 62: Carazie, of Paulina:

I would he had sent me
To the gallies or the gallows, when he gave me
To this proud little devil.

V., 3, 174: Mustapha, of Paulina:

A terrible little tyranness!

Parliament of Love, V., 1, 86: Perigot, of Leonora:

A confident little pleader.

Roman Actor, IV., 1, 15: Domitilla, referring to Domitia:

Who no sooner absent,
But she calls Dwarf! (so in her scorn she styles me)
Put on my pantofles, fetch pen and paper.

V., 2, 5: Domitilla speaks:

Could I make my approaches, though my stature
Does promise little, I have a spirit as daring
As hers that can reach higher.

Picture, I., 1, 96: Corisca speaks:

Your hand, or if you please
To have me fight so high, I'll not be coy,
But stand a-tiptoe for't.

III., 2, 27: Ricardo to Corisca:

Pretty one, I descend
To take the height of your lip.

II., 2, 197: And Pallas, bound up in a little volume.

Emperor of the East, II., 1, 388: Theodosius to Athenais:

By thyself,
The magazine of felicity, in thy lowness
Our eastern queens, at their full height, bow to thee.

Maid of Honour, I., 2, 46: Sylli to Camiola:

Nor I, your little ladyship, till you have
Perform'd the covenants.

II., 2, 117: Fulgentio to Camiola:

Of a little thing
You are a pretty peat, indifferent fair too.

Maid of Honour, IV., 3, 83:

BERTOLDO. Since she alone, in the abstract of herself,
That small but ravishing substance, comprehends
Whatever is, or can be wish'd, in the
Idea of a woman !

The Bashful Lover, I., 1, 116:

HORTENSIO. My little friend, good morrow.

(*Cf.* III., 1, 28, where "Ascanio" has to be carried.)

The part of Domitilla was taken by I. Hunniman; that of
Paulina by Theo. Bourne; that of Corisca (in *The Picture*) by
W. Trigge. It would appear, therefore, that these references
are not all due to the stature of any one individual actor,
but that Massinger took care to have actors of different height
brought into juxtaposition in his plays. He may here be
copying the well-known passages in *Midsummer Night's
Dream* (III., 2, 288-298, 324, 329). *Cf.* also *Antony and
Cleopatra*, II., 5, 118; III., 3, 13 ; *Much Ado*, I., 1, 172 and
216; *As You Like It*, I., 2, 284; *Twelfth Night*, I., 5, 219; II.,
5, 16; *King Lear*, I., 1, 201. *Cf.* Bradley's *Shakspearean
Tragedy*, p. 317, n. 1.

In Dekker's *Honest Whore*, Pt. 2, III., 1, the heroine,
Bellafront, is "a little tiny woman." So are Pretiosa in Middle-
ton's *Spanish Gipsy* (I., 5), and Isabella in *Women, beware
Women* (III., 2). *Cf.* also *The Case is Altered* (III. 3), "'Fore
God, the taller is a gallant lady." We find the same idea in *The
Fair Maid of the West*, II., 3; III., 1, 2. Celestina, in Shirley's
Lady of Pleasure (III., 2), is "a puppet." Spaconia in *A King
and no King* (III., 1) is "that little one"; Viola in *The Cox-
comb* (V., 3) is "not high." *Cf.* also *The Prophetess* (I., 3, 59),
a play which bears many marks of Massinger's work:

DIOCLESIAN. Thou know'st she is a prophetess.
MAXIMINIAN. A small one,
And as small profit to be hoped for by her.

The Spanish Curate (V., 1, 37), Jamie to Violante:

In stature you're a giantess: and your tailor
Takes measures of you with a Jacob's staff
Or he can never reach you: this by the way
For your large size.

Love's Cure (V., 3), Bobadillo to Lucio, speaking about Clara:

I put the longest weapon in your sister's hand, my lord,
because she was the shortest lady.

The Sea Voyage (IV., 3): MORILLAT: "This little gentlewoman
that was taken with us," referring to Aminta.   As Cleopatra
in *The False One* (II., 3) arrives in a parcel, she must have
been small.   Margarita in *Rule a Wife* (III., 4) is "of a low
stature."   Ismenia in *The Maid of the Mill* " was of the lowest
stature " (I., 2); *cf.* also V., 2, 7.   Evanthe in *A Wife for a
Month*, IV., 3 is "this little fort."   *Cf.* also *The Noble
Gentleman*, IV., 3.

APPENDIX II

DID Massinger know Greek ?   It is perhaps worth while
collecting the scanty evidence on the subject.   We find a pun
on the name Philanax in *The Emperor of the East*,[1] and Mathias
plays on the name of his wife Sophia.[2]   The phrase κατ'
ἐξοχήν is used in *The Guardian*.[3]   We find a Greek construction in *The Emperor of the East :*[4]

> And that before he gives he would consider
> The what, to whom, and wherefore.

On the other hand, we notice Theseus scanned as a trisyllable.[5]
There are one or two passages where the unexpected turn

---

[1] V., 3, 148:
> O Philanax, as thy name
> Interpreted speaks thee, thou hast ever been
> A lover of the King.

[2] *Picture*, I., 1, 6.

[3] III., 1, 7.   *Cf.* Ben Jonson's *Staple of News*, IV., 4
Pennyboy junior:

> Thou appears't
> κατ' ἐξοχήν, a canter.

[4] III., 1, 102-3.

[5] *Emperor of the East*, II., 1, 278 and 294.

of the thought rather suggests a Greek original. Thus, in *The Renegado*[1] we are reminded of *The Acharnians :*[2]

> GAZET. What places of credit are there ?
> CARAZIE. Chief gardener.
> GAZET. Out upon't ! 'Twill put me in mind my
> mother was an herb woman.

Another passage of *The Renegado*[3] reminds us of a famous fragment of Euripides,[4] often mistranslated:

> ASAMBEG.   At Aleppo
> I durst not press you so far: give me leave
> To use my own will and command in Tunis.

In *The Virgin Martyr*[5] we find a parallel to *The Hecuba :*[6]

> THEOPHILUS.   As a curious painter,
> When he has made some honourable piece,
> Stands off, and with a searching eye examines
> Each colour, how 'tis sweeten'd; and then hugs
> Himself for his rare workmanship.

In *The Emperor of the East*[7] occurs a parallel quoted by Dr. Walter Headlam in his notes to *Agamemnon :*[8]

> THEODOSIUS.   What an earthquake I feel in me !
> And on the sudden my whole fabric totters !
> My blood within me turns, and through my veins,
> Parting with natural redness, I discern it
> Chang'd to a fatal yellow.

It is the general opinion of scholars that our Elizabethan dramatists owed very little to the Greek drama directly, but we cannot forget that Massinger had had a good education at Oxford, and was a widely read man.[9] His forensic skill

---

[1] III., 4, 40.
[2] σκάνδικά μοι δός, μητρόθεν δεδεγμένος.   (l. 478).
[3] II., 5, 96.
[4] Telephus frag., 722:

> Σπάρταν ἔλαχες, κείνην κόσμει·
> τὰς δὲ Μυκήνας ἡμεῖς ἰδίᾳ.

[5] V., 1, 5.   [6] ὡς γραφεύς τ' ἀποσταθείς.   [7] IV., 5, 61.
[8] ἐπὶ δὲ καρδίαν ἔδραμε κροκοβαφὴς σταγών (l. 1121).
[9] *Cf. Shakspere's England*, Vol. I., ix., "Scholarship," by Sir J. E. Sandys.

often reminds us of Euripides; and if he did not know the works of his illustrious predecessor, he would have found in them a congenial spirit.[1]

The speech of Sanazarro to Giovanni in *The Great Duke of Florence*[2] reminds us of Creon's arguments in Sophocles' *Œdipus Tyrannus*, line 596 κ.τ.λ.

The scene in *The Bondman*,[3] when the senators frighten the mutinous slaves by shaking their whips, reminds us of the Scythians in *Herodotus*,[4] but it is also found in *Justin*,[5] and Gifford points out that it may really have been borrowed from a contemporary book of travels, Purchas's *Pilgrims*.[6]

Massinger had a good working knowledge of mythology; thus, references in his plays to Hercules and Alcides abound, as they do in Shakspere. We find several false quantities in proper names: Caesarěa, in *The Virgin Martyr ;* Archidǎmus, in *The Bondman ;* Eubŭlus, in *The Picture ;* Nomothētae, in *The Old Law*[7] *;* Cybēle, in *Believe as You List*.[8] We may compare Shakspere's *Andronĭcus*; Anthrŏpos in *Four Plays in One, The Triumph of Time;* and Euphānes in *The Queen of Corinth*.[9]

---

[1] It may be noted that the end of *The Knight of Malta* is modelled on the last scene of the *Alcestis*. The play has been attributed in part to Massinger, but the fact cited, though interesting, does not prove acquaintance either on the part of Fletcher or Massinger with Greek at first hand.

[2] III., 1., 92-106.   [3] IV., 2.   [4] IV., 3.   [5] II., 5.

[6] I have not succeeded in finding the passage referred to.

[7] I., 1, 47. (Chreocopia, in I., 1, 54, may be scanned with the accent on the penultimate.)

[8] I., 2, 21 and 29; III., 2, 110. Eudocia in *The Emperor of the East* is more doubtful. *Cf.* IV., 5, 83; V., 1, 122; V., 2, 105; V., 3, 170.

[9] Notice that in all these false quantities the stress is laid on the syllable which bears the Greek accent; that is to say, the words are scanned as a Byzantine Greek of the time would have pronounced them. *Cf.* in Marlowe's *Tamburlaine*, Pt. II., IV., 4: " As in the theoria of the world." A similar suggestion is anonymously made in *The Times Literary Supplement*, March 20th, 1919, for another line of Marlowe: "Our Pythagôras' Metempsýchosis."

"Academy," in *The Emperor of the East*, I., 1, 45, seems accented on the last syllable.

It seems scarcely worth while to collect the passages which show Massinger's knowledge of Latin; the authors he seems to have known best are Ovid, Juvenal, and Horace. Swinburne and others have commented on his indulgence in "the commonplace tropes and flourishes of the schoolroom or the schools."[1]

APPENDIX III

THE COLLABORATED PLAYS

THE plays in which Massinger is supposed to have collaborated with other authors are here set down, with the analyses made by Boyle (*D. N. B.*, xxxvii., pp. 10-16) and the views of Mr. A. H. Bullen in his article on Fletcher (*D. N. B.*, xix., pp. 303-311).[2]

1. *The Honest Man's Fortune.* (Field, Daborne, Massinger, Fletcher.)

   M.: Act III. or part of it.

   A. H. B. agrees.

   A. H. C.: I doubt whether Massinger had any share in this play. There are passages of ten-syllable lines in Act III., 1 which are quite unlike him, while 2 and 3 are interspersed with prose passages, a feature which Massinger as a rule avoids.

2. *Thierry and Theodoret.* (Massinger, Field, Fletcher, and possibly a fourth writer.)

   M : Act I., 2; Act II., 1, 3; Act IV., 2.

   A. H. B. attributes largely to Massinger, assigning Act III. to an unknown author.

   A. H. C. assigns to Massinger Act II., 1 and 3, and with some hesitation Act I., 2, ; Act IV., 2.

---

[1] *Cf.* p. 19, n. 2.

[2] Boyle's ascription is in each case printed first; M. signifies the portions of each play which he allots to Massinger. A. H. B. = Mr. Bullen, A. H. C. = the writer. Macaulay's views will be found in *The Cambridge History of English Literature*, vol. vi., Appendix to Chapter V.

3. *The Bloody Brother.* (Massinger, Field, Fletcher, and possibly a fourth writer.)

M.: Act I., Act V., 1.

A. H. B. thinks that Fletcher and Jonson wrote the play, and that Massinger revised it for a performance at Hampton Court in January, 1636-37.

A. H. C.: There are clearly three hands at work here, one of whom writes obscurely and uses a good deal of rhyme. Act I., 1 reminds us of Massinger in several touches, especially lines 269-70. The broken lines in this scene are complete, as is Massinger's unfailing practice, but the ten-syllable line is more common than is usually the case with him. While Act V., 1 has some sentences cast in the parenthetic form, the expressions used are less lucid than we expect from Massinger.

4. *The Knight of Malta.* (Massinger and Fletcher.)

M.: Act III., 2, 3; Act IV., 1; possibly part of Act V., 2.

A. H. B. agrees, assigning Act II. and Act III., 1 to Fletcher. "Some third person wrote Act I. and part of Act V."

A. H. C.: I trace Massinger only in Act III., 2.

5. *The Queen of Corinth.* (Massinger, Fletcher (?), Field.)

M.: Act I., Act V.

A. H. B. assigns Act II. to Fletcher, the rest to Middleton and Rowley.

A. H. C.: Massinger wrote Act I., 1, 2, 3 from "Enter Agenor," V., 2. Fletcher wrote Act I., 3; Act II., 1, 2, 3, 4; Act III., 1, 2; Act V., 3. As usual, he is responsible for the comic parts. Act V., 4 is a vigorous trial scene, not due, I think, to Massinger. The impression that I get from Act III. is that Massinger drafted it, and Fletcher worked over it.

6. *Sir John Van Olden Barnavelt.* (Massinger, Fletcher.)

M.: Act I., 1, 2; Act II., 1; Act III., 2, 3, 5; Act IV., 4, 5; Act V., 1 to "Enter Provost."

A. H. B. agrees on the whole.

A. H. C.: Act III., 5, and Act IV., 5 seem to me unworthy of Massinger. Perhaps a third hand wrote Act I., 3; Act II., 2-7; Act III., 1, as far as "will ripen the imposture"; Act III., 3; Act V., 1, as far as "Exeunt wife and daughter."

7. *Henry the Eighth.* (Massinger and Fletcher.)

A. H. B. agrees, attributing a few passages to Shakspere, notably the trial scene of Catherine.

Sir A. Ward thinks that Massinger and Fletcher wrote most of the play, Shakspere only a little (*H. E. D.*, ii., 246).

Macaulay ascribes it to Shakspere and Fletcher, "perhaps revised by Massinger."

For a fuller discussion of this problem, *cf.* pp. 84-91.

8. *The Two Noble Kinsmen.* (Massinger and Fletcher.)

M.: Act I.; Act II., 1; Act III., 1, 2; Act IV., 3; Act V., 1 from line 19, 3, 4.

A. H. B. thinks that Shakspere wrote additions for the revival of an old play, *Palamon and Arsett*, which came into the hands of Fletcher and Massinger after the death of Shakspere. Massinger has interpolated his own work in some of the Shakspere passages.

For a fuller discussion of this problem, *cf.* pp. 92-104.

9. *The Custom of the Country.* (Massinger and Fletcher.)

M.: Act II., 1, 2, 3, 4; Act III., 4, 5; Act IV., 1, 2; Act V., 1, 2, 3, 4.

A. H. B. agrees.

Macaulay adds part of Act V., 5 to Massinger.

A. H. C.: This play owes very little to Massinger. Boyle, in attributing Act II. to him, must have been guided solely by metrical considerations. There is not a trace of his style in the Act. No doubt it is true that Hippolyta is a type familiar in Massinger's plays; and her sudden change of mind in the last act reminds us of him. Again, the mental treatment to which Duarte owes his cure (Act IV., 1), and the praises of the medical profession (Act V., 4), recall *A Very Woman* (II., 2, 26).

But we have to set a good deal against these facts. The plot is more elaborate, bustling, and improbable than we expect from Massinger. It is improbable that the young men (Act II., 2) should leap into the sea and

leave Zenocia in the lurch.   It is improbable that they
should swim a league to shore with their swords erect
in the air, though swords no doubt they must have
if they are to behave as Fletcher's gentlemen behave.
It is improbable that Rutilio in his flight (Act II., 4)
should take refuge in a palace and find himself in the
bedroom of the lady of the house.   Difficulties of this
kind are familiar enough in Fletcher.   It need scarcely
be said that Sulpicia and her establishment are due to
Fletcher alone.

To sum up, if Massinger had any share in this play, he may
have given hints or added touches in connexion with
Hippolyta and Duarte.   The simplest supposition is
that he edited the play for a revival.   The Prologue
and Epilogue " at a revival " contain expressions which
remind us of him.   The Prologue ends thus (lines
18-20):

You may allow
(Your candour safe) what's taught in the old schools,
" All such as lived before you were not fools."

The parenthesis is in Massinger's manner.

Again, in the second Epilogue, line 7, we find "qualification,"
with which compare "fortification" in *A New Way*, I.,
2, 25.

10. *The Elder Brother*.   (Fletcher (?), Beaumont; probably
revised generally by Massinger.)

M.: Act I., 1, 2; Act V., 1, 2.

A. H. B. thinks that Massinger revised and completed it
after Fletcher's death, but says nothing about Beaumont.

A. H. C.: There are traces of Massinger in Act I., 1 and Act
V., 1, in which scenes we find careful metre and a good
many parentheses.   While Act I., 2 resembles Massinger, it seems to me to have a lighter touch than his.
In Act V., 1 we find a speech or two very much in
his manner, and characteristic also is the skill with
which an ambiguity is prolonged for some time in
this scene, and then dissipated.   I doubt if he wrote
Act V., 2.

11. *The Sea Voyage.* (Massinger, Fletcher.)

M.: Act II., 1, 2; Act III., 1, from "Enter Rosellia";
Act V., 1, 2, 3, 4.

A. H. B. says nothing about Massinger here. Macaulay
doubts if he had any share in the play.

A. H. C.: The metre is throughout too rough for Massinger.
The plot does not recall his work in any way.

12. *The Double Marriage.* (Massinger, Fletcher.)

M.: Act I., 1; Act III., 1; Act IV., 1, 2; Act V., 2, to "Enter
Pandulfo."

A. H. B. agrees.

Macaulay assigns all Act I. to Massinger.

A. H. C.: I find no trace of Massinger in this improbable
play.

13. *The Beggars' Bush.* (Massinger, Fletcher.)

M.: Act I., 1, 2, 3; Act V., 1, latter part; V., 2, lines 1-110.

A. H. B. does not think Massinger's part is clearly marked.

Macaulay assigns to Massinger Acts I., II., III., and V.

A. H. C.: I find no trace of Massinger. Neither the plot is
lucid nor the expression. The commercial scenes and
the beggars' slang are both unlike anything in Massinger, and alien to his courtly mind.

14. *The False One.* (Massinger, Fletcher.)

M.: Act I.; Act V.

A. H. B. agrees.

A. H. C.: Massinger wrote Act I., a good deal of Act IV.,
and Act V. There is hardly a scene except the Masque
in Act III., 4 which reads like Fletcher's unaided work.
The dignified rhetoric throughout the play has the
stamp of Massinger; more than that, the character-
drawing is like his. The outspoken Sceva reminds us
of the old courtier Eubulus in *The Picture.* The rudeness of Eros to Septimius in Act III., 2, reminds us of
Donusa in *The Renegado.* The continual changes of
mind on the part of Septimius are an effect which Massinger loves. (*Cf.* also Arsinoe and Photinus in Act
V., 4.)

15. *The Prophetess.* (Massinger and Fletcher.)

M.: Acts II., IV., V., 1, 2.

A. H. B. thinks Massinger's share " very considerable."

A. H. C.: Fletcher wrote Act I., 1, 2, and the Geta scenes (Act I., 3; Act III., 2; Act IV., 3, 5; Act V., 3). Perhaps some hack wrote the choruses (Act IV., 1; Act V., 1) or are they inherited from an old play ? The main part of the play is due to Massinger. He certainly had a hand in Act III., 1. Maximinian is a skilfully drawn character on his lines.

16. *The Little French Lawyer.* (Massinger and Fletcher.)

M.: Act I.; Act III., 1; Act V., 1, from " Enter Cleremont," with traces of his hand in other scenes.

A. H. B. agrees.

A. H. C.: Massinger can be traced at the beginning of Act I., 1 and in Act III., 1 and Act IV., 5. The resemblances are rather slight, and it is possible that they are due to the fact that Fletcher occasionally imitated Massinger.

17. *The Lover's Progress.* (Massinger and Fletcher.)

M.: Act I., 1, 2 (to " Enter Malefort "); Act II., 2; Act III., 4, 6 (last two speeches); Act IV.; Act V.

A. H. B. thinks it is " by Fletcher, with large alterations by Massinger." He refers to the explicit statement in the Prologue where the reviser declares himself to be—

ambitious that it should be known
What's good was Fletcher's, and what ill his own,

a statement in harmony with Massinger's well-known modesty.

A. H. C.: Massinger wrote Act I., 1, Act II., 2. There are traces of his work in Act III., 4, 6; Act IV., 2, 4; Act V., 1, 3. The improbabilities of the plot—*e.g.*, the action of Clarangé—are due to Fletcher. It is clear from the Prologue that the original play was too long. Massinger probably cut it down, by leaving out, among other things, scenes in which Lisander killed his two foes. The play is probably to be identified with *The*

Wandering Lovers or *The Picture*, entered as by Massinger in the Stationers' Register, September 9th, 1653.

18. *The Spanish Curate.* (Massinger and Fletcher.)
M.: Act I.; Act III., 3; Act IV., 1, 4; Act V., 1, 3.
A. H. B. agrees.
Macaulay adds Act IV., 2 to Massinger.
A. H. C.: Massinger can be clearly traced in Act I., 1, Act V., 1; not in Act V., 3. The trial scene (Act III. 3), though on slighter lines than he uses as a rule, may be due to him.

19. *The Fair Maid of the Inn.* (Massinger and Fletcher.)
M.: Act I.; Act III., 2; Act V., 3.
A. H. B. attributes to Rowley and Massinger, and thinks Fletcher's share very small.
Macaulay assigns to "Massinger and another (not Fletcher)."
A. H. C.: Massinger wrote Act I., Act V., 3 as far as Clarissa's speech. Fletcher wrote Act II., Act III., Act IV., Act V., 1, 2. The mother's device to save her son is the sort of improbability from which Fletcher does not shrink.

20. *A Very Woman.* (Massinger and Fletcher.)
M.: Act I.; Act II., 1, 2, 3 down to "Enter Pedro"; Act IV., 1, 3.
A. H. B. identifies this play with *The Woman's Plot*, acted at Court in 1621. In its present state it is a version of a play by Fletcher, revised for a revival by Massinger in 1634.
Macaulay assigns Act III. and Act IV., 1, 2, 3 to Fletcher.
For a discussion of this play *cf.* pp. 129-131.

21. *The Second Maiden's Tragedy.* (Massinger, Tourneur.)
M.: Act I., Act II.
In *Eng. Stud.*, ix. 234, Boyle, with some hesitation, regards this play as "an early, anonymous, and unsuccessful attempt of Massinger's." Whoever wrote it, the work is immature.
A. H. C. I find no trace of Massinger in this play, but a great deal of Tourneur's manner. *Cf.* Appendix XIII.

22. *Love's Cure.*   (Massinger and (?) Middleton.)
    M.: Act I.; Act IV.; Act V., 1, 2.
    A. H. B. agrees that the play is due to Massinger and Middleton.
    Fleay thinks that Massinger altered a play by Beaumont and Fletcher.
    A. H. C.: It is to be noted that the Prologue expressly attributes the play to Beaumont and Fletcher.   I find nothing like Massinger except a few touches in Act I., 1 and 3.   The lightheartedness of the play reminds us alike of Fletcher and Middleton; the romantic atmosphere reminds us of the former, the inferiority of the metre of the latter.

23. *The Fatal Dowry.*   (Massinger and Field.)
    M.: Act I.; Act III. (to " Enter Novall junior "); Act IV., 2, 3, 4; Act V., 1, 2.
    For further discussion *cf.* Appendix XI.

24. *The Virgin Martyr.*   (Massinger and Dekker.)
    M.: Act I.; Act III., 1, 2; Act IV., 3; Act V., 2.
    For a discussion of this verdict *cf.* Appendix X.

25. *The Old Law.*   (Massinger, Middleton, Rowley.)
    Massinger's share was slight, and can only have consisted in revision for a later performance.   *Cf.* supra, pp. 141-2.

OTHER PLAYS ATTRIBUTED IN PART TO MASSINGER.

26. *The Laws of Candy.*
    A. H. B. thinks a large part was written by Massinger, and that Fletcher cannot be traced.
    Boyle (*Eng. Stud.*, vii. 75) thinks that though the metrical treatment is like Beaumont's, the play is evidently later in date, perhaps due to Shirley.   Fleay (*Eng. Stud.*, ix. 23) assigns it to Massinger and Field.
    Macaulay says " probably by Massinger and another author (not Fletcher)."
    A. H. C.: I find no trace here of the Massinger that we know.

27. *The Captain.*
    Macaulay: " By Fletcher and another, perhaps Massinger."

A. H. C.: This is one of the many plays in the Fletcher corpus which begins admirably and falls away into improbability. I find no trace of Massinger here, though the incident in Act IV., 5 reminds one of the banquet in *The Guardian*, Act III., 6.

28. *The Cure for a Cuckold*, "a pleasant comedy written by John Webster and William Rowley; London, 1661."

It has been supposed by Fleay that the first act is due to Massinger. It must be pointed out that a large part of the play is written in prose, and that the verse parts are not like Massinger. If one or two phrases remind us of his style the stage is too crowded to make it likely that it is his design. The real reason, no doubt, for the assumption is that the incident of Clare and Lessingham is similar to one in *The Parliament of Love*. Clare sends a letter to Lessingham in which she tells him she will marry him if he will kill his dearest friend.

Prove all thy friends, find out the best and nearest,

Kill for my sake that friend that loves thee dearest.

But even so the incident is worked out with much variety in detail.

Mr. Rupert Brooke in his *Study on Webster* (Appendix J) arrives at the conclusion that Webster's play is subsequent to Massinger's, both of them bearing a general resemblance to Marston's *Dutch Courtesan*. The stinging and incisive vigour of Marston's play is a great contrast to the romantic treatment of the subject in *The Parliament of Love*.

29. *The Island Princess*.

This is rather a dull play, though it contains some fine passages and isolated lines. It is well constructed, and contains one or two touches, such as "I love a soldier" (I., 2) and "something shall be thought on" (II., 7), which recall Massinger. And compare "When the streams flow clear and fair, what are the fountains ?" (V., 2) with *The Bondman*, I., 3, 282. The King in gaol reminds us of *Believe as You List ;* the attempt of the Queen Quisara to convert Armusia to her faith reminds us of *The Renegado*. On the other hand, the metre is singularly like Fletcher's throughout; the diction in many details is unlike Massinger, and there are no parentheses. Perhaps Fletcher was helped in this play by some young man such as Brome who was acquainted with Massinger's style.

30. *The Double Falsehood, or The Distressed Lovers.*
This play scarcely deserves serious consideration. *Cf.* Appendix XV.

It will at once be seen how precarious and subjective is much of this attribution. For example, to trace four styles in a play is a difficult feat, yet Boyle does this in (2) and (3). Brander Matthews, in discussing the relation of Massinger and Fletcher, has some interesting remarks, illustrated by modern parallels. He points out that collaboration may be either a chemical union or a mechanical mixture of the authors' qualities, so that it is hard to decide which process has taken place in a particular play. These considerations lead him to doubt the finality of Boyle's distribution of scenes.

Boyle's strong points are his argument from metrical details and his intimate knowledge of the texts. I feel, however, that the metrical test is open to the charge of being mechanical when weighed against the impressions which we gain from the evidence of construction, style, and expressions. Massinger constructed his plays well, and modelled his characters carefully, whereas Fletcher, while excelling in isolated scenes, shrank from no improbability which might be necessary to carry the plot through. I am more conservative, therefore, than Professor Gayley, who says that "in *The Spanish Curate*, *The Little French Lawyer*, *The Prophetess*, and *The Beggars' Bush* Massinger's contribution was fully as important as Fletcher's. The general design appears to be the work of the former. Fletcher fills in the details of comic business";[1] and that

---

[1] *R. E. C.*, p. lxxxii.

"he has no doubt about Massinger's part in *The Knight of Malta*, *The Lover's Progress*, and *The Elder Brother*."[1]

Next, with regard to style and expression, when we remember the intimacy of the two men, it is quite possible that Massinger imitated Fletcher consciously or unconsciously at some time of his life, and *vice versa*. Or we may put it in this way: there was a certain amount of conventional stock-in-trade common to the two writers, such a phrase, for instance, as, "To the temple" when the inevitable marriage ceremony is to take place. It would be absurd to suppose that Fletcher never used such a phrase as "write nil ultra," which is no doubt a distinguishing mark of Massinger's style. Again, Fletcher may have worked over drafts of scenes in the first instance written by Massinger, and there is evidence for supposing that in many cases revision for a revival rather than co-operation is the clue. Massinger's good judgment would make him an excellent reviser.

It must, however, be allowed that the large amount of agreement between two experts such as Boyle and Bullen is remarkable. We cannot acquit those who produced the Folio of Beaumont and Fletcher in 1647 of negligence in omitting to give their due to Massinger and other collaborators. On the other hand, it might be argued that if Massinger's share in Fletcher's plays were as large as Boyle believes it to have been, the Folio would for very shame have acknowledged it; and it must be pointed out that the large mass of commendatory verses prefixed to the Folio entertains no doubt of the traditional authorship.[2]

Believing that the matter of first importance is to estimate Massinger from the plays which he undoubtedly wrote, I have not given above my evidence in full for the impressions which I have formed of the "collaborated" plays. The results of my study of these plays may be

---

[1] *R. E. C.*, pp. lxxxiii-lxxxiv.
[2] In particular G. Hill's poem deserves attention.

summarised as follows: Massinger wrote considerable portions of *The Prophetess, The False One,* and *Sir John Van Olden Barnavelt.* His work can be traced in *Thierry and Theodoret* and *The Bloody Brother.* He wrote the greater part of Acts I. and V. of *The Queen of Corinth,* and of Acts I. and V. of *The Elder Brother.* He wrote much of the same acts in *The Little French Lawyer, The Spanish Curate, The Fair Maid of the Inn.* He may have assisted in *The Knight of Malta.* He revised for subsequent performance *The Custom of the Country* and *The Lover's Progress.* He had nothing to do with *The Honest Man's Fortune, The Sea Voyage, The Double Marriage, The Beggars' Bush, Love's Cure, The Laws of Candy, The Captain, The Cure for a Cuckold, The Island Princess.* In my opinion, Massinger's hand can be most clearly discerned in (1) serious plays; (2) the serious parts of plays; (3) the first and last acts of a joint composition.[1]

---

[1] I have read with interest and care E. H. C. Oliphant's articles in *Englische Studien* (xiv., xv., xvi.). He finds more work of Beaumont in the plays than other scholars. Though his knowledge of the whole subject is great, his analysis seems to me too subtle; thus in *The Fair Maid of the Inn* we find, according to Mr. Oliphant, scenes written by (1) Massinger, (2) Massinger and Rowley, (3) Beaumont and Massinger, (4) Beaumont, Fletcher, and Massinger. Fletcher's part in the play is ultimately reduced to a few lines in IV., 1! I cannot agree with him that Massinger wrote any of *The Coxcomb, The Faithful Friends,* or *Love's Pilgrimage.* In *The Faithful Friends* the metre is very careless, and the occasional bursts of bombast are not like Massinger. There are touches of his style in the play, which suggest that a pupil may have helped Fletcher. *The Coxcomb* and *Love's Pilgrimage* seem to me very characteristic works of Beaumont and Fletcher. Mr. Oliphant has also discovered (*Modern Language Review,* III., pp. 337-355) that Massinger wrote a considerable portion of *The Tempest* and *Cymbeline.* It is not long since that we were reminded, in other departments of art, of Lucas and Leonardo, of Ozias Humfrey and Romney. The critical scent which Mr. Oliphant requires of his readers postulates a super-dog careering through the literary thickets of the English language. Let us rather read and enjoy our composite plays, without meticulous analysis.

APPENDIX IV

ON THE INFLUENCE OF SHAKSPERE

The instances quoted in the text can be supplemented by many others. Compare the diction and thought of the following passages:

Maid of Honour, IV., 3, 61:
> Ministers of mercy,
> Mock not calamity.

Hamlet, I., 4, 39:
> Angels and ministers of grace defend us!

Maid of Honour, V., 1, 133:
> And I to make all know I am not shallow,
> Will have my points of cochineal and yellow.

Twelfth Night, II., 5, 169:
> Remember who commended thy yellow stockings.

Virgin Martyr, I., 1, 177:
> All kind of tortures; part of which they suffer'd
> With Roman constancy.

Julius Caesar, II., 1, 226:
> Let not our looks put on our purposes,
> But bear it as our Roman actors do,
> With untired spirits and formal constancy.

(*Cf. Duke of Milan*, V., 1, 128.)

Parliament of Love, II., 2, 37:
> Yet since thou art
> So spaniel-like affected.

Midsummer-Night's Dream, II., 1, 205:
> Use me but as your spaniel, spurn me, strike me.

Two Gentlemen of Verona, IV., 2, 14:
> Yet, spaniel-like, the more she spurns my love,
> The more it grows and fawneth on her still.

Emperor of the East, IV., 5, 105:
> Methinks I find Paulinus on her lips.

Othello, III., 3, 341:
> I found not Cassio's kisses on her lips.

Emperor of the East, V., 2, 103:
> Can I call back yesterday, with all their aids
> That bow unto my sceptre ? or restore
> My mind to that tranquillity and peace
> It then enjoyed ?

Othello, III., 3, 330:
>   Not poppy, nor mandragora,
> Nor all the drowsy syrups of the world,
> Shall ever medicine thee to that sweet sleep
> Which thou owedst yesterday.

Othello, III., 3, 347:
>   O, now for ever
> Farewell the tranquil mind ! farewell content !

Virgin Martyr, I., 1, 342:
> An humble modesty, that would not match
> A molehill with Olympus.

Great Duke of Florence, IV., 2, 305:
> As the lowly shrub is to the lofty cedar,
> Or a molehill to Olympus, if compar'd,
> I am to you, Sir.

Roman Actor, III., 1, 3:
>   If you but compare
> What I have suffered with your injuries
> (Though great ones, I confess), they will appear
> Like molehills to Olympus.

(*Cf.* also *Duke of Milan,* I., 3, 193.)[1]

Coriolanus, V., 3, 29:
>   My mother bows;
> As if Olympus to a molehill should
> In supplication nod.

---

[1] *Cf. A Woman killed with Kindness,* III., 1:
> And in this ground, increased this molehill
> Unto that mountain which my father left me.

The Maid in the Mill, V., 2, Bustopha:
> Oh mountain, shalt thou call a molehill a scab upon the
> face of the earth ?

Duke of Milan, III., 1, 204:
> Thou didst not borrow of Vice her indirect,
> Crooked, and abject means.

2 Henry IV, IV., 5, 184:
> God knows, my son,
> By what by-paths and indirect crook'd ways
> I met this crown.[1]

Great Duke of Florence, II., 2, 12:
> Yes, and drink more in two hours
> Than the Dutchman or the Dane in four and twenty.

Hamlet, I., 4, 18:
> This heavy-headed revel east and west
> Makes us traduced and tax'd of other nations.
> They clepe us drunkards, and with swinish phrase
> Soil our addition.

(*Cf.* also *Othello*, II., 3, 78-87.)

Parliament of Love, IV., 5, 137:
> Now, as a schoolboy,
> Does kiss the rod that gave him chastisement.

Richard II, V., 1, 31:
> And wilt thou, pupil-like,
> Take thy correction mildly, kiss the rod ?

Two Gentlemen of Verona, I., 2, 58:
> That, like a testy babe, will scratch the nurse,
> And presently, all humbled, kiss the rod.

Unnatural Combat, IV., 2, 6:
> Let his passion work, and like a hot-reined horse
> 'Twill quickly tire itself.

Henry VIII, I., 1, 132-4:
> Anger is like
> A full-hot horse, who being allow'd his way
> Self-mettle tires him.

Emperor of the East, III., 1, 2:
> A sudden fever
> Kept me at home.

---

[1] *Cf. False One*, III., 1, 28:
> Let indirect and crooked counsels vanish.

Henry VIII, I., 1, 5:
                    An untimely ague
Stay'd me a prisoner in my chamber.

A Very Woman, II., 1, 20:
          The furnace of your father's anger.

Bondman, III., 3, 170:
                         Or yield up
Our bodies to the furnace of their fury,
Thrice heated with revenge.

Henry VIII, I., 1, 140:
     Heat not a furnace for your foe so hot
That it do singe yourself.

Virgin Martyr, V., 2, 158:
                    And now, in the evening,
When thou should'st pass with honour to thy rest,
Wilt thou fall like a meteor ?

Henry VIII, III., 2, 226:
                         I shall fall
Like a bright exhalation in the evening,
And no man see me more.

Guardian, V., 4, 115:
                    In this casket are
Inestimable jewels.

Richard III, I., 4, 27:
     Inestimable stones, unvalued jewels.

Picture, I., 2, 17:
               Since this bubble honour
(Which is indeed the nothing soldiers fight for)
With the loss of limbs or life, is in my judgment
Too dear a purchase.

As You Like It, II., 7, 152:
          Seeking the bubble reputation
Even in the cannon's mouth.

Picture, II., 2, 136:
               It continuing doubtful
Upon whose tents plum'd victory would take
Her glorious stand.

Othello, III., 3, 349:
     Farewell the plumèd troops, and the big wars,
That make ambition virtue !

Virgin Martyr, V., 2, 82:
> There is a scene that I must act alone.

Romeo and Juliet, IV., 3, 19:
> My dismal scene I needs must act alone.

Great Duke of Florence, III., 1, 57:
> What you deliver to me shall be lock'd up
> In a strong cabinet, of which you yourself
> Shall keep the key.

Hamlet, I., 3, 85.
> 'Tis in my memory locked,
> And you yourself shall keep the key of it.

Believe as You List, I., 2, 18:
> When he smiles, let such
> Beware as have to do with him, for then,
> Sans doubt, he's bent on mischief.

Hamlet, I., 5, 107:
> Meet it is I set it down,
> That one may smile, and smile, and be a villain.

Old Law, IV., 1, 36:
> Besides, there will be charges saved too; the same rosemary
> that serves for the funeral will serve for the wedding.[1]

Hamlet, I., 2, 180:
> Thrift, thrift, Horatio! the funeral baked meats
> Did coldly furnish forth the marriage tables.

Parliament of Love, III., 3, 133:
> A hurtful vow
> Is in the breach of it better commended,
> Than in the keeping.

Hamlet, I., 4, 15:
> It is a custom
> More honour'd in the breach than the observance.

---

[1] Compare also *Eastward Ho!* Act II.: GOLDING. Let me beseech you, no, sir: the superfluity and cold meat left at their nuptials will with bounty furnish ours.—Act III., 2: QUICKSILVER. Your father, and some one more, stole to church with them in all the haste, that the cold meat left at your wedding might serve to furnish their nuptial table.

Guardian, V., 1, 44:

These woods, Severino,
Shall more than seem to me a populous city.

Othello, I., 1, 77:

The fire is spied
In populous cities.

(*Cf.* also IV., 1, 64.)

We may infer that Massinger studied the Folio of 1623 carefully.

APPENDIX V

WARBURTON'S LIST

(*Lansdowne MSS.*, *B.M.*, 807.)

This volume contains three plays, the only survivors of Warburton's collection: *The Queen of Corsica*, by Fran. Jaques, *The Second Maiden's Tragedy*, and *The Bugbears*, together with a fragment of a fourth, R. Wild's *Benefice*.

On the back of the first leaf of this volume is attached the list of Warburton's collection, in his own hand. The entries referring to Massinger are as follows: I preserve the spelling.

> *Minerva's Sacrifice.* Phill. Masenger.
> *The Forc'd Lady a T.* Phill. Massinger.
> *Antonio & Vallia,* by Phill. Massinger.
> *The Woman's Plott.* Phill. Massinger.
> *The Tyrant, a tragedy,* by Phill. Massenger.
> *Philenzo and Hipolito,* a C. by Phill. Massenger.
> *The Judge,* a C. by Phill. Massenger.
> *Fast and Welcome,* by Phill. Massinger.
> *Believe as You List,* C. by Phill. Massinger.
> *The Honour of Women,* a C. by P. Massinger.
> *Alexius or the Chaste Gallant,* T. P. Massinger.
> *The Noble Choise,* T.C. P. Massinger.

The Parliament of Love is attributed to Wm. Rowley. The versification of the play which we have under that name is far above Rowley's powers, nor are there signs of collaboration in the play, as far as we can tell.

The list has been carefully discussed by Mr. W. W. Greg in his article, "The Bakings of Betsy," in *The Library* (July, 1911).

He puts the matter thus: Warburton enters *Minerva's Sacrifice* and *The Forc'd Lady* as above. In the *Stationers' Register*, Sept. 9, 1653, these titles are given as alternatives for the same play. This might mean that Moseley was trying to smuggle through two plays for a single fee. Mr. Greg is inclined to give Moseley the benefit of the doubt, and to suppose that there were plays existing in divergent versions, which would justify the double titles. If, however, Moseley was honest, Warburton cannot be correct. Mr. Greg suggests that Warburton, being interested in old plays, and having access to the *Stationers' Register*, drew up for his own use a list, mainly based on Moseley's entries, containing the titles of such pieces as he thought it might be possible to recover, and added the names of those in his possession. The cook destroyed some of the plays, and Warburton, discovering his loss, added the famous memorandum to the text without remembering that it contained the names of plays which he did not possess. In this case the damage done by " Betsy " would not be so extensive as has been believed.

APPENDIX VI

A METRICAL PECULIARITY IN MASSINGER

Our dramatic writers must have often felt that their metre required variety to relieve it from the dangers of facility and monotony. No doubt the same problem suggested itself to Homer and the Greek dramatists. In the former, the frequent pauses after the first foot or in the middle of the second foot, in the latter, the much-discussed pauses after the first foot, are as likely to be due to a desire for variety as to any special emphasis on the particular words thus singled out.[1]

In what ways did the Elizabethans secure variety ?[2]

---

[1] For this frequent effect in Homer cf. *Iliad*, I., lines 100, 103, 132, 139, 144, 160, 184, 195, etc. In the *Agamemnon* and *Alcestis*, to take no other plays, note the following: *Agamemnon* 15, 1047, 1079, 1123; *Alcestis*, 154, 181, 203, 339, 347, 619.

[2] The quadrisyllabic scansion of such a word as "remission"

1. By the use of rhyme. This was the early solution. Massinger does not often resort to rhyme, though in some of his plays, notably in *The Roman Actor*, he several times employs the well-known couplet at the end of a scene.

2. By the free use of the eleven-syllable line. This was Fletcher's solution. It is astonishing how the pleasure which the occasional use of this licence gives us turns to a feeling of satiety and weakness when it is too freely employed, so that many passages in Fletcher sound like a horse with a fit of roaring.

3. In the free use of trisyllabic feet. This fact has been recently brought before the public by Mr. Bayfield in connexion with Shakspere. There is no need to quote instances of this common and easy expedient.

4. By the occasional use of short lines. As has been pointed out above,[1] Massinger is a strict metrist, and does not often resort to this liberty, even in rapid conversation.

5. By skilful variation of pauses, such as we find in Milton, Tennyson, and most of our modern writers of blank verse. Massinger's flexible and meandering sentences contain many examples of such variation.

I believe that he had another shaft in his quiver. He occasionally suppressed a short syllable at the close of the line, and more rarely in the early part, with the result that an anapaestic lilt of some effectiveness makes its appearance. An example from *The Emperor of the East* will make this clear.

> PULCHERIA. What ís thy náme ?
> ATHENAIS. The forlórn⌒Áthenáis (I., 1, 342).

If the stresses are placed as above, it is clear that there is a syllable suppressed after the word "forlorn," a three-syllable foot in the third place, and an anapaestic lilt, " the forlorn."

Nor is Massinger alone in this device; instances from other poets are quoted below. This theory conflicts with the dic-

---

(*Parliament of Love*, II., 2, 107) has not, in my opinion, any metrical significance in Massinger. It is, indeed, very frequently found, so frequently as to be no criterion of his style. I fancy that it may be more often found in passages which he wrote against time, or when his head was tired.

[1] Page 59, n. 1.

tum of Schmidt in his Shaksperian lexicon, that words like "forlorn," "complete," "supreme," "conceal'd," can be stressed either on the first or second syllable, the stress being on the first syllable when the stress in the following word falls on the first syllable. Presumably Schmidt would have scanned the line in question thus:

> What ís thy náme ?   The fórlorn Áthenáis.

Schmidt's dictum, however, will not explain all the cases quoted below, and it is worth considering whether it is not a simpler solution of the problem to suppose that our Elizabethan poets combined uniformity of accent with variety in the metre, sometimes applied more than once in the same line. It is clear that lines which contain a past participle like "condemned" cannot be used for the purposes of this argument, as such words may have been scanned as two syllables or three.

The following cases will support my suggestion. The list does not profess to be a complete summary of the evidence.

1. *The Emperor of the East*, III., 4, 139:
> To búild me úp a compléte⌒prínce, 'tis gránted.

2. *The Duke of Milan*, III., 1, 32:
> Mónkeys and páraquíttos consúme⌒thóusands.
>
> (Here the first foot is a trochee. *Cf. infra*, Nos. 6, 8, 20, 21, 36, 43, 48.)

3. *The Bondman*, I., 1, 65:
> Of stránge and resérved párts; but a gréat⌒sóldier.

4. *The Bondman*, II., 1, 143:
> Which súllied wíth the tóuch of impúre⌒hánds.

5. *The Bondman*, III., 3, 89:
> Were thís sad spéctaclé for secúre⌒gréatness.

6. *The Bondman*, IV., 3, 192:
> Máde for your sátisfáction, the póor ⌒wrétch.

7. *The Bondman*, V., 2, 20:
> All éngines tó assáult him.   Indéed⌒vírtue.

8. *The Renegado*, I., 1, 81:
> Ín a relígious schóol, where divíne⌒máxims.

9. *The Renegado*, I., 3, 152:
> Have cálled your ánger ón, in a frówn⌒shów it.

10. *The Renegado*, II., 4, 58:
   Displéasures agaínst∧thóse, withóut whose mércy.

11. *The Renegado*, III., 2, 36:
   I é'er had íreful fiérceness, a stéel'd∧héart.

12. *The Renegado*, IV., 3, 79:
   Forsáke a sevére,∧náy, impérious místress.

13. *The Renegado*, V., 1, 7:
   That wíll for éver árm me agaínst∧féars.

14. *The Great Duke of Florence*, I., 1, 127:
   And íf my grácious úncle, the gréat∧dúke.

15. *The Great Duke of Florence*, I., 2, 29:
   To thínk her wórthy of yóu, besídes∧chíldren.

16. *The Great Duke of Florence*, II., 1, 133:
   And máke a pláin discóvery. The dúke's∧cáre.

17. *The Great Duke of Florence*, II., 3, 66:
   The swéetness óf her bréath. Such a bráve∧státure.

18. *The Great Duke of Florence*, III., 1, 66:
   On whát desígn, or whíther, the dúke's∧wíll.

19. *The Great Duke of Florence*, IV., 1, 102:
   And píety bé forgótten. The dúke's∧lúst.

20. *The Great Duke of Florence*, V., 2, 3:
   In the great státes it cóvers. The dúke's∧pléasure.

21. *The Great Duke of Florence*, V., 3,.127:
   Équal offénders, whát we shall spéak∧póints.

22. *The City Madam*, III., 3, 78:
   Relígious chárity; to'sénd∧ínfidéls.

23. *The Bashful Lover*, III., 3, 90:
   And sénsual báseness; íf thy profáne∧hánd.

24. *The Bashful Lover*, IV., 2, 60:
   'Tis impióus in mán to prescríbe∧límits.

25. *The Bashful Lover*, V., 3, 179:
   There's nó conténding agáinst∧déstiný.

26. *A Very Woman*, II., 3, 42:
   Not fár off dístant, appéars∧dím with énvy.

27. *The Unnatural Combat*, IV., 1,'35:
   Yet wáking, I' ne'er chérished obscéne∧hópes.

28. *Believe as You List*, I., 1, 144:
And secúre∧gréatness wíth the trúe relátion.

29. *Believe as You List*, I., 2, 10:
A póint of jústice, his wórds∧fúll in méasure.

30. *Believe as You List*, II., 2, 265:
Undergó the sáme∧púnishmént which óthers

31. *The Guardian*, I., 1, 285:
This profáne∧lánguage. Práy you, bé a mán.

32. *The Guardian*, I., 2, 21:
Your hónour detésts∧fláttery, Í might sáy.

33. Epilogue 2:
Tó the still dóubtful áuthor, at whát ∧ráte.

34. *The Parliament of Love*, II., 3, 26:
You nów expréss yoursélf a compléte ∧lóver.

35. *The Parliament of Love*, III., 2, 149:
To háve the gréatest bléssing, a trúe∧fríend.

36. *The Parliament of Love*, IV., 1, 95:
Cást yourself ón her cóuch. Oh, divíne∧dóctor !

37. *The Parliament of Love*, V., 1, 69:
The módern víces. Begín;∧réad the bílls.

38. *The Parliament of Love*, V., 1, 184:
The ápplicátion, ánd in a pláin∧stýle.

39. *The Parliament of Love*, V., 1, 520:
Led thríce through Páris; thén at the cóurt∧gáte.

40. *The Picture*, I., 1, 48:
Of the sóuls∧rávishing músic; the sáme∧áge.
(A highly irregular line.)

41. *The Picture*, I., 2, 73:
Are búried in hér; the lóud∧nóise of|wár.

42. *The Picture*, I., 2, 106:
Her kíngly cáptive abóve∧áll the wórld.

43. *The Picture*, I., 2, 184:
Dóted on thís Semiramís, a kíng's∧wífe.
(The third foot here is ∪ ∪ ∪ ∪.)

44. *The Picture*, I., 2, 248:
Beyónd my júst propórtion. Abóve∧wónder !

45. *The Picture,* II., 1, 35:
     Appéar, and, what's móre, appéar⌃pérfect, híss me.

46. *The Picture,* II., 1, 66:
     Their fáirest íssue to méet ⌃sénsuálly.

47. *The Picture,* II., 1, 165:
     My énd must bé to stánd in a córn⌃fíeld.

48. *The Picture,* II., 2, 286:
     Í should fix hére, where bléssings beyónd⌃hópe.

49. *The Picture,* III., 2, 40:
     They thánk'd the bríngers óf it.   The póor⌃lády.

50. *The Picture,* III., 5, 161:
     What cán you stáke agaínst it.   A quéen's⌃fáme.

51. *The Picture,* IV., 4, 64:
     If thís take nót, I am chéated.   To slíp⌃ónce.

52. *The Picture,* V., 3, 11:
     Befóre he góes to súpper.   Ha! Is my hóuse⌃túrn'd.
     (The fourth foot is ∪ ∪ ∪ –.)

53. *The Picture,* V., 3, 40:
     And néed no tútor.   Thís is the gréat⌃kíng.

It will be noted that the rhythm often occurs in a broken line—*i.e.,* a line divided between two speakers. *Cf.* Nos. 7, 20, 36, 44, 50, 51, 52, 53. (*Cf.* also *The Emperor of the East,* I., 1, 342.)

Cf. The False One, I., 1:
     What néarer plédges chállenge: resígn⌃ráther.

The False One, V., 4:
     The stóry óf a supréme⌃mónarchŷ.

The Prophetess, I., 3:
     Chéerful and gráteful tákers the góds⌃lóve.

The Prophetess, I., 3:
     Nor múst I revéal⌃fúrther, tíll you cléar it.

The Prophetess, III., 1:
     For ládies of hígh⌃márk, for divíne⌃beáuties.

The Lover's Progress, I., 1:
     To Cúpid agáinst⌃Hýmen!   Óh, mine hónour.

The Fair Maid of the Inn, I., 1:
A compléte⌢cóurtier ! máy I livé to sée him.

Thierry and Theodoret, IV., 2:
Thou dóst throw chárms upón me, agáinst⌢whích.

Thierry and Theodoret, IV., 2:
Añd the place whére, the pálace, agáinst⌢áll.

Jew of Malta, I., 2:
And extréme⌢tórtures óf the fíery déep.

Dr. Faustus, I., 1:
And Í that háve with concíse⌢sýllogísms.

Nero, I., 4:
O sevére⌢ánger óf the highest góds.

Rule a Wife, I., 1:
For thére I dáre be bóld to appéar⌢óften.

The Maid in the Mill, I., 3:
Now by' the sóul of lóve, a divíne⌢créature.

Henry VIII, II., 1, 11:
I'll téll you ín a líttle.   The gréat⌢dúke.

I believe that many of the rhythms from Shakespeare quoted by Schmidt and by Mr. R. Bridges in his "Milton's Prosody," can be explained in this way.

APPENDIX VII

" BELIEVE AS YOU LIST "

This play was edited by Mr. T. Crofton Croker, with a short Preface, in the Percy Society's Publications, Vol. XXVII., 1849. The Tudor Society has published a photographic facsimile of the MS., now in the British Museum (Egerton MSS., 2828). *Cf.* B.M. Catalogue of Additions, 1907, p. 384. The MS. was purchased for the Museum at a sale on November 27, 1900, for £69. It is of paper. The original document, measuring 12½ inches by 7½ inches, comprises folios 5 to 29; folios 2 and 3 are the old vellum cover.

Mr. Croker's account of the MS. (Pref., p. ix) runs as follows:
"The MS., from its commencement to the termination of the licence, was written on forty-eight pages of foolscap paper, in a small hand, sometimes not easy to be read. Of the second leaf only an inconsiderable portion remains, and the top and bottom of the paper have been injured in some places by damp. In four additional pages after the licence, the Pro logue, Epilogue, and property directions are preserved. The MS. is stitched up in a parchment cover, which appears to have been a cancelled "Indenture" of Elizabeth's reign. On the outside page of this parchment, or back of the cancelled indenture, is written the title, in what I agree with Mr. Beltz in regarding as Massinger's autograph."[1]

From the letter of Mr. S. Beltz, given by Mr. Crofton Croker, we learn that Gifford had more than once lamented to Mr. Croker the disappearance of this MS., which Colley Cibber had seen;[2] and that the MS. had formerly been in David Garrick's hands. Mr. S. Beltz also says: "It is well known from other sources that the play was acted on May 7, 1631."

The MS. had belonged to George Beltz, Lancaster Herald, and executor of Garrick's widow. His brother Samuel found it among "a mass of rubbish." It was in the possession of J. O. Halliwell Phillips at one time. This well-known Shaksperian scholar inserted a note about it on p. 1, in which he says, inter alia : "This is one of the few play-house copies of any English plays before the suppression of theatres known to exist. I strongly suspect it has some corrections in Massinger's own autograph."

---

[1] The autograph and Herbert's Imprimatur are reproduced in facsimile in the Percy Society volume. But would Massinger have referred to himself as *Mr.* Massenger [*sic*] ?

[2] *Apology*, ii. 203. C. Cibber, in a list of dramatic authors, makes reference to Massinger's plays. He says: "Mr. Massinger, I believe, was author of several other dramatic pieces: one I have seen in MS., which I am assured was acted, by the proper quotations, etc. The title runs thus: ' Believe as you list, written by Mr. Massinger, with the following licence: "This play, called ' Believe as you list,' may be acted this 6th of May, 1631. Henry Herbert." ' " Malone (*Shakspere*, vol. iii., p. 230) gives the date (*i.e.*, of the actual performance) as May 7th, 1631.

His Grecian Expedition, what the
with his own hands presents you as a labour
was their man by to witness it?

Marcellus: eight miles round
to recollect my self. yes — five leagues off.
the your miles round.

Antiochus: 43 leagues, and you
bound under to part from it. is it still
in your possession.

Marcellus: the Roman power & ...
and visible & civil will Europe.

Antiochus: will you not say
it brings under and twenty five years ...
new master of his grist; & now I know it
amongst a profane offspring; that & some
as a ... of ...

Marcellus: I shall receive it.
is not common height. ...

II. BELIEVE AS YOU LIST, ACT V, SCENE 2, LL. 85-116*b* See page 117

Sir George F. Warner, in the *Athenæum* (January 19, 1901) discusses the MS. He believes it is in Massinger's own hand, as the alterations are made *currente calamo*. This fact can easily be verified from a perusal of the MS. Sir G. Warner, after comparing the MS. with the Henslowe document at Dulwich, arrived at the conviction that the writing was Massinger's. He considers that the title and marginal stage-directions are due to the manager, and that the Prologue and Epilogue are in a third hand. He points out that "Carthage" is written over "Venice" (Crofton Croker, p. 41), "Affricque" over "Europe" (p. 44), and "Berecinthius" over "Sampayo" (p. 79).[1] He proceeds to explain the reason for these alterations, and then emends some of Mr. Croker's mistakes.

With all due deference to the great authority of Sir G. Warner, I do not feel certain that this hand is that of the appeal to Henslow. On the other hand, we must remember that seventeen years had elapsed, and that it is unlikely that a poor man like Massinger would have employed an amanuensis. Capital "I," "s," "f," and "e" are alike in the two documents; but "ve" in "have ever" did not seem to me to be the same, nor did any of the "r's" at Dulwich resemble the hand in the play.[2]

---

[1] The references are as follows: II., 2, 368; III., 1, 20; IV., 3, initial stage direction.

[2] Beside the Henslow document there are to be seen at Dulwich College four signatures of Massinger, in a beautiful clear hand; three of these are attached to leases of Alleyn's, and the fourth is added to Daborne's signature to the document mentioned by Cunningham in his Preface (p. xii.). The poem "*Sero sed serio*" is to be found in B.M. Royal MSS. XVIII., A. 20. The signature is identical with the Dulwich signatures. The poem itself is in another hand, with many flourishes.

The only reason for supposing it to be the poet's, besides his poverty, is an erasure in line 14, which runs thus:

then
"Being∧silent then,"

which looks like a correction made by the author himself, *currente calamo*. The hand of *The Second Maiden's Tragedy* does not resemble that of *Believe as You List*. The hand of *Sir John Van Olden Barnavelt* is uniform throughout. It is neat and full of flourishes, especially in the letter L. It is,

There are few mistakes in the MS. beyond those which the
writer has corrected himself. The corrections and additions
all appear to be in the same hand. The simplest explanation
of the MS. is to suppose that Massinger had before him the
MS. of the play which had been condemned by the Censor,
and that he copied it out again, making the necessary changes
of name, etc. This would account for one or two mistakes
which the writer has corrected.[1] In other passages we can
see his judgment at work, altering the phraseology,[2] or ex-
panding one line into two.[3] Sometimes a word is repeated
from a previous line and then cancelled,[4] as if the writer had
been tired, as he might well be. The writing combines German
and Italian forms.

The play was remodelled from its original form by order of
the Censor.[5] Sir G. Warner has pointed out that it is derived
from " the strangest adventure that ever happened, either
in the ages passed or present: containing a discourse concerning
the successe of the King of Portugal, Dom Sebastian. London:
printed for Frances Henson, dwelling in the Blackfriers, 1601."[6]

---

of course, possible that Massinger wrote this in 1619. The
stage directions are in a bolder hand and deep black ink.
They are plainly part of the MS., and not later insertions like
those in *Believe as You List*. I incline to think the writing
is all due to an amanuensis. There is very little correction
in the play, except that several long passages are very thor-
oughly scrawled out.

    [1] *Cf.* Appendix VIII.: I., 1, 26; I., 2, 186; II., 1, 51; II., 2,
217; II., 2, 368; III., 1, 20; IV., 3, stage direction.

    [2] *Cf.* Appendix VIII.: I., 1, 60; I., 2, 67; I., 2, 72; II., 2,
52; II., 2, 56; III., 3, 151; III., 3, 234; IV., 1, 7.

    [3] *Cf.* Appendix VIII.: II., 2, 285; IV., 1, 5; IV., 3, 44.

    [4] *Cf.* Appendix VIII.: II., 2, 98; II., 2, 240; III., 3, 166;
IV., 4, 45.

    [5] *Cf.* p. 15, n. 1.

    [6] Koeppel (*Quellen-Studien*) traces the story to P. V. P.
Cayet's *Chronologie Septenaire*, Paris, 1605. He does not
seem to have consulted *The Strangest Adventure*, a copy of
which may be seen in the British Museum. *The True History
of the Late and Lamentable Adventures of D. S.* (London, 1602)
begins with the imprisonment at Naples, and agrees with
Cayet almost verbally until the latter part. *The Continua-
tion of the Lamentable Adventures* (London, 1603) is very dull,

This book is the story of a claimant to the throne of Portugal. On p. 78 we have " the markes and signes which the King of Portugall Dom Sebastian beares naturally on his body." Twenty-two in all are given. Among them are:

(1) He hath the right hand greater than the left.
(2) The right arme longer than the left.
(5) The right legge is longer than the left.
(6) The right foote greater than the other.

Compare these statements with the words erased in the MS., folio 8.[1]

1 MARCHANT:
> His verie hand legge and foote, and the lefte side
> Shorter than on the right.

(12) He hath little pimples on his face and hands.

Cf. 2 MARCHANT:
> The moles upon
> His face and hands[2]

(21) Another marke or wound upon the head.
(22) Another upon the right eye-brow.

Cf. 3 MARCHANT:
> The scarres, caused by his hurts,
> On his right browe and head.[3]

(14) He lackes one tooth on the right side in the neather jaw.

Cf. BERECINTHIUS:
> The hollownesse
> Of his under jawe, occasion'd by the losse
> Of a tooth pull'd out by his chirurgion.[4]

---

and contributes nothing except the advice of an old man to Sebastian, which may have suggested the first scene of the play. The two tracts are to be found in Harleian Miscellany (iv., 403; v., 443). *Cf*. also Scott-Saintsbury's *Dryden*, vii., p. 309, *n*. The English pamphlets are based on the *Aventure Amirable*, published in 1601. (*Cf*. Bullen's *Peele*, i., 227.) Massinger must have used Cayet for the incidents in the latter part of the play.

[1] After Berecinthius says " His stature ! speech ! " in I., 2, 186.

[2] I., 2, 187.   [3] I., 2, 188.   [4] I., 2, 189.

(18)   The lip of Austriche,[1] like his
Grandfather Charles the Fift, Emperor,
Father to his mother, and of his
Grandmother, Catherine, Queen of
Portugall, mother to his father, sister
To the said Charles the Fift.

Compare the original reading in the play,[2] " His nose ! his
German lippe !" Over German "very" has been written, and
underneath is traceable the " A " of Austrian.

These passages leave no doubt as to the derivation of the
earlier part of the story which Massinger dramatised.

On p. 45 of *The Strangest Adventure* we read that Dom
Sebastian comes to Venice " very poorly, and robbed by five
of his own servants, which he entertained in Cicilie." This
incident occurs in *Believe as You List*, Act I. At Venice he
was persecuted by the " embassadour of Castile," whose name
is not given, but whose place in the play is taken by Flaminius.
On p. 49 he is said to have been beaten by the Moors in Africa
in 1578, and to be now (1600) a prisoner at Venice. In *Believe
as You List* the period of twenty-two years is referred to as
the interval during which Antiochus has been travelling about
the world.[3] On p. 50 Dom Sebastian arrives at Venice with
" but one poor gazete." In the play Antiochus, after being
robbed by his servants, finds " a waste paper " lying near him,
and speaks as follows:

There is something writ more.
Why this small piece of silver ?   What I read may
Reveal the mystery: " Forget thou wert ever
Called King Antiochus.   With this charity
I enter thee a beggar."[4]

On p. 67 Sebastian is set free, and on p. 86 he goes to
Florence, on his way to Marseilles, with some talk of trying
to establish his identity in Holland. But the narrative closes
abruptly, and we know no more of the claimant to the Portu-
guese throne from *The Strangest Adventure*.

The ineffectiveness of the play may be partly due to the
necessity of altering the original modern setting to an ancient

---

[1] The " Austrian lip " is one of the features Mistress Carol
ascribes to Fairfield in Shirley's *Hyde Park* (III., 2).
[2] I., 2, 186.   [3] I., 1, 64.   [4] I., 1, 135.

one. It is hard, for example, to see how the monk Sampayo was metamorphosed into Berecinthius, the fat priest of Cybele.

Mr. Croker's reprint was the cause of a very pretty literary quarrel between the Shakespeare Society and the Percy Society. A writer who signed himself "A Member of both Societies" published a pamphlet animadverting on Mr. Croker's abilities as an editor,[1] and Mr. Croker replied in no measured terms. The documents may be seen at the British Museum.

The anonymous writer, working on the many indications given in the marginal notes, reconstructed the cast of *Believe as You List*.[2] "My cast," he says, "has been a work of difficulty, and, in the case of some of the minor performers, a matter of considerable doubt, more especially as a few of them doubled or even trebled their parts; and as we here see (the only instance of the kind I am acquainted with), perhaps exchanged characters during the progress of the play.

Antiochus	J. Taylor.[3]
Flaminius	J. Lowin.[3]
Lentulus	R. Robinson.
Marcellus	R. Benfield.
Berecinthius	T. Pollard.
Chrysalus	E. Swanston.
Demetrius	W. Patrick.
Amilcar	— Rowland.
1 Merchant..	J. Honeyman.
2 ,, ...	W. Penn.
3 ,, ...	— Curt.
Calistus	T. Hobbes.
Titus	R. Baxter.
Queen to Prusias	— Ball.
Cornelia	— Nick.
Courtesan	— Boy.

"With regard to the three female parts, and another of a Moorish woman,[4] we are left much in the dark, and I have placed names against them with considerable hesitation.

---

[1] *Shakespeare Society's Papers*, vol. iv., art. xiv.

[2] *Shakespeare Society's Papers*, p. 138.

[3] Famous names. "Taylor acted Hamlet incomparably well." Colley Cibber's *Apology*, 2, 142,

[4] V 2, 139

"The actors who doubled their parts were W. Penn, who was also a Jailor; Rowland, who was also King Prusias; Patrick, who was also a Captain; and Baxter, who was also an officer and a servant, besides, as well as we can judge, delivering a speech or two as Demetrius. Rowland must also have trebled his small parts. Besides these, we hear in the course of the play of W. Mago, Gascoine, Herbert, and Harry Wilson; the last was a singer. . . . It need hardly be added that the 'tragedy' was got up and acted by the Company called the King's Players, all the names being those of performers in that association in 1631."

APPENDIX VIII

COLLATION OF MS. OF "BELIEVE AS YOU LIST"

This play is accessible to the general public at present in Colonel Cunningham's edition of Massinger, and in Mr. Arthur Symons's edition in "The Mermaid Series." An examination of the original MS., now in the British Museum, shows that Cunningham's text is not always correct. Though an exhaustive collation of the MS. is not necessary, several points of interest emerge from a study of the original document, which I have digested here. (C.=Cunningham's edition; MS.= Manuscript reading. Brackets signify Cunningham's conjectural additions, which he has not always taken the trouble to indicate.)

Page 595. There is no list of dramatis personae in MS.

I., 1.—C.: Enter Antiochus and a Stoic. The three servants enter after line 118.

> MS.: Antiochus Stoic in philosopher's habits; Chrysalus with a writing, Syrus, Geta, bondmen.

I, 1, 26.—C.: Stoic.
> MS.: Stoic: Hermit (cancelled).

I., 1, 56.—C.:

Old (He) sper with his fierce beams (scorch)ing in vain
Their (wives, their sisters and their tender daughters).

> MS.: The line is much damaged, being the last on the page. A mention of the old after the young (lines 52 to 55) seems to be required.
>
> I read it thus: Olde men with sil . . . in vain. There is no trace of 57, but it is required by the sense.

I., 1, 60.—MS.: The soldiers' greedy lusts. "Greedy" deleted.

I., 1, 85.—C.: A prey so precious and so dearly purchased.

> MS.: A prey so precious and dearly purchased. "Precious" is scanned as a trisyllable.

I., 1, 117.—C.:

> The imperious waves
> (Of my) calamities have already fallen.
>
> MS.: "Of my" is not in MS. The last word of 118 is "Swollen." The word "Marvell" can be seen at the end of a line after 118.
>
> Here comes a hiatus of two pages. No doubt Antiochus had a fairly long soliloquy. It is impossible to tell how many lines are lost here, as the characters seem to be conducting a rapid dialogue, in which it is not necessary to suppose that a whole line was assigned to each speaker at a time.

I., 1, 119.—C.:

> Despair with sable wings
> (Sail-stretch'd ab)ove my head.
>
> MS.: Ore my head. A verb is wanted. (?) Sail-stretch'd flies o'er my head.

I., 1, 121.—MS.: . . . ius furnished me. The line begins with a name to which there is no clue, probably introduced in the part now lost.

I., 1, 122.—C.: (And) make my first appearance like myself.
> MS.: Made   ? Which made, etc.

I., 1, 123.—C.: (Have these) disloyal villains ravished from me. Addition required by sense.

I., 1, 124.—C.: (Wret)ch that I was.
> MS.: "ch" at end of a word which has disappeared. "Wretch" gives the sense.

I., 1, 125.—C.: (With) such a purchase.

    MS.: Such a purchase. The first word in the line has disappeared.

I., 1, 126.—C.: Without (the) gold to fee an advocate.

    MS.: Without gold to fee an advocate. The first word in the line has disappeared. (?) And.

I., 1, 127.—C.: (To) plead my royal title, nourish hope.

    MS.: Plead my royal title, nourish hope. The first word in the line has disappeared. "To" is required.

I., 1, 129.—C.: Wanting the outer gloss.

    MS.: Wanting the outward gloss.

I., 1, 153.—C.:

    Bids me become a beggar. But complaints are weak
    And womanish. I will like a palm-tree grow
    Under my (own) huge weight.

    MS.: Bids me become a beggar. But complaints
    Are weak and womanish. I will, like a palm-tree,
    Grow under my huge weight.

I., 1, 155.—C.:

    Nor shall the fear
    Of death or torture that dejection bring
    Make me (or) live or die less than a king!

    MS. has: To make me live or die less than a king!—*i.e.*, "that" in 156 is the demonstrative, not the relative.

I., 2, 2.—C.: Keeps us at such (a) distance.

    MS.: Keeps us off at such distance.

I., 2, 20.—C.: Sans doubt, he's bent on mischief.

    MS.: Sans doubt he's bent to mischief.

I., 2, 24.—C.:

    He shall find I can
    Think, and aloud too.

    MS.: Chant, and aloud too.

I., 2, 53.—C.: 'T had perfected thy life.

    MS.: It had.

I., 2, 66.—C.: (to task). Not in MS. Traces of a word in the beginning of a line now lost at the foot of 66.

I., 2, 67.—C.:

   If arrogantly you presume to take
The Roman government, your goddess cannot
Give privilege to it, and you'll find and feel
'Tis little less than treason, Flamen.

  MS.: If arrogantly you presume to tax
  The Roman government, you'll find and feel your
   goddess cannot
  Give privilege to it, and you'll find and feel
  'Tis little less than treason, Flamen.

   " You'll find and feel" cancelled in line 68—*i.e.*,
  the author changed his mind as he wrote.

I., 2, 72.—C.: These Asiatic merchants whom you look on.

  MS.: These Asiatic merchants whom you look upon.

   "Merchants" added afterwards above the line,
  and the first syllable of "upon" deleted.

I., 2, 90.—C.: To it again.

  MS.: To it again now.

I., 2, 139.—C.: Yet you repine and rather choose to pay.

  MS.: Yet you repined and rather chose to pay.

I., 2, 151.—C.: And this is my last caution.

  MS.: Since this is my last caution.

I., 2, 161.—C.: (On) which.

  MS.: Mutilated at beginning. " On " makes sense.

I., 2, 186.—C.: His nose, his very lip.

  MS.: His nose, his German lip. " German " scratched
   out, and underneath appears a word beginning
   with " A," Asian or Austrian ?[1] " Very " is
   written above " German."

I., 2, 187.—C.:

  His very hand, leg and foot !
          The moles upon
  His face and hands.

  MS.: His own (?) hand, leg and foot, and the left side
   Shorter than on the right.
          The moles upon
  His face and hands.

  "His own" down to "the right" is cancelled in MS.

---

[1] See p. 180, n. 1, and *cf. The Alchemist*, IV., 1.

I., 2, 191.—C.: 1 M. To confirm us, tell us your chirurgeon's
name
When he served you.
A.   You all knew him as I
Do you, Demetrius Castor.
2 M.   Strange.
3 M.   But
Most infallibly true.
MS.:   1 M.   To confirm us,
Tell us his name when he served you.
A.   You all know him,
As I do you : Demetrius Castor.
2 M.   Strange.
3 M. But most infallibly true.
In line 192 " his " has been altered to " the
chirurgeon's " to the detriment of the métre.

I., 2, 196.—C.: We'll pay for our distrust.
MS.: We sin in our distrust.

II., *ad initium*.—Stage-manager's note in left-hand margin,
" Long."

II., 1, 6.—C.: I will exact
MS.: 'Twill exact.

II., 1, 47.—MS.:
We hold it fit you should have the first honour
notice,
That you may have the honour to prevent iᵗ.
" Honour " in 47 deleted.

II., 1, 51.—MS.: In the shape of King Antiochus.
Under King can be seen " Don Sebastian."

II., 2, 45.—C.: With due invitation, and remember.
MS.: With a due invitation and remember.

II., 2, 49.—C.:
And though the Punic faith is branded by
Our enemies, our confederates and friends
And seventeen kings, our feodaries found it
As firm as fate.
MS.: And though the Punic faith is branded by
Our enemies, our confederates and friends
Found it as firm as fate, and seventeen kings
Our feodaries.

II., 2, 52.—MS.:
Our strength at sea superior upon the sea
Exceeding theirs.
  " At sea superior " deleted.   A clear case of the
  author's alteration as he went.

II., 2, 56.—C.:
And then for our cavallery, in the champaign
How often have they brake their piles.
  MS.: And then for our cavallery, how often, in the
  champaign
  How they brake often have they brake their piles.
      " How often" in line 56. and the first " they
      brake " deleted.   Author's alterations again.

II., 2, 59.—C.: If so we find it.
MS. If so, as we find it.

II., 2, 67.—MS.: By yielding up a man.
      Written over something of which the first words
      are " in a," the last word " king."

II., 2, 98.—MS.: By the conquered Asiatics this impost in
      their hopes.
      "This impost" deleted.   "This impostor" oc-
      curs just above in line 97.

II., 2, 108.—C.: By her.
MS.: By his.

II., 2, 138.—C.: He bears him like a king.
MS.: He bears himself like a king.

II., 2, 142.—MS.: Ceutha deleted before Afric.

II., 2, 165.—C.: Cannot near you.
MS.: Cannot hear you.

II., 2, 205.—C.: Filled.
MS.: Filed.

II., 2, 209.—MS.: And hath keeps a whore in Corinth.
      " Hath " deleted.

II., 2, 217.—MS.: In the royal monument of Hib the Asian
      kings.
      (?) The author started to write " Hiberian kings."

II., 2, 240.—MS.: Rebellion delivery or restoring.
     "Rebellion" deleted; it occurred in the previous line.

II., 2, 253.—C.:
     With reverence to
     This place, thou liest.
    MS.: Setting aside, with reverence to
     Thy place, the state, thou liest.
      "Setting aside" and "thy place" deleted.

II., 2, 255.—C.: By being . . .
    MS.: By being libb'd, and my disability
     To deflower thy sisters.

II., 2, 256.—C.: I (bow to) your goddess.
    MS.: Thank your goddess.
      "Thy" deleted under "your."

II., 2, 285.—MS.:
     Of brave and able men that might have stood
     In opposition for the defence.
      "That might" down to "opposition" inserted in same hand above the line.

II., 2, 289.—C.: For my confed'rates.
    MS.: For my confederates.
      Required by metre.

II., 2, 328.—MS.: Word deleted before Antiochus. Sebastian would scan.

II., 2, 335.—MS.: With your accustomed clemency wisdom you'll perceive.
     "Clemency" deleted.

II., 2, 346.—MS.: Such depositions as they pleased knew would make.
     "Pleased" deleted.

II., 2, 368.—MS.: Word deleted under "Carthage." (?) Venice.

III., 1, 20.—MS.: "Europe" deleted under "Afric."

III., 1, 22.—MS.: "To the good king Hiero" deleted under "To the pro-consul Marcellus."

III., 1, 47.—C.: You'll find there that they .
    MS.: You shall find there that .
      (A nominative is wanted; unless for "there" we read "them"

III., 1, 62.—C.: To my (aid).
MS.: To my wish.

III., 1, 91.—MS.: There's thy reward.
Underneath "there's," "take" deleted.

III., 1, 103.—C.:
Your travail's ended, mine begins; I take my leave.
Formality of manner now is useless.
MS.: Your travail's ended, mine begins, and therefore
Sans ceremonie I will take my leave.
"Sans ceremonie" deleted, and "formality
... useless" added at the end of the line. The
author omitted to cancel "I take my leave."

III., 2, 31.—C.: Thou thin gut!
MS.: You thin gut!

III., 2, 35.—MS.: Cancels from "Jove! if thou art" to 38,
"They come."

III., 2, 36.—C.: Change not Jove's purpose.
MS.: Change not you Jove's purpose.

III., 2, 106.—MS.:
I will conjure him
If revenge hath any spells.
Cancelled in MS.

III., 3, 132.—C.: Will but—I spare comparisons.
(?) Punctuate: Will—but I spare comparisons.

III., 3, 150.—MS.: Of such such as are.
Second "such" deleted.

III., 3, 151.—MS.: Bithynia covered with our knights armies.
"Knights" deleted.

III., 3, 166.—MS.: And more than my his caution to you; but
now peace or war.
"And more than my" deleted. The previous
line had begun with these words. Was the author
copying a former draft of the scene?

III., 3, 229.—C.: To cross your purpose.
MS.: To cross your purposes.

III., 3, 234.—MS.: The warrant and authority of a wife your
queen.
"A wife" deleted.

III., 3, 244.—C.: These (eyes) pull'd out.
    MS.: These pulled out.
        "Eyes" is required by the sense, and "these"
        and "eyes" are much alike in this hand.

Ibid.—C.: Do then.
    MS.: Do you then.

III., 3, 248.—C.: Born deaf.
    MS.: Born dumb.

Act IV.—Stage-manager's note in left-hand margin of 186,
        "Long." *Cf.* Act II.

IV., 1.—C.: A street in Callipolis.
        Not in MS.
    MS.: Sempronius a Capturion—*i.e.*, "captain" altered to
        "centurion."

IV., 1, 2.—MS.: I heard such.
        "Such" deleted. It begins the next line.

IV., 1, 5.—MS.: He promised me a visit, if his designs as I
        desire they may.
        "He" deleted and "who by his letters"
        written above it.
        For similar expansion of one line into two,
        cf. II., 2, 285.

IV., 1, 7.—MS.: Till he arrive you behold him.
        "He arrive" deleted.

IV., 1, 23.—MS.: "My" deleted before "yourself."

IV., 1, 29.—C.: Lips.
    MS.: Lip.

IV., 1, 34.—C.: Tacks on "he" to this line.
    MS.: "He" begins line 35.

IV., 1, 45.—Enter Flaminius.
        (?) "Ferdinand" deleted below.

IV., 1, 90.—C.: And may prove fortunate.
    MS.: And it may prove fortunate.

IV., 2, 5.—C.: (Why), the sufferings of this miserable man.
    MS.: No trace of "why."

IV., 2, 11.—C.: Tacks on "to" at the end.
    MS.: It begins line 12.

IV., 2, 29.—C.: And know that not the reverence that waits.

MS.: And though I know the reverence that waits.

IV., 2, 33.—C.: Or iron.

MS.: Or fire.

IV., 2, 58.—C.: They aim at.

MS.: They aimed at.

IV., 2, 60.—C.: A few more hours.

MS.: A few hours more.

IV., 2, 66.—MS.: For the pretty tempting friend I brought; my life on't.

Under " tempting," " beauty " (?) deleted.

IV., 2, 87.—MS.: Crack not with the weight of deer, and far-fetched dainties.

"Not" spoils the metre and the sense; it occurs in line 88. " Dispute not with heaven's bounties."

IV., 2, 90.—C.: Homely cakes.

MS.: Homely cates.

IV., 2, 96.—MS.: I have already

Acquainted her with her cue. The music ushers

Her personal appearance.

Scratched out at top of 20*b*, and inserted at foot of 20*a*.

IV., 2, 127.—C.: Pray, what are you ?

MS.: Pray you, what are you ?

IV., 2, 147.—C.: That, (sir), is.

MS.: " Sir " not visible owing to mutilation. (?) Sir, that is.

IV., 2, 158.—MS.: And met your wishes.

"And met " deleted before " and met."

IV., 2, 226.—MS.: To pluck your eyes out.

Last half of line deleted. Last word (?) "thoughtes."

IV., 2, 228.—MS.: Add a deleted line:

Dieted with gourd water.[1] Oh ! the furies !

C.: leaves out.

---

[1] *Cf. The Sea Voyage*, III. 1.

IV., 3, 1.—MS.: Officers leading in Berecinthius.
" Sampayo " deleted under " Berecinthius."
C.: Place of execution at Callipolis.
MS.: Does not mention Callipolis.

IV., 3, 28.—MS.: My bark you see wants stowage.
" Balance " deleted before " stowage."

IV., 3, 29.—C.: But give me half a dozen hens.
MS.: But give me half a dozen of hens.

IV., 3, 39.—MS.: " Helped me " *bis.* The first one deleted.

IV., 3, 44.—MS.: To make three sops for his three heads; may
serve for a breakfast.
" that " inserted after " heads," and " something more than an ordinary " after " serve for."
One line converted into two, as above, IV., 1, 5.

IV., 3, 46.—MS.: The cur is vengeance devilish hungry.
" Vengeance " deleted.

IV., 3, 48.—C.: Provided for my frame.
MS.: Provided for my fame.

IV., 3, 53.—MS.: That no covetous Roman, after I am dead.
" Needie " deleted under " covetous."

IV., 4, 13.—C.: His faults are inscribed.
MS.: His fault's inscribed.

IV., 4, 22.—C.: But in one thing most remarkable.
MS.: But one thing most remarkable.

IV., 4, 45.—MS.: Of kings deposed, and some in triumph led.
" Read " deleted before " led." It is the last
word of line 44.

IV., 4, 48.—C.: Is of worse condition, and Rome.
MS.: Is of a worse condition, and Rome.

V., 1, 28.—MS.: " rows " deleted before " is chained."

V., 1, 98.—C.: In the world.
MS.: Of the world.

V., 1, 102.—C.: Since I am term'd a soldier.
MS.: Since I am turn'd soldier.

V., 1, 116.—C.: Grant you like (opportunity, but why).
MS.: Grant you like;
C.'s addition required by the sense.

V., 1, 137.—C.: In which, my lord being a suitor with (me).
MS.: In which, my lord being a suitor with. Addition required.

V., 1, 143.—C.: And though it needs not, for further proof.
MS.: And though it needs it not, for further proof.

V., 1, 157.—C.: They find.
MS.: May find.
"May" required by the sense.

V., 1, 172.—MS.: Swim down the torrent stream but to oppose the torrent.
"Torrent" before "stream" deleted.

V., 2, 14.—C.: I will make this good.
MS.: I will mock this good.

V., 2, 30.—C.: That noble Roman. By h(im you are sent for).
MS.: That noble Roman. By h . . . Addition required.

V., 2, 33.—C.: Though I grand him.
MS.: Though I grac'd him.

V., 2, 46.—C.: ANTONIUS. Forbear.
MS.: MARCELLUS. Forbear.

V., 2, 59.—MS.: "Marcell" deleted before "King Antiochus."

V., 2, 124.—C.: (The armlet).
Koeppel points out that in Cayet it is a ring.[1]

V., 2, 125.—C.: Which you wear on your sl(eeve).
MS.: Which you wear on your——slight traces of "sl."

V., 2, 125.—C.: I ack(nowledge).
MS.: I ack . . .

V., 2, 155.—C.:
My power to justify the ill, and pressed
You with mountainous promises of love and service.
MS.: My power to justify the ill, and pressed you
With mountainous promises of love and service.

V., 2, 166-7.—MS.: As far as "faithfully" in one line, but all written at the same time.

V., 2, 173.—C.: The violence of your passion.
MS.: . . . . 1 . . ce of your passion.

---

[1] *Cf.* 178, n. 6.

V., 2, 174.—C.: Cornelia. (Do) but (expre)ss.

    MS.: Cornelia has a line which has disappeared; towards the end are traces of " but " and " ss."

V., 2, 175.—C.: Your thankfulness for his so m(any favours).

    MS.: Your thankfulness for his so m . . .

V., 2, 176.—C.: And labour that the senate may restore h(im).

    MS.: And labour that the senate may restore h . . . Addition required.

V., 2, 212.—C.: Yield an account without appeal for wha(t).

    MS.: Yield an account without appeal for wha . . .

V., 2, 213.—C.: You have already done. You may p(eru)se. (Does it.)

    MS.: You have already done. You may p . . . se. No need for " Does it."

V., 2, 214.—C.: Do you f(i)nd I ha(ve).

    MS.: Do you f . . nd e I ha . . . Addition required.

V , 2, 215.—C.: (The warran)t. (C)all in the Asian merchants.

    MS : . . . all in the Asian marchants. (?) " The document " would scan better.

V., 2, 216.—C.: 2 Merchant. Now to be hanged.

    MS. has space above 216 for half a line to be said by someone else.

V., 2, 217.—C.: 3 Merchant. Him that pities thee.

    MS. gives no clue to the speaker.

Ibid.—C.: Flaminius. Accusers.

    MS. . . . sers. It is the last word of line 217 ?

V., 2, 218.—C.: . . . die, and will prove that you took bribes.

I suggest as restoration of lines 215–218:

              Call in the Asian merchants;
Let's hear them speak.

1 Merchant:
         'Tis thy turn now to be hanged.
And shame to him that pities thee.

Marc: Th' accusers
    Are ready, and will prove, etc.

V., 2, 232.—C.: ('Tis) a Roman.
　　MS.: A Roman.
　　　(C.'s addition required by the sense.)
PROLOGUE—1.—C.: (So far our) author.
　　MS.: . . . author.

APPENDIX IX

"THE PARLIAMENT OF LOVE"

The MS. (No. 39 in the Dyce Collection, Victoria and Albert
Museum) comprises nineteen leaves of the same size as those
of *Believe as You List*.　It has suffered much from damp, and
is in a brittle, dilapidated state.　In several passages the MS.
has suffered since Gifford's collation (*e.g.*, II., 2, 15).　The
lacunae in the text—*e.g.*, at I., 4, 55; I., 5, 7; and I., 5, 74—
are all caused by the mutilation of the lower edge of the MS.
The hand seems to be the same throughout, but bears no resemblance to that in which *Believe as You List* is written, nor
is it so easy to decipher.　There are very few corrections in the
text, and no marginal notes of any kind except the customary
entrances and departures of the characters, which are dupli-
cated as in *Believe as You List*, but in the same hand.　The
licence on folio 19*a* has been cut off.　On folio 19*b* is written
in a largish hand, *The Parliament of Love*, without any author's
name.　Gifford believed that this MS. was in Massinger's
hand, and says " this has since been confirmed."　He does not
say how.　One thing is certain; the same hand did not write
The Parliament of Love and *Believe as You List*.　One instance
out of many can be give in proof of this: the letter C, small
and capital, in *The Parliament of Love* is constantly written
thus, ⊕.　A marked feature of the MS. is the doubling of
consonants—*e.g.*, tollerable, vallor, quallities, cullors.　It
looks as if, while it was in Gifford's hands, ink had been used
to restore letters here and there, and towards the end of the
play there are several substitutions of words in a later ink
Gifford's collation where I have tested it is correct in the main
but I noted one or two mistakes—*e.g.* :

I., 5, 87.—MS.: Sudainely.
  G.: Speedily.

II., 3, 58.—MS.: The graces from the Idalian greene [*sic*].
  G.: The Loves and Graces. This would make the line scan.

III., 2, 15.—MS.: If I compared it to an Indian slave's.
  G.: with.

V., 1, 158.—MS.: Have.
  G.: Had.

V., 1, 292.—"To" in MS. begins line 293.

The sort of mistake which we find in this MS. lends support to two hypotheses, between which, as far as I can see, there is nothing to decide; either, as we saw there was ground for supposing in *Believe as You List*, the author altered his diction as he composed, or he was dictating to an amanuensis. The earlier corrections are all made in the same ink. In favour of the former hypothesis are such passages as the following:

I., 4, 84: "May you ~~sue~~ prosper." "Succeed" was the original word, but cancelled for one which scans better.

I., 5, 23: "Clarindore" cancelled at end of line, "Cleremond" substituted. Clarindore is mentioned in the next line.

I., 5, 66: "Summer's sunne": "heate" substituted for "sunne."

II., 1, 81: "That" deleted after "assurance"; the line thereby runs more smoothly.

II., 3, 5: "Thy selfe": "selfe" deleted before "strengthe."

III., 2, 16: "That with incessant labour to searche out." After "labour" "searche" is deleted. In other words, the construction is changed: the main verb being "dives" in the next line, instead of the original intention, "searches."

III., 3, 124: "Perform'd" deleted before "expir'd."

V., 1, 111: "In hell's most uglie cullors." "Horrid coullors" is deleted before the last two words.

V., 1, 189: "Nor did I scorn": "him" after "scorn" is deleted, as if the syntax had been changed.

V., 1, 206: "Acknowledged" deleted before "appointed."

passage. Thus, Romont's speech, beginning at line 201, seems to show traces of Massinger; likewise Pontalier's, beginning at line 370. It is probable that Field wrote the prose scenes in the play, and possibly the songs; nor would I deny that the regular ten-syllable blank verse of such passages as Act II., 2, 178-187 (ROCHFORT. Why, how now, Beaumelle ? . . . nothing but good and fit), and Act II., 2, 318-328 (This is my only child . . . were multiplied tenfold), is Field's work. In the two plays which have come down to us from Field there is much passable blank verse. It is important to remember, however, that we have so little of Field left that it is hazardous to base material tests on it; and secondly, the authors may have collaborated in individual scenes in such a way as to escape analysis. This is what probably has taken place in Act II., 2. Nor do I feel certain that the latter part of Act III. is wholly due to Field; lines 438-478 contain much that is like Massinger, though the ugly line 464 is not in his style.

> " I not accuse thy wife of act, but would
> Prevent her precipice to thy dishonour."

On the other hand, the rhymed couplet (lines 375-6) is probably Field's.

The pert page in Act IV., 1, reminds us of a similar character in *Woman's a Weathercock*, and is probably Field's handiwork. On the other hand, Pontalier's speech in the same scene (lines 119-140) reads to me like Massinger.

These instances may serve to show how hard it is to dissect the play satisfactorily.

APPENDIX XII

THE TRAGEDY OF "SIR JOHN VAN OLDEN BARNAVELT"

This play is to be found in Bullen's *Old Plays*, vol. ii. It was printed from B.M. Add. MSS. 18653, a folio of thirty-one leaves in a small clear hand.

Mr. Bullen thinks that Massinger wrote III., 2; III., 6; IV. (the trial scene); V., 1. He ascribes the concluding scene

to Fletcher.   These ascriptions seem to me correct.   There is
much fine poetry in the play, notably in the Leidenberg scene.
But Fleay goes too far when he calls the play " magnificent."
It is a " piece of occasion,"[1] written shortly after the tragic
death of Barnavelt, in such a way, however, that it would
not interest a later generation, who had forgotten the sensa-
tion of the time.   In the second place, it has no unity, a fact
no doubt partly due to the dual authorship.   We do not know
if we are intended to sympathise with Orange or Barnavelt.
Such a specimen of the historical drama pure and simple
makes us feel that more than a mere narrative of events is
needed in a play; we look to the author to guide our sympathies, and have a view of his own about his theme.[2]

APPENDIX XIII

"THE SECOND MAIDEN'S TRAGEDY"

This play was reprinted by the Malone Society in 1909.[3]
The writing of the original MS. in the British Museum is
remarkably good.   It is No. 807 in the Lansdowne Collection,
and comes to us from the famous Warburton MSS.   The play
was licensed by Sir George Buck, October 31st, 1611, and acted
by the King's men.   At the end is inscribed: "by Thomas
Goffe,[4] George Chapman, by Will Shakspear.   A tragedy
indeed !''

---

[1] Mr. Bullen (vol. iv., App., p. 381) shows that the play was
produced in August, 1619, after some objections had been
raised to it by the Bishop of London.

[2] Old Plays, vol. ii., App. 2, contains much information
from Boyle about Massinger's style.   Inter alia, he says,
"Fletcher as usual spoiled Massinger's fine conception of
Barnavelt, and made him whine like Buckingham in Henry
VIII."

[3] It is also to be found in Dodsley's Old English Plays, ed.
W. C. Hazlitt, 1875, vol. x.

[4] The name Goffe is so carefully obliterated that it is
uncertain; but it is curious to note that Goffe and Massinger
are in juxtaposition in the passage of Don Zara del Fogo
referred to supra, p. 77 n. 3.

The last phrase is true. The first two names are erased; the third name has been added by a late seventeenth or eighteenth century hand.

The underplot, according to Boyle, is derived from Cervantes' *Curious Impertinent*, and in Acts I. and II. passages "are literally taken from that novel." There is an incident at the end of the play which reminds us of *The Duke of Milan*. The "Tyrant" removes the body of the heroine from her tomb, and sends for a painter to give colour to her face and lips. Govianus, her husband, comes in disguise to do the deed, and the Tyrant is killed by the poison which Govianus has put on the lips of the corpse.

Massinger may therefore have known the play, but I differ entirely from Boyle's estimate. He thinks Massinger wrote Acts I. and II., Tourneur Acts III., IV., V. I see no trace of Massinger in Act I., except the reference in line 541 to a "cup of nectar." The sudden repentance of the heroine's father Helvetius, in Act II., 1, 253, reminds us of a trait of Massinger referred to above;[1] but the style of the first two acts is too feeble and vague, and the metre too halting for him.[2] I cannot suppose that at the age of twenty-seven Massinger could have taken part in writing a play where "A voice from within" the tomb says to the mourning husband, "I am not here!"[3]

APPENDIX XIV

"THE POWERFUL FAVORITE"[4]

"*The Powerful Favorite*, or the life of Aelius Sejanus, by P. M., printed at Paris, 1628." So runs the title in the English translation.

---

[1] *Supra*, p. 74.

[2] Mr. Phelan (pp. 48-49) argues that this play is really the lost play by Massinger, entitled *The Tyrant*. Tieck translated the play as being by Massinger. Mr. P. Simpson has pointed out to me that *The Second Maiden's Tragedy* is entered on the Stationers' Register for September 9th, 1653, immediately after several of Massinger's plays. He justly observes that the juxtaposition is fortuitous.

[3] Act IV., 4.   [4] *Cf.* Phelan, *op. cit.*, p. 3.

Two translations of Pierre Matthieu's book, "Histoire d'Aelius Sejanus," appeared in the same year. One is padded out with additions; in the shorter and more exact translation, the initials on the title-page of the Bodleian copy have been filled out thus: P. Massinger.

We know that Massinger's political sympathies were against the Duke of Buckingham, and it is probable that a Life of Sejanus may have attracted attention at a time when the parallel was drawn and the unpopularity great; but it is simpler to suppose that P. M. stands for the French author. It would require some courage to publish under one's own name or initials a translation of the book.

It is noteworthy that in 1632, after Buckingham's death, a translation appeared by Sir T. Hawkins. The title which he gave his book was "Unhappy prosperitie expressed in the histories of Aelius Sejanus and Philippa, the Catanian." Underneath he adds the words: "Written in French by P. Matthieu."

APPENDIX XV

"DOUBLE FALSEHOOD"

In 1728 there appeared at London a play with the following title: "Double Falsehood, or The Distressed Lovers; written originally by W. Shakespeare, and now revised and adapted to the stage by Mr. Theobald, the author of *Shakespeare Restor'd.*"

It was dedicated to the Rt. Hon. George Dodington, Esq. In the Preface Theobald states that one of the copies in MS. is of above sixty years' standing. He goes on to say that there is a tradition that Shakspere wrote it—"in the time of his retirement from the stage." The story is taken from a novel in *Don Quixote*, which appeared in 1611, five years before Shakspere's death. Theobald professes to allow that the colouring, diction, and characters come nearer to the style and manner of Fletcher.

Some writers[1] have supposed that Theobald in compiling

---

[1] Sir A. W. Ward (II., 528[2]) seems disposed to assign it to Shirley.

this play used materials from a lost play by Massinger. The first thing we notice in it is that there are a good many prose scenes. This is unlike Massinger. In the second place, the metre is unlike Massinger's; it is simple and regular, and contains very few double endings or run-on lines. In Act II., 4, Leonora gives an important letter to her lover Julio, out of a window, to a "citizen" whom she does not know, by night. Is this improbable incident the sort of thing that Massinger would write ?[1]

The whole play is an eighteenth-century effusion in the manner of Rowe. There is no trace of Fletcher or Massinger here.

APPENDIX XVI

MIDDLETON'S "A TRICK TO CATCH THE OLD ONE"

A Trick to catch the Old One is a lively play, mainly written in prose, in which an air of plausibility is skilfully cast around a farcical plot. There can be no doubt that Massinger borrowed the idea of *A New Way* from Middleton, as well as a few expressions.[2] In both plays there are an uncle who has strained the law to deprive his nephew of his lands, a rich widow whose supposed affection for the nephew converts the uncle to make reparation, and creditors who have to be satisfied. The ser-

---

[1] Compare this with the scene in Ford's *Tis Pity She's a Whore* where Annabella gives the Friar a letter from an upper window.

[2] Compare *A Trick*, I., 1:
      What trick is not an embryon at first ?
" Embryon " is a favourite word of Massinger's.

I., 1: Witgood. I shall go nigh to catch that old fox, mine Uncle; though he make but some amends for my undoing, yet there's some comfort in't, he cannot otherwise choose, though it be but in hope to cozen me again, but supply any hasty want that I bring to town with me.

II., 1: Lucre. There may be hope some of the widow's lands too may one day fall upon me if things be carried wisely.

vants (*A Trick*, IV., 4) who are to discharge their duties in Hoard's new household may have suggested the group in Lady Allworth's house who supply a comic element. On the other hand, the two plays are constructed on very different lines. The central point of *A Trick* is the hatred of the two usurers, Lucre and Hoard, for one another, both being in the end cheated by the hero Witgood. In *A New Way* there is only one usurer, Sir Giles. *A Trick*, though well constructed, has a lame and hurried conclusion; and it is overloaded with minor characters, who help the action but little—in particular, the usurer Dampit seems to be introduced for no particular reason except to fill up the time with mediocre fun. The part played by the heroine, Joyce, is small and obscure. Then again, there can be no comparison between the slight figure of Hoard and the powerful creation of Sir Giles Overreach. Wellborn does nothing in the play that misbecomes a gentleman; the ingenuity with which he frames a plan to deceive his uncle leads us to believe that when he has repented his

---

A New Way, IV., 1, 77:
    OVERREACH.   'Tis not alone
The Lady Allworth's land, for these once Wellborn's,
As by her dotage on him I know they will be,
Shall soon be mine.

A Trick, I., 2: WITGOOD. Thou knowest I have a wealthy uncle, i' th' city, somewhat the wealthier for my follies.

A Trick, I., 3: HOARD. Thou that canst defeat thy own nephew, Lucre, lay his lands into bonds, and take the extremity of thy kindred's forfeitures.

A New Way, I., 1, 48:
    TAPWELL. Which your uncle, Sir Giles Overreach,
        observing
(Resolving not to lose a drop of them)
On foolish mortgages, statutes, and bonds,
For a while supplied your looseness, and then left you.

II., 1, 81:
    OVERREACH. And 'tis my glory, though I come from
        the city,
To have their issue whom I have undone,
To kneel to mine as bondslaves.

A Trick, II., 1: LUCRE. You've a fault, nephew; you're a stranger here; well, heaven give you joy.

wild life he has the capacity to make good. His prototype, Witgood, on the other hand, is merely an amusing adventurer. Indeed, Middleton seems throughout to be pursuing with his vengeance the sharp practices of those who lend money to fast young men, and we certainly sympathize with his castigation of Lucre, Hoard, and Dampit. Massinger's widow is a lady of birth and title; Middleton's is a courtesan in disguise. When she marries Hoard, though we feel some satisfaction at the deception which has been practised on him, we cannot help asking ourselves as the characters retire to the conventional " wedding dinner " of an Elizabethan comedy, whether the solution would have worked in real life. The answer is, that while we have been much amused, we have been cheated by the author's great skill and vivacity into accepting an improbable plot. Massinger's play, on the other hand, contains little that might not have happened, and the conclusion is so arranged that there is every prospect of the characters living happily hereafter. While Middleton's play is a charm-

---

A New Way, III., 2, 276:
> OVERREACH. My nephew !
> He has been too long a stranger; faith you have !
> Pray, let it be mended.

A Trick, III., 1: I would forswear . . . muscadine and eggs at midnight.

A New Way, IV., 2, 84:
> CREDITOR. Your worship broke me
> With trusting you with muscadine and eggs.

A Trick, IV., 4: Hoard's anticipations of his future pomp may have suggested the thoughts which Sir Giles entertains about his daughter's future estate when married to Lord Lovel.

Cf. A New Way, IV., 3, 130-141.

A Trick, IV., 5:
> SIR LAUNCELOT. I would entreat your worship's device
>   in a just and honest cause, sir.
> DAMPIT. I meddle with no such matters.

A New Way, II., 1, 23:
> OVERREACH. The other wisdom,
> That does prescribe us a well-governed life,
> And to do right to others, as ourselves,
> I value not an atom.

ing extravaganza, Massinger's has held the stage ever since. The one play can be acted now, the other cannot. This is not merely due to the fact that *A New Way* has more dignity and refinement than its predecessor, but it is because Massinger's characters behave like real beings.[1]

APPENDIX XVII

These two poems are copied from a folio MS. in the library of Trinity College, Dublin (G, 2, 21), containing compositions of Donne and other poets of the seventeenth century. They are to be found on pages 554-559. The handwriting is that of the seventeenth century. I have reproduced the original punctuation and spelling. Mr. Grosart published the poems in *Englische Studien*, No. xxvi. He says that the librarian of Trinity, Dr. T. K. Abbot, had grounds for supposing that the MS. had been in the possession of Trinity College for a century; he does not, however, state what the grounds are. As far as the dates go which are indicated in the volume, it might have passed into the library with other books from Archbishop Ussher's collection.

From the tone of line 16 of the first poem we may assume that it was addressed by Massinger when quite young to William, the third Earl of Pembroke.

I

The Copie of a Letter written upon occasion to the Earle of Pembrooke
Lo: Chamberlaine

My Lord   p. 554
    Soe subiect to the worser fame
    Are even the best that clayme a Poets name:
    Especially poore they that serve the stage
    Though worthily in this Verse-halting Age.

---

[1] Compare the way in which Massinger, in *The Great Duke of Florence*, transfers to Italy *A Knacke to Know a Knave*. (Hazlitt's *Dodsley*, vi.)

And that dread curse soe heavie yet doth lie
W^{ch} the wrong'd Fates falne out wth Mercurie
Pronounc'd for ever to attend upon
All such as onely dreame of Helicon.
That durst I sweare cheated by selfe opinion
I were Apolloes or the Muses Mynion   10
Reason would yet assure me, 'tis decreed
Such as are Poets borne, are borne to need.
If the most worthy then, whose pay's but praise
Or a few spriggs from the now withering bayes
Grone underneath their wants what hope have I
Scarce yet allowed one of the Company—   16
                                        Of
                                   p. 555
*When thou sighst, thou sigh'st not wind, but sigh'st my
     soule away
When thou weep'st unkindly kind, my lifes blud doth
     decay
It cannot bee
That thou lov'est mee as thou sai'est, if in thine my life
     thou wast,
Thou art the best of mee.†
†Note in left-hand margin: [T]his verse is ye 5the in ye
[   ] vi page.

Of better fortune, That with their good parts   p. 555
Even want the wayes the bold and thriving arts
By wch they grow remarkable and are priz'd
Since sure I could not live a thing despiz'd   20
Durst I professe t'were in my power to give
A patron that should ever make him live—
Or tell great Lords that the maine Reason why
They hold A Poets prayses flatterie
Is their owne guilt, that since they left to doo
Things worthy praise even praise is odious too—
Some few there are that by this boldnes thrive
W^{ch} yet I dare not follow; others strive

---

* Lines in another hand inserted in a space left blank at the
top of p. 555.
† Marginal note in a third hand.

In some high mynded Ladies grace to stand
Ever provided that her liberall hand   30
Pay for the Vertues they bestow upon her
And soe long shees the miracle and the honor
Of her whole Sex, and has forsooth more worth
Then was in any Sparta e're brought forth
But when the Bounty failes a change is neare
And shee's not then what once shee did appeare
For the new Giver shee dead must inherit
What was by purchase gott and not by merit
Lett them write well that doo this and in grace
I would not for a pension or A place   40

                        Part

Part soe wth myne owne Candor, lett me rather   p. 556
Live poorely on those toyes I would not father
Not knowne beyond A Player or A Man
That does pursue the course that I have ran
Ere soe glow famous: yet wth any paine
Or honest industry could I obteyne
A noble Favorer, I might write and doo
Like others of more name and gett one too
Or els my Genius is false.   I know
That Johnson much of what he has does owe   50
To you and to your familie, and is never
Slow to professe it, nor had Fletcher ever
Such Reputation, and credit nonne
But by his honord Patron, Huntington
Unimitable Spencer ne're had been
Soe famous for his matchlesse Fairie Queene
Had he not found a ~~Spencer~~ Sydney to preferr [sic]
His plaine way in his Shepheards Calender
Nay Virgills selfe (or Martiall does lye)
Could hardly frame a poore Gnatts Elegie   60
Before Mecænas cherisht him; and then
He streight conceiv'd Æneas and the men
That found out Italic   Those are Presidents[1]
I cite wth reverence: my lowe intents
Looke not soe high, yet some worke I might frame

                        That

---

[1] *I.e.*, precedents.

That should nor wrong my duty nor your Name.   p. 557
Were but your Lo^{pp} pleas'd to cast an eye
Of favour on my trodd downe povertie
How ever I confesse myselfe to be
Ever most bound for your best charitie   70
To others that feed on it, and will pay
My prayers wth theirs that as y^u doe y^u may
Live long, belov'd and honor'd doubtles then
Soe cleere a life will find a worthier Penn.
For me I rest assur'd besides the glory
T'wold make a Poet but to write your story.   76

Phill: Messinger.

p. 557

II

A New yeares Guift presented to my Lady and M:^{rs} the then Lady Katherine Stanhop now Countesse of Chesterfield.

By Phill: Messinger.

Madame
Before I ow'd to you the name
Of Servant, to your birth, your worth your fame
I was soe, and t'was fitt since all stand bound
To honour Vertue in meane persons found
Much more in you, that as borne great, are good
W^{ch} is more then to come of noble blood
Or be A Hastings; it being too well knowne

An

p. 558

An Empresse cannot challenge as her oune
Her Grandsires glories; And too many staine
Wth their bad Actions the noble straine   10
From whence they come.   But as in you to be
A branch to add fresh honor to the tree
By vertue planted, and adorne it new
Is graunted unto none or very few

To speake you further would appeare in me
Presumption or a servants flattery
But there may be a tyme when I shall dare
To tell the world and boldly what yᵘ are
Nor sleight it Madame, since what some in me
Esteeme a blemish, is a guift as free   20
As their best fortunes. this tooke from the grave
Penelopies chastitie, and to it gave
Still living Honors; this made Aiax strong
Ulisses wise: such power lies in a Song
Wᶜʰ Phaebus smiles on, wᶜʰ can find noe Urne
While the Sea his course, or starrs observe their turne
Yet 'tis not in the power of tinckling Rime
[1] That takes rash iudgments and deceive the tyme
Wᵗʰ Mountebanke showes a worke that shold indure
Must have a genius in it, strong, as pure   30
But you beginne to smile, as wondring why
I should write thus much to yᵘ now since I
Have heretofore been silent may yᵘ please

              To know

To know the course it is noe new disease   p. 559
Groune in my iudgment, nor am I of those
That thinke good wishes cannot thrive in prose
As well as Verse: but that this New yeares day
All in their loves and duties, what they may
Present unto you; though perhaps some burne
Wᵗʰ expectation of a glad returne   40
Of what they venture for. But such I leave
To their deceiptfull guifts given to deceive
What I give I am rich in, and can spare
Nor part for hope wᵗʰ ought deserves my care
He that hath little and gives nought at all
To them that have is truly liberall.   46

---

[1] ? To take.

APPENDIX XVIII

ALLITERATION IN MASSINGER

The art with which Massinger employs alliteration escapes all but the most careful perusal; but once noticed, it attracts attention as one of his favourite expedients. Perhaps the best way to exemplify its use is to give a complete collection of instances from one of the plays: I take for this purpose *The Unnatural Combat.*

I., 1, 150: Impartial judges, and not sway'd with spleen.

,, 158: Not lustful fires, but fair and lawful flames.

,, 189: Our goods made prize, our sailors sold for slaves.

,, 217:   He that leaves To follow as you lead, will lose himself.

,, 286: Their lives, their liberties.

,, 308: Both what and when to do, but makes against you.

,, 309: For had your care and courage been the same.

,, 342: He may have leave and liberty to decide it.

II., 1, 14: With my best curiousness and care observed him.

,, 23: A sudden flash of fury did dry up.

,, 94: But dare and do, as they derive their courage.

,, 143: In a moment raz'd and ruin'd.

,, 157: In one short syllable yield satisfaction.

,, 170: With scorn on death and danger.

,, 177: But what is weak and womanish, thine own.

,, 183: As a serpent swoll'n with poison.

,, 226: Marseillés owes the freedom of her fears.

,, 241: That will vouchsafe not one sad sigh or tear.

,, 267: And with all circumstance and ceremony.

II., 3, 67: Nor should you with more curiousness and care.

III., 1, 10: It being a serious and solemn meeting.

,, 17: I'll undertake to stand at push of pike.

,, 21: When the dresser, the cook's drum, thunders, Come on !

III., 1,   23: As tall a trencher-man.

     ,,   32: The only drilling is to eat devoutly
And to be ever drinking.

     ,,   57: Delay is dangerous.

     ,,   88: Continue constant
To this one suit.

     ,,   90: Every cast commander.

     ,, 100: And so by consequence grow contemptible.

     ,, 117: For his own sake, shift a shirt !

III., 2,   46: The colonels, commissioners, and captains.

     ,,   78: That losing her own servile shape and name.

     ,,   85: Believe my black brood swans.

     ,,   95: As I have heard, loved the lobby.

     ,, 150: Of her fair features, that, should we defer it.

     ,, 160: And serves as a perpetual preface to.

III., 3,   43: The curiousness and cost on Trajan's birthday.

     ,,   78: I've charged through fire that would have
singed your sables.

     ,,   82: Such only are admired that come adorn'd.

     ,,   93: Does make your cupboards crack.

     ,, 114: For want of means shall, in their present pay-
ment.

     ,, 149: With my son, her servant.

III., 4,   89: And he shall find and feel, if he excuse not.

IV., 1,   53: And liked and loath'd with your eyes, I beseech you.

     ,,   91: A loathsome leprosy had spread itself.

     ,, 101: Sir, you have liked and loved them, and oft
forc'd.

     ,, 119: My ranks of reason.

     ,, 132: Thy virtues vices.

     ,, 133: Far worse than stubborn sullenness and pride.

     ,, 206: In your fame and fortunes.

IV., 2,   47: Against my oath, being a cashier'd captain.

     ,,   68: Your lords
Of dirt and dunghills.

     ,, 118: My corslet to a cradle.

     ,, 120: Or to sell my sword and spurs, for soap and
candles ?

IV., 2. 135: Fair France is proud of.
  „   148: Such as have power to punish.

V., 2, 35: Or our later laws forbid.
  „   38: And solemn superstitious fools prescribe.
  „   57: Into some close cave or desert.
  „   58: Our lusts and lives together.
  „   165: But to have power to punish, and yet pardon,
          Peculiar to princes.
  „   248: Accuse or argue with me.
  „   307: To season my silks.

APPENDIX XIX

By the kindness of Mr. Edmund Gosse I have been enabled
to examine and collate the manuscript notes in copies of the
first quartos of the following plays in his possession: *The Duke
of Milan, The Bondman, The Roman Actor, The Renegado,
The Picture, The Fatal Dowry, The Emperor of the East, The
Maid of Honour.* The dates of these quartos range from
1623 to 1632. The poet Swinburne had no doubt that the
manuscript notes were due to Massinger himself; the resemblance of the handwriting is certainly indubitable, but
as we have no other evidence than that of the corrections
themselves, we are forced to be content with the conclusion
that the insertions are of a contemporary date. I take the
plays in the above order.

The Duke of Milan

I., 1, 23.—This, the last line on the page, has suffered from
the binding, and is written in the margin.[1]

I., 1, 56.—The same thing has happened here.

In both cases the writing resembles that of the poet. It
may be argued, on the other hand, that it is unlikely that the
play should have suffered so soon from binding; it is, however,

---

[1] In the Malone copy in the Bodleian line 23 has disappeared, and at the end of line 22 rather less of the letters
is preserved than at the beginning.

of course not impossible that the eight plays were bound up together shortly after the year 1632.

V., 2, 203.—Forza. S. inserted before F. (So *infra*, 218, 234, 256.)

At the end of the play occurs a symbol ω)/ which might represent the poet's initial.

The Bondman

I., 1:	Timagorus bis in stage-directions, and also in I., 1, 5	us corrected to as	
I., 1,	37: I love	live	
I., 2,	2: I cannot brooke with gadding	this	
I., 3,	83: As to the supreame Magistrates surely tenders	Sicilie	
,,	161: And yet the chu	rl added	
,,	181: made glorious by Achon	Action	
,,	182: gave warrant to her couns	ailes added	
,,	183: hand	heard	
,,	206: nor defence	noe	
,,	295: ? at end	? deleted	
,,	319: of slaves	our	
II., 1,	71: fam'd	fann'd	
,,	87: vayle	y deleted	
,,	144: loose both sent and beauty	th inserted after "loose," and c in "sent"	
,,	153: owe	awe	
II., 2,	16: manners; yet this morning	for	
,,	57: cunning	cominge	
,,	62:	? added	
III., 3,	99: too too large	second "too" deleted	
,,	135: leave her off	stand her of	
,,	165: during	daring	
III., 4,	29: Timandra	Timag	
,,	51: cares	feares	

IV., 1, 21: still	you
IV., 2, 128: when	where
„ 140:	"Pray you, leave mee" added at end to complete the line
IV., 3, 145: tempter	second t deleted
V., 3, 19: not be deni'de	to inserted before "be"
„ 38: howsoere the fortune	thy
„ 103: gods and fautors	his
„ 193:	) inserted after devices
„ 245:	Gra. inserted at beginning of line. (*i.e.*, Graccho)

All these corrections are manifestly right, except possibly III., 3, 135 and IV., 1, 21. The addition in IV., 2, 140, though not especially appropriate to the situation, presents us with a type of line much favoured by Massinger.

The Roman Actor

I., 1, 6: stocke	socc (*i.e.*, sock)
„ 25:	parenthesis inserted after " vice "
„ 37: gald	l added after " l "
„ 44: The Catta and the Dacie	Catti . . . Daci
„ 46: Jove hasten it	? added
„ 49: we obey you	full stop added
„ 51: the sceane	Scaene
„ 79: is to eb* guilty	bee
„ 115: grieve	greive ("give" is required by the sense)
I., 2: Enter Domitia and Parthenius	" with a letter " added
I., 2, 33: for to be thankfull	I woulde
„ 44: his plea	its
„ 86: new workes that dare not do	Monarches. Pa: added, (*i.e.*, Parthenius)
„ 88: Parth. Will you dispute	Parth. deleted and ? added
I., 3, 44:	( ) added

* The misprint is in the original.

I., 3, 53-4 :   (   ) added

„   67 : condemne   condemnd

„   78 : which   with

„   78 : redde (*i.e.*, read)   ) added

„   86 : Cancillus   Camillus

I., 4,   13 : Fulcinius and prisoners   "and" deleted
               led by him

II., 1,   4 : yours   ; added

„   16 : though   (added

„   21 : purple   ! added

„   22 : my heyre   ? added

„ 182-3 :   (   ) added

„   217 : promped   prompted

„   372 :   (   ) added

„   386 :   (   ) added

III., 1,   30 : words   swordes

„   52 : retch   reach

„   58 : the mortall powers   im̄ortall

„   78 : tyrannie   tyrant

„   163 : steepie   steep

„   205 :   ! added

IV., 1,   8 : I thinke not   "not" deleted, and
                                 added after "re-
                                 spects" in 9

„   95 : compliant   complaint

„   149 :   ? added

IV., 2,   12 : lesse;   ; deleted

„   27 : pe   bee

„   28 : you command to me   ever you com̄and me

„   39 : tremele   tremble

„   44 : geeat   great

„   70 : Hypollitus   one l substituted

„   123 : express thee   stop added

„   127 : To render me that was   (   ) added   before
                 before I hugg'd thee   "t h a t"   a n d
                 An adder in my bosome   "before," and after
                                 "t h e e"   a n d
                                 " bosome "

IV., 2, 130: Thy pomp and pride—163 Perpetual vexation
shall not fall.

Note at top of p. 31 *b*: "This page follows the later."

Note at top of p. 32*a*: "This page misplac'd."

,, 182: would	coulde
,, 190: the iu ice	st inverted inserted here between "iu" and "ice"
,, 191: had with h inverted	had
,, 196: if	yf
,, 229: act	are
,, 242: grim death	"grim" deleted
,, 295:	( ) added
V., 1, 115: assure	as sure
,, 142: still'd	stil'd
,, 228: pinn'd	pinion'd
V., 2, 22: iumpe	impe
,, 78: this murther	'tis
,, 85: to sentence	her inserted after "to"

I have compared the Malone quarto in the Bodleian Library and find that the mistakes are identical. In other words, *The Roman Actor* was carelessly printed. Nearly all the corrections made, alike of sense and punctuation, are improvements. The emendation at IV., 2, 28 reads like one made by the author. On the other hand, a careful study of IV., 2, 127 will reveal the fact that the writer's sense has been mistaken, and the omission of "grim" in IV., 2, 242 spoils the rhythm. The curious thing is that the play is full of misprints, which have not been corrected—*e.g.*, III., 2, 143, Anaxerete (and in several other lines); line 154, "Epethite," for "epithet"; 258, Heccuba. Take again IV., 2, 181: An e is inverted and not corrected; 188, "bttchered" stands for "butchered"; and 189, "lacriledge" for "sacrilege."

The Renegado

I., 3, 159: receive least losse	"the" inserted after "least." It spoils the metre

II., 5,	46: up to the bre a c	breache
,,		? added
III., 3,	1: I will	'Twill
,,	89: like a neighing gennet to her stallion	mare to her proud stallion
III., 5,	114: well made galley	mann'd
IV., 1,	114: witnesse of my change	" of " deleted: "good" inserted after " my "
V., 2,	79:	Franci. inserted (= Francisco)
V., 3,	111:	Vitelli inserted

III., 3, 89 reads like an author's emendation. On the other hand, the alteration in IV., 1, 114 is not in Massinger's style.

The Picture

Line 37,	Poem by T. Jay: of to heare	or
,,	38: write neere	writ
,,	40: admir'd	admire
I., 1,	31: satisfie	satietie
,,	40:	( ) added
,,	53: If I am so rich or	Sir
,,	120: wone him	o inserted after " o "
,,	154: wracke	w deleted
,,	190: ere the fight begun	s added after " fight " (=is)
I., 2,	13: bravel	ye added
,,	71: but	deleted and added again in margin
,,	170: examp	le added
II., 1,	82: A post.	deleted
,,	83:	" Aside. A Post." added in margin
II., 2,	98: " In one here " printed in a separate line after this line	" In one here " deleted (*vide* Gifford)
,,	103: resolve	s added

II., 2, 103: lords of her, like   acres

,,   174: fierce dame   n inserted before "m."
                           dame=dam

,,   255: solder   soldier

,,   260: tosses   trifles

Here it will be noted that two good emendations are made—
I., 1, 53 and II., 2, 103. On the other hand, no notes are
made on the last three acts: such a misprint as " ijgobobs "
in V., 3, 161 escaping comment.

The Fatal Dowry
Nil.

The Emperor of the East

I., 1,   83: musicke ?   ? deleted, and " Sir ? "
                           added

I., 2, 169: too   to

,,   178: Constantinople   courte

,,   242: them feare   their

,,   291: care   feare

,,   323: Nimph   Umph

,,   347: wooned   d deleted

II., 1, 114: in knowledge   " the " inserted after
                           " in "

III., 2,   62:   ( ) added

,,   93: heaven is most gratious   " to you " deleted
         to you, madam

,,   111: with a kinde impotence   " of " inserted after
                           " kinde "

,,   138: I speak it   ) added

,,   139: 1   I (so III., 4, 145, 163;
                           IV., 1, 13)

,,   199: ransone   m

III., 4,   19: how . sister: ! ! added

,,   29: str   stirre

,,   44: beg pardon   a inserted after " beg "

,,   60: my pity   t added above " t "

,,   80:   ? added

III., 4,	132: observe	handle
,,	146: royall sir	comma added
IV., 1,	14: Princesse	Empresse
IV., 3,	36: they	hee
,,	43: fraide	defray'd
,,	62: camer	cancer
,,	132: this admiration	thie
V., 3,	47: flights	s deleted
,,	85: niggle	iuggle
,,	111: I fever	if ever
,,	190: my grace on all	cancelled

The corrections in this play are nearly all good: thus the metre is restored at I., 2, 178, and III., 2, 93, and improved in III., 4, 132. V., 3, 85 is an excellent emendation. On the other hand, I do not think the author would have made such a stupid mistake as the one found at IV., 1, 14, for Chrysapius is there addressing the Empress, about Pulcheria.

The Maid of Honour
Nil.

NOTE BY MR. EDMUND GOSSE.

In 1877, when he was breaking up his home at Clifton, and disposing of his books, John Addington Symonds gave Mr. Edmund Gosse a thick volume containing eight first editions of plays by Massinger. The book was bound in worn old calf of the period, and had stamped on the back the author's name. Symonds, in giving the book to Mr. Gosse, called his attention to the contemporary corrections in ink, and said there was "a tradition" that they were in the handwriting of Massinger himself. Mr. Gosse, unfortunately, broke up the volume and had the eight plays separately bound, but the old binding had contained no further indication. In 1882 Swinburne made a careful examination of the corrections, and again in 1883, when he urged that they should be published. He became persuaded that they were made by Massinger himself. Nothing, however, has until now been done with them. The volume came from the Harbord library at Gunton in Norfolk, and was sold, with other old books, at the death of the fourth Lord Suffield in 1853. Symonds bought it of an Oxford bookseller when he was an undergraduate.

APPENDIX XX

BIBLIOGRAPHY

W. ARCHER: "The Elizabethan Stage" (Quarterly Review, No. 415, April, 1908).

R. BOYLE: Dictionary of National Biography: "Massinger."
,, Englische Studien (Heilbronn): "On Beaumont, Fletcher, and Massinger," v. 74, vii. 66, viii. 39, ix. 209, x. 383.
,, New Shakespeare Society Transactions, part ii., 1880-85, xviii., pp. 371-399: "Massinger and The Two Noble Kinsmen." (*Cf.* Discussion on March 9, 1883, p. 66.)
,, New Shakespeare Society Transactions, 1880-86, xxi., pp. 443-488; "Henry the Eighth."
,, New Shakespeare Society Transactions, 1886, xxvi., pp. 579-628.

A. C. BRADLEY: Oxford Lectures on Poetry: "Shakespeare the Man, and Shakespeare's Theatre and Audience."

A. H. BULLEN: Dictionary of National Biography: "Fletcher."

H. COLERIDGE: Preface to Massinger and Ford. 1840.

S. T. COLERIDGE: Lectures on Shakespeare and the Poets (T. Ashe, 1883), pp. 403-407, 427, 432, 437, 534, 540.

W. T. COURTHOPE: History of English Poetry, vol. iv., pp. 348-369.

T. COXETER: The dramatic works of P. Massinger: 1761.

LIEUT.-COL. F. CUNNINGHAM: The plays of P. Massinger: Chatto and Windus: 1870.

DOWNES: Roscius Anglicanus.

EDINBURGH REVIEW, No. 23, 1808. (Review of Gifford's edition.)

F. G. FLEAY: Biographical Chronicle of the English Drama.
,, Chronicle History of the London Stage, 1559-1642.

F. G. FLEAY: Chronicle History of W. Shakespeare.

,,   New Shakespeare Society Transactions, 1874, vol. i., No. 2: " On Metrical Tests as applied to Dramatic Poetry " (Fletcher, Beaumont, Massinger.)

,,   Shakespeare Manual.

GARDINER: "The Political Element in Massinger." (Contemporary Review, August, 1876): reprinted in New Shakespeare Society Transactions, 1875, No. xi., pp. 314-332. (*Cf.* also History of England, 1884, vol. vii., pp. 327 and 337)

GARNETT AND GOSSE: English Literature: an Illustrated Record. Heinemann.

GAYLEY AND BRANDER MATTHEWS: Representative English Comedies, vol. iii. New York, 1914.

W. GIFFORD: 1805. Second edition, 1813.

W. W. GREG: Henslowe's Diary, vol. ii., pp. 165, 171, 224. 1904-08.

,,   Henslowe Papers, pp. 66, 70, 74, 85. 1907.

,,   List of English Plays written before 1643 and printed before 1700. Bibliographical Society, 1900.

HALLAM: Literature of Europe, part iii., chap. vi.

HAZLITT: Lectures on Elizabethan Literature, pp. 131-136.

E. KOEPPEL: Cambridge History of English Literature, vol. vi., chap. vi.: " Massinger."

,,   Quellen Studien zu den Dramen George Chapman's, Philip Massinger's, und John Ford's.

C. LAMB: Specimens of English Dramatic Poets.[1]

G. C. MACAULAY: Cambridge History of English Literature, vol. vi., chap. v.: " Beaumont and Fletcher."

J. MONCK MASON: Dramatic Works, 1779.

E. H. C. OLIPHANT: Englische Studien, xiv., xv., xvi.

,,   Modern Language Review, iii., 337-355; iv., 190-199, 342-351.

,,   Problems of Authorship in the Elizabethan Drama. Chicago, 1911.

---

[1] Add references in Letters, edited by C. Ainger, vol. i., pp. 23, 24, 136, 154.

J. PHELAN : Dissertation (Halle), 1878. This careful performance contains information about Massinger's family. (*Cf.*, however, Furnivall's Protest in Anglia, ii., p. 504.)

J. M. ROBERTSON : The Baconian Heresy, chap. iii.

G. SAINTSBURY : Cambridge History of English Literature, vol. v., chap. viii.: " Shakespeare."

SCHELLING : Elizabethan Drama, 1908.

SHAKESPEARE'S ENGLAND : Oxford University Press, 1916.

L. STEPHEN : Hours in a Library, vol. ii.

A. C. SWINBURNE : Contemporaries of Shakespeare (Gosse and Wise).

,,   Fortnightly Review, July, 1889.

,,   Letters (Gosse and Wise), Nos. lxii. and lxxiii.

A. SYMONS : Mermaid Series, two volumes.

ASHLEY H. THORNDIKE : Tragedy. Constable, 1908.

L. WANN : Shakespeare Studies (University of Wisconsin), vii.: "The Collaboration of Beaumont, Fletcher, and Massinger."

SIR A. W. WARD : Cambridge History of English Literature, vol. v., chap. xiv.

,,   History of English Dramatic Literature, especially vol. iii., pp. 1-47. -

INDEX

A

AESCHYLUS, 149 169
Alliteration in M., 121 *n*. 1, App. XVIII.
Aristophanes, 61, 70, 149
Aristotle, 27 *n*. 1, 28 *n*. 2, 75, 76, 110 *n*. 1, 140
Armada, 18
Aubrey, 5 *n*. 2
A Wood, A., 2, 6

B

Bashful Lover, The, 48, 50, 57, 58, 75, 98, 131, 147, 199
Beaumont, 21 *n*. 5, 25, 57, 59 *n*. 1, 70, 94, 99 *n*. 2, 110, 129 *n*. 1
Beethoven, 76
Believe as You List, 15, 54, 93, 140, App. VII., App. VIII.
Besant, Sir W., 7
Boccaccio, 9 *n*. 1, 11 *n*. 1, 76 *n*. 3
Bondman, The, 15, 24, 27, 31, 32 *n*. 1, 35, 36, 48, 61, 73, 75, 104, 108, 134, 145, 150
Boyle, 2 *n*. 3, 20, 21, 25, 55, 56, 62 *n*. 1, 70 *n*. 1, 88, 96, 97-104, 109, 122 *n*. 3, 129, 131, App. III., 198, 200
Bradley, A. C., 14, 26 *n*. 3, 28 *n*. 4, 65 *n*. 3, 80 *n*. 16
Bridges, R., 69 *n*. 1, 175
Brooke, R., 111, 159
Brooke, Tucker, 95-97
Browne, Sir T., 82, 119
Buckingham, Duke of, 16, 204
Bullen, A. H., 70, 95 *n*. 2, App. III., 178 *n*. 6, 201
Bunyan, 108 *n*. 1

C

Catalogue lines, 54, 91 *n*. 1
Cayet, 178 *n*. 6, 193
Cervantes, 5 *n*. 5, 203
Chapman, 15 *n*. 2, 66 *n*. 2, 117, 139, 202

Charles I., 7, 15
Cibber, Colley, 176, 181 *n*. 3
City Madam, The, 10, 11, 13, 31, 32 *n*. 1, 43, 53, 54, 55, 73, 113, 116, 133
Cokaine, Sir A., 22
Coleridge, S. T., 55, 64, 71, 76 *n*. 3
Collier, J., 24
Corneille, 43
Courthope, 96
Croker, T. Crofton, 175
Cunningham, F., 7 *n*. 1, 24, 133 *n*. 1, 182

D

Daborne, 2
Davies, 123
Dekker, 20, 44 *n*. 1, 123, 135 *n*. 2, 147, App. X., 199, 200
Diderot, 110 *n*. 1
Dostoevsky, 61
Double Falsehood, The, App. XV.
Downes, 24 *n*. 3
Dryden, 24, 116
Dublin MS., App. XVII.
Duke of Milan, The, 16, 31, 32 *n*.1, 41, 52, 81, 82, 135, 145, 203

E

Emperor of the East, The, 17, 27, 28, 32 *n*. 1, 43 *n*. 2, 48, 51, 54, 72, 82, 101, 102, 108, 128, 146, 148, 149, 170
Euripides, 27, 32, 33, 75, 77, 110 *n*. 1, 169 *n*. 1

F

Fair Penitent, The, 137
Fatal Dowry, The, 8, 20, 28 *n*. 4, 36, 49, 53, 56 *n*. 2, 119, App. XI.
Field, 21, 138, App. XI.
Fielding, 63, 77
Fleay, F. G., 5 *n*. 5, 20, 33 *n*. 2, 56 *n*. 2, 57 *n*. 1, 159, 202

Fletcher, 3, 10, 19, 21 *n.* 1, 28, 59 *n.* 2, 66, 71, 84 *n.* 1, 91, 97, 98, 109, 123, 129, 130, 133, 135, 147, App. III., 170
Ford, 8, 13 *n.* 5, 13 *n.* 6, 33 *n.* 2, 59 *n.* 1, 62, 63 *n.* 3, 65 *n.* 3, 81, 120, 205 *n.* 2

G

Gardiner, 7
Garrick, 124 *n.* 4, 176
Gayley, 26 *n.* 4, 141 *n.* 1, 160
Georgian Poets, The, 61
Gibbon, 28
Gifford, 7 *n.* 1, 25, 176, App. IX., 198, 220
Goffe, 77 *n.* 3, 202
Gosse, E., App. XIX.
Gounod, 109 *n.* 1, 137 *n.* 3
Great Duke of Florence, The, 16 *n.* 1, 25, 47, 54, 102, 103, 150
Greene, 102 *n.* 5
Greg, W. W., 24 *n.* 2, 67 *n.* 2, 168
Grosart, 6 *n.* 1, 208
Guardian, The, 4, 12, 24, 27, 28, 49, 74, 120, 134, 148

H

Hallam, 70
Hazlitt, 25, 124 *n.* 4, 137 *n.* 3
Henry VIII., 11 *n.* 5, 20, 22, 71, 73 *n.* 1, 84-91, 128, 141 *n.* 1
Henslowe, 4, 177
Herbert, Sir H., 15
Heywood, 117
Homer, 169
Hroswitha, 124 *n.* 3

J

James I., 7
Johnson, S., 121 *n.* 2
Jonson, Ben, 6 *n.* 2, 12, 43 *n.* 2, 69 *n.* 4, 70, 72, 77 *n.* 3, 113-116, 118, 128, 133, 185 *n.* 1

K

Kean, 124 *n.* 4
Kemble, 124 *n.* 4
Knacke to Know a Knave, A, 208 *n.* 1
Koeppel, 28, 178 *n.* 6, 193
Kyd, 127

L

Lamb, C., 25, 33, 122 *n.* 3, 199
Langbaine, 2 *n.* 2, 34
Lee, Sir Sidney, 77 *n.* 2, 112
Love Lost in the Dark, 24
Lyly, 117

M

Macaulay, G. C., 21 *n.* 5, 65 *n.* 1, App. III.
Maid of Honour, The, 16, 18, 27, 28, 40, 74, 103, 132, 146
Malone, 15 *n.* 1, 15 *n.* 3, 24, 176
Marlowe, 29 *n.* 1, 110, 117, 150 *n.* 10
Marston, 62, 112 *n.* 1, 159
Massinger, Arthur, 1
Massinger, Philip: life, 2; religion, 3; knowledge of Spanish, 5 *n.* 5; death, 7; politics, 14; stagecraft, 26; style, 33; versification, 55; faults, 60; imitation of Shakspere, 77; introduction of doctors, 81; method, 104; favourite words, 106; character, 118; use of epithets, 120 *n.* 5; use of assonances, 121 *n.* 1; knowledge of Greek, App. II.; a metrical peculiarity, App. VI.; use of alliteration, App. XVIII.
Matthews, Brander, 25, 45, 64, 71, 123 *n.* 4, 142 *n.* 3, 160
Matthieu, P., 6 *n.* 2, App. XIV.
Middleton, 21, 28, 62, 65 *n.* 3, 124, 127, 141 *n.* 1, 147, 158, App. XVI.
Milton, 32 *n.* 3, 51, 55, 69
Monck Mason, 25, 123, 134
Montgomery, Philip, Earl of Pembroke and, 5, 14
Mozart, 76, 88

N

New Way to Pay Old Debts, A, 12, 20, 25, 47 *n.* 3, 48, 52, 70, 108, 115, 122, 124, 142 *n.* 3
Nichol Smith, 77 *n.* 1

O

Old Law, The, 21, 141, 158
Oliphant, E. H. C., 59 *n.* 2, 162 *n.* 2
Ovid, 34, 105 *n.* 3, 151

P

Parliament of Love, The, 42, 50, 59, 60, 82, 83, 92, 139, 146, App. IX.
Peele, 142 *n.*
Pembroke, second Earl of, 2
Pembroke, third Earl of, 6
Pepys, 24
Phelan, 137 *n.* 3, 203 *n.* 2
Philipps, Halliwell, 24 *n.* 2, 176
Picture, The, 8, 9, 29, 50, 54, 73, 74, 82, 111 *n.* 1, 140, 146

Plautus, 2, 67 *n.* 2, 104
Powerful Favourite, The, 6 *n.* 2,
App. XIV.
Prince of Tarent, The, vide *A Very
Woman*
Prynne, 65 *n.* 3
Puritans, 10, 45

R

Renegado, The, 3, 13, 24, 27, 31,
53, 65, 74, 75, 134, 145, 149
Repetition of words and phrases,
54, 197 *n.* 1
Richardson, 135
Roman Actor, The, 28, 33, 38, 52,
66, 72, 82, 116, 126, 137, 146
Rosenbach, 5 *n.* 5
Rowe, 56 *n.* 2, 137
Rowley, W., 21, 141 *n.* 1, 142, 168

S

Schelling, 5 *n.* 5, 65 *n.* 1
Schmidt, 43 *n.* 2, 171, 175
Scott, Sir W., 68
Sea scenes, 28
Second Maiden's Tragedy, The, App.
XIII.
Sero sed Serio, 5 *n.* 1
Shakspere, 3, 12 *n.* 3, 18, 20, 29,
32, 33 *n.* 1, 43 *n.* 1, 43 *n.* 2, 45,
49, 56 *n.* 2, 63, 69, 70, 72, 73,
77-80, 83, 85, 87, 90, 91, 98, 99,
101, 109, 113, 118, 121-123, 125,
128, 130, 135 *n.* 1, 137, 147, 153,
App. IV.
Shelley, 31
Shirley, 116, 126 *n.* 2, 147, 180 *n.* 1
Signorelli, Luca, 61
Simpson, P., 65 *n.* 3, 133 *n.* 1,
203 *n.* 2
Sir J. V. O. Barnavelt, 8, 9, 52,
139 *n.* 3, 177 *n.* 2, App. XII.
Sophocles, 150

Stephen, Sir Leslie, 45, 68, 76 *n.* 2,
76 *n.* 3, 132
Stevenson, 64
Strangest Adventure, The, 178
Subordinates combined, 29
Swinburne, 52, 151, 215
Sykes, Dugdale, 93, 94, 96
Symonds, J. A., 222

T

Taylor, J., 124 *n.* 2
Theobald, 204
Torture on stage, 28
Tourneur, 20, 55, 62, 157, 203
Turks, 9
Two Noble Kinsmen, The, 20, 22,
23 *n.* 1, 92-104

U

Unnatural Combat, The, 8, 28, 31,
54, 69, 138, App. XVIII.

V

Very Woman, A, 21, 42, 50, 81,
82, 84, 100, 102, 108, 129
Virgil, 127 *n.* 3
Virgin Martyr, The, 3, 18, 20, 24,
31, 32, 33, 46, 47 *n.* 3, 62, 72,
73, 81, 120, 123, 142, 149,
App. X.
Vocabulary of M., 106

W

Warburton, 23, App. V.
Ward, Sir A., 25, 65 *n.* 1, 110
Warner, Sir G. F., 177
Weber, 21 *n.* 6
Webster, 5, 29 *n.* 2, 111-113, 159
Wit and Fancy in a Maze, 77 *n.* 3

Z

Zielinski, 50